Soviet Economic Planning

STUDIES IN *Soviet*
Economic
Planning

Iosifovich

ARON KATSENELINBOIGEN

M. E. Sharpe INC., WHITE PLAINS, N.Y.

Translated by Arlo Schultz.

Library of Congress Catalog Number: 77-90277
International Standard Book Number: 087332-112-X

Printed in the United States of America.

In memory of my parents,
Ida and Josef Katsenelinboigen

Contents

Preface   xi

I.   SOME GENERAL PROBLEMS IN THE DEVELOPMENT
OF SOVIET ECONOMIC SCIENCE

    1. Methodological Problems in the Study of Soviet
Economics   3

      Economic invariants   3
      Causes of "schizophrenia" in the mechanism of
      functioning of the Soviet economy   9
      On the relationship between economics and
      mathematics 16

    2. The Role of Marxism in the Formation and
Development of the Soviet Economic System   23

      Communist society and the perpetual motion
      machine   24
      The Marxists' rejection of experimentation in
      the social sciences   30
      The demand for the destruction of old institutions:
      a highly important trait of Marxism   36
      His majesty the working class   41

    3. Conflicting Trends in Soviet Economic Science   48

      The status of Soviet economic science   48
      The structure of Soviet economic science and rela-
      tions between economists of various schools   57
      The relations of Soviet economists with the party
      leadership   65

II.   ECONOMIC INVARIANTS AND THEIR USE IN
      THE SOVIET PLANNING SYSTEM

   4. Methods of Describing Economic Systems and
      Representation of the Soviet Economy   77

      Macrodescription of economic systems   78
        Production functions   78
        Structural models   81
      A microdescription of an economic system   89

   5. Value Parameters and Their Use in the Soviet
      Economic Mechanism   97

      Value invariants in production systems   97
        Price and profit   98
        Subsidies and superprofits   104
        Productivity of the system   107
        Penalties   110
        Money   112
      Value invariants in production systems with
      human participation   118
        Excise taxes, subsidies, and limited
        commodities   118
        Contour money   120
      Soviet experience in the use of the price
      mechanism   122
        Theoretical substantiation of the price
        mechanism by Soviet economists   122
        The practice of using the price mechanism   127

   6. Economic Incentives and the Soviet Experience
      in Using Them   138

      Incentives and the nature of workers' activity   139
        On the relationship between expenditures to
        maintain a worker and incentives for his
        greater efficiency   139
        Incentives and "flation"   143
        Incentives, envy, and manipulation of
        personnel   148

Incentive and anticipation   151
  Contract, plan, and incentives   151
  The plan and incentives in the USSR   154
  The contract-and incentives in the USSR   160

7. Market Colors and the Soviet Economy   165

Legal markets   170
  The red market   170
  The pink market   173
  The white market   175
Semilegal markets   178
  The gray market   178
Illegal markets   186
  The brown market   186
  The black market   192

Notes   203

Index   227

About the Author   229

Preface

The expanding scale of economic market systems and the acceleration of the pace of the processes in them more and more urgently raise the question of improving the economic mechanisms of their functioning. As shown by experience in the development of indicative planning in a number of Western countries and discussion of the introduction of planning in the United States, this improvement is associated to a large degree with the introduction of the institution of planning. Hence it is understandable that particular interest has attached to studying the mechanism of the functioning of the planned economy of the USSR, which is a large-scale industrial system.

A great number of books and articles devoted to analyzing the positive and negative aspects of the economic mechanism of the Soviet economy have been published in the West. One can boldly state that many of these works far exceed in depth of treatment those published in the USSR. This is due both to the fact that Western experts on Soviet economics have at their disposal a more powerful analytical apparatus based on modern advances in economic science, as well as to the fact that they enjoy more freedom in their research.

The majority of Soviet economic studies show a comparatively low level of organization of the material, since the overwhelming majority of Soviet economists are unable to use Western research methodology. They are not familiar with Western theories formulated in the last hundred years. Nor are they familiar with Western research on Soviet economics which, because of its secrecy in the USSR, is accessible only to individual economists concerned primarily with "criticizing our critics," as the saying goes in the USSR.

At the same time, Soviet economists feel ideological pressure.

They must make the existing material fit the Marxist framework or at least must adapt it to conventional Marxist phraseology. Current political events play a dominant role for economists, compelling them to create strictly within the framework of decisions made by the party.

In no way do I mean to cancel out Soviet economic literature with the foregoing remarks. That literature is undoubtedly a valuable source for data on processes taking place in the Soviet economy, particularly since the latter is closed to Western researchers for all practical purposes. Especially valuable are individual original studies that have appeared specifically thanks to the use of mathematical methods and under their cover.

Nor by these comments do I in any way want to paint a black picture of all Soviet economists. There are many able people among them. The described style of work of many economists is more their misfortune than their fault.

But I needed this preface to call attention to the difficulties that I, as a recently emigrated Soviet economist, encountered in making my decision to write a book for the Western reader — a book about Soviet economics or, more precisely, a series of essays united by the common idea of using economic invariants.

Exactly why did I undertake to write such a work? First, it seems to me that the West still has unused reserve capacities in the realm of methodology that can be applied to the study of Soviet economics.

Second, my personal experience allows me to call attention to a number of aspects in the functioning of the Soviet economy which, because of their informal character, have been illuminated to a lesser degree in Western literature.

Third, the book may be of some interest to a historian of science: it allows him to see what an economist can do who has spent a good half of his life in a Soviet-type system and who has been recently "transplanted" to the West.

True, the two years I have spent working on the present book in the United States could not but affect its contents.

Thanks to the efforts of a group of professors at the University of Pennsylvania, and especially Professors H. Levine, A. Riasanovsky, and A. Rieber, I was able to give the following lecture courses at that university: "Soviet Economics," "Mathematical Models of Planned Systems," "Introduction to Marxism: Marx and His Soviet Interpreters."

Experts on Soviet economics — J. Berliner, G. Grossman,

Preface

H. Levine, A. Nove, and V. Treml in particular — discussed with
me various questions dealt with in the work. Naturally, they bear
no responsibility for the present book.

Finally, in preparing the manuscript for publication, I also considered the numerous comments made by a "captious" and, at the
same time, very well-meaning reviewer. The remarks were aimed
primarily at improving the work by utilizing the attainments of
Western economic science and deleting from it various principles
that are considered quite well known to the Western reader.

But, of course, this book mainly reflects the knowledge I amassed
in the USSR. What is more, since I accumulated this knowledge in
the corresponding political atmosphere, reaction to it is now inevitable. That is why the critical aspect predominates in this book.

I would be very glad if this book helped the Western reader gain
a better understanding of the mechanism by which the Soviet economic system functions.

Acknowledgments

Chapter 3 has been presented in various forms to several audiences, including a seminar on socialist economics in Berkeley for associates of the Russian Institute of Columbia University, at a meeting of American economists and former associates of the Central Economic Mathematical Institute of the USSR Academy of Sciences who have emigrated to the United States, and at the annual conference of the American Association for the Advancement of Slavic Studies held in Atlanta in 1975. A short version of the chapter was published in The Russian Review, 1976, no. 3, and an expanded version will appear in my Limited Diversity: The Renaissance of Economics, Soviet Style. I am grateful to A. Yanov for very important discussions we had about the problems dealt with in this chapter.

A Ford Foundation Grant No. 750-0578 enabled me to write and prepare for press the majority of the chapters in Part II of the book.

For Chapter 5, the section on money (pp. 112-18), Professors F. Balderston and G. Grossman gave the author a great deal of support in his work. The experimental calculations were made by W. Ingram of the Computer Center at the University of California, Berkeley.

Chapter 6 is based in part on a paper that I prepared jointly with H. Levine for a conference of the American Economics Association, Dallas, December 1975. I am grateful to R. P. Sheinman for discussions on a number of points dealt with in the section on incentives and anticipation (pp. 151-64) in this chapter.

I would also like to thank Professor V. Treml for his contribution to Chapter 7 and for his valuable comments in general.

I

*Some general problems in the
development of Soviet economic science*

1

Methodological Problems
in the Study of Soviet Economics

Economic Invariants

In our study we assume that there is one economic science.
There are no capitalist, socialist, feudal, servile, etc., economic
sciences. Just as there is no bourgeois and socialist physics, so
there is no bourgeois and socialist economics.[1]

Here economic science is similar to any other science that
studies processes taking place in the system reflected by it and
that reveals the laws governing its dynamics. On the basis of properties perceived by science, existing processes are reproduced artificially or new ones are created. Just as biology is related to
medicine and physics to engineering, so theoretical economic science is related to economic practice. In this regard the difference
between the natural sciences and economics lies in the following.
The natural sciences study a given world that reflects an incredibly
long experience of nature. The science of economics finds itself in
a more difficult situation, however, for the object of its study has
amassed comparatively little experience: developed economic relations that are accessible to its examination became known only in
the seventeenth century. This is also reflected in the fact that developed economic theories appeared only in the eighteenth century.

Conceiving economics as a single science makes it possible to
analyze specific economic systems from unified positions. Of
course, the mechanisms of functioning of various systems have
their specific features. These features should not be exaggerated,
however. At the outset it is more important to see common features. The general theory of systems, based primarily on the experience of mathematics and the natural sciences, teaches such an
interpretation of economic science. The discovery of invariants,
of the common features that are preserved during the transforma-

3

tion of one system into another, makes it possible to minimize the efforts required in solving many problems. Separation of the general from the specific in analyzing a certain system allows one to concentrate on its specific features. When the invariants are lacking, both general and specific features will be mixed together in the analysis of a given system, which naturally makes it much more difficult to solve the problems posed.[2]

The idea of invariants and the methodology of searching for them in economic systems can make it much easier to analyze various economic systems and more effectively transform one system into another depending on changes in conditions.

The absence of a developed general theory of economic systems essentially means that the idea of economic invariants has not yet been adequately elaborated. The search for economic invariants can be conducted in breadth and in depth. Comparing one economic system with other systems makes it possible to see common features in these systems and to separate the specific features of some economic systems from those of other systems. In this way economic invariants cease to be such and become invariants of more general systems. Naturally, it is very difficult to carry out such a study of economic invariants on a broad scale. The present work will make only certain steps in this direction. These will concern the development of general production invariants, that is, invariants in production systems in general that may function with or without human participation.

In searching for invariants in the economic systems themselves one can distinguish between invariants belonging to all these systems — that is, global invariants — and invariants within specific parts of a system — or local invariants. Later it will be better to speak of the spectrum of invariants, for individual parts in the system follow a hierarchy of specificity.

In this connection let us note the following. By investigating economic systems it is possible, first of all, to isolate invariants that are common to all economic systems.

Given the numerous planned economies that exist in the world at the present time, a comparative analysis is particularly interesting. Although all these planned systems differ significantly in the methods used to search for goals for the plan, in information about production possibilities, and in the responsibility of participants in the economic systems for the fulfillment of the plan, these systems also have properties in common. It is apparently possible to isolate

invariants for all planned systems, invariants for those planned
systems with a command economy, and so on.

Planned economic systems with command economic mechanisms
will be the subject of our study. The economic system in the USSR
will be examined first and foremost. The reason is that, in the
first place, the USSR is a very large country, its economy is more
closed, internal factors of development play a large part in it, and
it is easier to determine their influence on the development of the
economic system. Second, the USSR has a great deal of experience
in organizing the processes of functioning of the economy and has
more developed economic mechanisms than the other major socialist country, China.

In Western economics considerable attention is devoted to the
search for invariants. They are used both to ascertain methods
of describing an economic system (see Chapter 3 for greater detail) and to analyze its development. At the macrolevel one can
speak of the search for invariants in the following sense. Researchers have been confronted with a multitude of economic systems in
different states and with different mechanisms of functioning. They
have tried to select macroparameters that characterize all economic systems and to establish relations between them — that is,
the laws governing their development. Essentially, it is these general laws of development that are the invariants of economic systems.[3]

At the microlevel the search for invariants is characterized by
the identification of common economic institutions. A great deal
of work in this direction has been done by Western researchers, especially by those engaged in the comparative study of
economic systems.[4]

In the Soviet economic literature very modest attention has been
devoted to the search for invariants. Invariants are investigated
primarily in the description of production processes and the informational aspects of management problems.[5]

At the same time, generally speaking the idea of invariants does
not contradict Marxism. Thus, for example, in Chapter 5 of
the first volume of Capital, Marx studied economic relations
between workers and capitalists based on the use of the idea
of invariants. He first examined the structure of the labor
process as such and then its specific characteristics under capitalism.

Such methodological devices are not typical of Marxism, however.
In Marxism the emphasis falls mainly on the specific features of

5

various modes of production. Hence the denial by Soviet Marxists of the existence of a single economic science and their emphasis on the existence of a class-oriented socialist and bourgeois political economy.[6]

Once the invariants have been identified, the particular features of the economic system under investigation can begin to be analyzed. Combined study of the general and specific features of the corresponding part of the economic system makes it possible to develop adequate mechanisms for the functioning of that part of the system. One can then begin to synthesize the system and to integrate the heterogeneous mechanisms of functioning of various parts of the system.

A real economic system is the synthesis of mechanisms of functioning, each of which reflects specific features of its corresponding structure. This synthesis encompasses both the ways in which the structure of the system is formed and the mechanism of its functioning. At the same time, under certain conditions these can be studied separately.

Much experience has been amassed in this area in biology. From the general biological point of view, the creation of organs is inseparably linked to the functioning of the system, if only because organs are developed to fulfill certain functions. Since in the study of any system some structural formations must be adopted as initial, one is justified in breaking down knowledge of the system in terms of its structure and the mechanism responsible for coordinating their actions. Moreover, this type of study is also promoted by the fact that, because the structure of the system and the mechanism of its functioning are so stable, in a certain sense their improvement occurs independently.

In an economic system, as in a biological system, there is also a single process by which new structures and the mechanisms for coordinating their actions are formed. But after the type of economic system has been identified, it is admissible within this framework to make a segment-by-segment study of the structure of the system and the mechanism of its functioning.

As with anatomy and physiology, in economics a distinction can be made between econotomy and econology, respectively. In the present work we will be studying primarily econology — the processes involved in the functioning of an economic system — taking the existing structure as given.

We will be still more justified in drawing on images from biology to define various segments of economic science if we use the further division of the segments existing in biology. As we know, both anatomy and physiology are divided into normal and pathological.

By analogy we will examine normal and pathological econology. In analyzing concrete systems such a division of econology makes it possible to separate the internal failures and errors that are permissible for a normally functioning system from pathological situations that are generally accompanied by pronounced derangement of the system.

Naturally, in every system, its motive forces inevitably collide with obstacles generated by these same forces. Such is the immanent character of any mechanism of functioning. Every improvement usually generates negative aspects as well. The effectiveness of the system consists in the degree to which it successfully reduces negative consequences and generally increases efficiency.

It is also natural for malfunctions to occur in every system for one reason or another. How effective a system is can be seen in how able it is to correct errors and eliminate malfunctions arising in it.

Systematically repeated disruptions in the operation of the system are evidence of a pathological situation. The reasons for such pathology may be quite varied. In my opinion pathological phenomena in the Soviet economic system are generated primarily by the disjunction between the value and physical aspects of the mechanism of its functioning.

At the same time, in the Soviet economic system there are managers endowed with common sense. These people usually have enough common sense to set logically formulated goals (the nature of these goals from the standpoint of humaneness, etc., is another matter). At the same time, their common sense is not sufficient to formulate a relatively effective, internally unified mechanism of functioning; they have created instead a disjunct, schizophrenic mechanism.

The common sense of these people is sometimes enough to avoid the absurdities engendered by the disparity between the goals set and the schizophrenic mechanism of actions toward their attainment. Sometimes they, or at least their subordinates, become the victims of the mechanism they themselves have created. The following example, somewhat sketchy but based on facts taken from Soviet practice, can serve to illustrate this point (the figures cited are arbitrary).

In the USSR at one time there arose an urgent need to increase the production of plastic wares, which are very important to the country. The government instructed one of the plastics plants to increase production approximately one and a half times in a very short period. It was impossible to meet this target using an extensive approach — the expansion of production capacities through installation of additional presses — because all this would require time: the plant would have had to construct new production buildings, order presses, and wait for them to be manufactured. The realization of the target might have been drawn out for several years.

The plant's engineers took another course that enabled them to meet the target in a very short time. As we know, pressing is the limiting link in the production of plastics. The initial temperature of the molding powder significantly influences the length of this process. For this reason the engineers decided to install high-frequency current generators near the presses, use them to preheat the powder, and thus raise the productivity of the presses. And indeed press productivity was increased and production rose approximately one and a half times. The management and engineering-technical personnel of the enterprise had successfully coped with the important task and were awarded the State Prize.

But when the plant's economic indicators were analyzed, it was found to be deep in the hole. First, output per press operator had declined. Under the previous, longer pressing cycle, one person tended two presses; but under the new conditions, with the shorter period of pressing, a press operator was unable to operate two units and additional labor had to be hired. Since the number of press operators doubled while the productivity of the presses increased only one and a half times, output per operator fell.

Second, the enterprise cost of production increased, since the wages of the press operator remained the same although the output per operator dropped. The wage level remained unchanged because the intensity of the operator's labor was not decreased, since additional operations involved in heating the molding powder had to be performed. The enterprise cost of production was also increased by the rise in expenditures on electric power (per item): expenditures on technological power for preheating the molding powder had to be made. Even though overall output at the plant expanded, the reduction of so-called fixed expenditures per item could not compensate for the rise in expenditures listed above. Since the transfer prices remained the same while the enterprise cost of production increased appreciably, the plant started operating at a loss, with all the ensuing negative consequences (absence of the director's fund, etc.).

Thus a single measure received two different assessments: the plant had to be simultaneously "pardoned" and "executed."

The government agency that set the target of increasing production in a short time because the product was vitally needed by the national economy, that is, had a high degree of utility, realized that the plant producing this product had to be "pardoned."

At the same time, the overall economic mechanism of functioning created by the government demanded that the plant be "executed" — after all, the plant had begun operating at a loss. At an important conference organized in the course of a government campaign to improve the economic indicators of enterprises, I myself witnessed a tongue-lashing administered to the management of a plastics plant by district party authorities for poor economic performance. [7]

Causes of "Schizophrenia" in the Mechanism of Functioning of the Soviet Economy

From my point of view the schizophrenic nature of the mechanism of functioning of the Soviet economy stems directly from the fact that this mechanism is based on the principle of a "complex of models" rather than one complex model that would unify the myriad aspects of the economic system.

Historically and logically, a planning system based on an "aggregate of models" emerged in response to the urgent demands of practice in the absence of a developed general theory of the functioning of planning systems. At the very dawn of Soviet power it became a priority task to elaborate unified state plans for the development of the socialist economy and to organize the activity of all links of the single national economic organism on a planned basis. But the extraordinary complexity of the economy and the lack of experience in its planned management, in the absence of any design for a planning system (see Chapter 2), made it impossible in the early stages to create a single model of the functioning of the national economy that would encompass all the processes in the production, distribution, and exchange of material and nonmaterial goods.

In the course of development of national economic planning, two types of model emerged that can conditionally be called block and functional.

By block models we mean models that are meant to be used in elaborating the plan for an individual economic cell (shop, enterprise, ministry) or territorial unit (economic region, republic, etc.). In solving these problems there has been increasingly broad application in recent years of the ideas and methods of optimal planning, which is unquestionably of great importance. Such models are used to develop and improve methods for calculating optimal plans; at the same time, in many instances they produce a direct economic effect (increase in output, reduced expenditure of materials, etc.).

To be sure, the area of application of block optimal models is still limited, since the results obtained with their aid frequently fail to agree with the existing mechanism of functioning. For example, due to the solution of optimal transport problems, the volume of shipping can be reduced. But if the plan for transport organizations is established in ton-kilometers, and if they are rewarded for the overfulfillment of this plan, the practical significance of such optimization problems is reduced. Accordingly, effective use of the results of the solution of local block problems requires the appropriate economic and organizational conditions and a definite mechanism of functioning — in particular, material incentives for those indicators reflected in the formulated criterion of optimality of the economic object. Where it is possible to combine the rational optimality criterion of the object that is contained in the model with the existing practice of planning and material incentives, block models yield a clear effect.

So-called functional models are of a completely different nature. We can classify various models of price formation, wages, financial flows, rate of interest (called in the USSR "normative of effectiveness of capital investment"), and so on, under this heading. These models are used to find the corresponding economic parameters prior to the establishment of the production plan or in parallel with, but independently of, the plan's elaboration.

Naturally, I do not intend to exclude the analysis of individual functional aspects of economic development from the arsenal of economic research. Nonetheless, in my opinion this analysis should not be conducted using functional models that are created specifically for each individual aspect and are not interconnected with one another. It can be most effective if it is performed on the basis of a complete concept of the mechanism of the functioning of the economy.

Let us try to describe in general terms the "complex of models" of the planning and management of the national economy. I shall say from the very outset that the point here is not any detailed study or description of the existing mechanism of national economic planning and all its myriad aspects, but only a rather simplified scheme, whose sole purpose is to show how an executive in the Soviet planning system might conceive of this mechanism in principle. Let this executive be an official like the chairman of USSR Gosplan. Let us call the model describing his train of thought "Bai-ba" (by association with Baibakov, who has been chairman of USSR Gosplan for many years).

Our official is a person with common sense and an engineering education. We note that the country's economic leadership, including the personnel of USSR Gosplan, is made up mostly of engineers. (A similar situation exists with regard to the country's political leadership, i.e., the Politburo.) Leading economic cadres tend to have such a composition because, on the one hand, primary attention in the existing planning process is focused on physical input-output indicators; value indicators do not play a leading role. On the other hand, an engineering background is very important for management when there is a "power struggle." "Power struggle" refers to a method of management in which the leader of the upper level of the hierarchy obligates the leader of a lower level to meet the highest possible target. The latter, in turn, resolutely resists the adoption of this target, since his fate depends largely on whether the target is met. To be qualified to figure out the validity of these refusals, one must first and foremost perceive their technical justification.

And so our executive undertakes the compilation of the plan. He knows that the major factor on which his career depends is his ability to satisfy the demands of the leadership — that is, the Politburo.

The point of departure in the plan target set by them is that the highest national economic agencies formulate for him in the most general terms the goals and basic directions of development of the economy in the planned period. In particular, they set specific targets for developing the most important branches of the national economy and for raising the people's living standard.

One of the major tasks of the central planning agency is to compile a balanced plan.[8] This is necessary because the directives of the highest agencies of management establish production indicators for only the basic types of products (coal, oil, steel, electric power, meat, textiles, etc.); these are significantly fewer in number than

11

the total of all aggregated products — final and intermediate — produced in the national economy. For this reason the central planning agency must establish a structure of production that takes into account the production of all intermediate products necessary for fabricating the basic products. This is achieved through the elaboration of physical (natural) balances.

The heart of all the work of our official lies in solving this problem. For physical balances to be compiled, however, there must be "norms": the need for corresponding intermediate products and for natural and labor resources depends on input coefficients per unit of output. For example, to determine the amount of lumber required to extract a given quantity of coal, one must know the expenditure of these materials per ton of output.

But how can input-output coefficients be determined, since there are many methods for producing a given product?

Let us assume that these coefficients have been established for every production method (in our example, for various methods of extracting coal) through scientific and experimental work. But the question arises, what is the proportion between these different methods as envisaged in the plan? Obviously the proportion adopted will directly determine the magnitude of input-output coefficients. If the open-pit method of extracting coal is predominant in the planned period, less lumber will be required. There will be less expenditure of lumber if the plan makes provision for the broader application of metal roofing in underground mining, but the need for metal will increase.

A multitude of ways to solve this problem open up before our imaginary official. One way is the creation of methods for constructing input-output coefficients based on branch production functions, that is, without penetrating the structure of processes occurring in the branch or changing the proportions of production methods employed. The official creates special scientific research institutions to devise methods of constructing such functions. It never occurs to the staff of these institutions, or to the official, that there are production functions and other apparatus for constructing consolidated norms. They try in some way to find the methods for constructing input-output coefficients on the basis of statistical data.

However, it is very difficult to expect that the dynamics of change in the coefficients can be taken into account in this way: technical progress here is not amenable to accounting. Our official is not concerned with these difficulties; he does not have the time to wait for the results of these elaborations — he is a man of action and he actually has to compile the plan today. Moreover, he realizes that "life is complex" and that "scientific" input-output coefficients are still not so well founded in fact. For this reason he chooses an entirely realistic way to construct these coefficients — through the "power struggle." Even if "scientifically substantiated" coefficients are available, he uses them as merely one device in the "power struggle."

Thus our official sees himself confronted with three real problems, which we will scientifically call models, that he must combine: (1) the model of the elaboration of targets by executive agencies, on the understanding of which his career primarily depends; (2) the model of the balancing of the plan for the production of final and intermediate products with the available resources; (3) the model of the "power struggle" with agencies in formulating the plan, which is expressed in the assigning of input-output coefficients.

The official sincerely believes that all other economic problems are independent problems lying outside the domain of these models. Determining the effectiveness of new production methods, of prices, of rent, and so on, is not the most important problem for our official. He is certain that a national economic plan can be compiled without solving these problems, and he compiles such a plan. He is also convinced of this by the structure of the government agencies. For example, a special State Committee on Prices of the USSR Council of Ministers deals with prices.

Thus if you tell this official that compiling the plan also means at the same time solving the problem of the normative effectiveness of capital investments, prices, and other economic parameters — that is, simultaneously resolving the direct and dual extremal problems of economic development — he will at the very least think that you are frivolous or "touched." After all, the common sense of this person and his daily practice convince him of the correctness of his opinion. (An official similar to our imaginary one once had a talk with a representative of economic science, who was also an official, although he had a high academic title. The "academic" official had already "picked up" a little from economic scholars. He tried to explain to the highly placed official that compiling an output plan also meant simultaneously obtaining the norms, prices, and other parameters corresponding to this plan. The highly placed official said that he had heard about this sort of nonsense. But he was astonished that his companion, whom he had known for a long time to be a person with common sense, could surrender himself to such drivel.)

Naturally, our official realizes that these other problems must be resolved. He is even forced to participate to some degree in their solution, since he represents the country's supreme economic headquarters.

Thus the previously mentioned problem of choosing the best proportions of production methods, which our official was solving in the "power struggle," still requires a response to the question of the economic effectiveness of these methods.

This is an independent problem within the framework of the complex of planning models being investigated. In order to solve it special scientific institutions are created. They work out standard methods for determining the economic effectiveness of various production methods and calculate the recoupment period of investments. Some of these institutions may be subordinate to our official, while some are in other eparchies. The latter particularly traumatize our official and "divert him from his basic work," since the corresponding methods cannot be put into operation without his leave as representative of the country's economic headquarters.

But solving the problem of selecting economically substantiated technical variants of production of a given product runs into a new problem: price formation. Indeed, without knowing prices it is impossible to determine which method of production is better. After all, different products — or the same products in different proportions — are used in different methods. Clearly, without considering the prices of individual products, it is impossible to compare different variants and select the most effective ones.

But to solve the problem of prices on the basis of common sense, one must have one's own models and research institutes, and even one's own organizations. According to Marxist theory price must first and foremost reflect socially necessary expenditures. Moreover, these must be average expenditures of labor. But how can these average expenditures be found if the given product can be produced by different methods and if their optimal proportions in the plan are unknown? The result is a vicious circle. The volume of production of intermediate products and the expenditure of resources cannot be determined without knowing the optimal proportions among production methods; these proportions, in turn, cannot be set without a knowledge of prices; and prices, according to accepted theory, cannot be determined unless the proportions of production methods are known.

What is more, practical workers feel the need to use prices to rationally expend natural resources and capital, calculate shortages of various means of production, stimulate the production of high-quality products, and so on. In practice attempts are made to solve these problems. They are made in isolation, however, and are not coordinated with the plan in physical terms. They are not based on a foundation of strict theory. Their theoretical basis is equilibristics, the external aspect of coordination with adopted economic theory. The result is inconsistency and ambivalence in the measures for using prices to take into account the diversity of conditions in various situations.

This is the way the Soviet planned economic system functions. The very logic of its functioning requires that the process of compiling the national economic plan be truncated and that much of what concerns the price mechanism be separated from it. Given the existing methods of planning, the attempt to elaborate norms of effectiveness of investment, prices, and other parameters in the course of compiling the plan would lead to logical insolubility. But since in the real mechanism of functioning of the economy it is difficult to dodge the problem of combining its physical and value aspects, many insidious problems lie in wait for our official. He is able to solve some of them in such a way that the goals do not suffer. In a number of cases the existing economic mechanism seizes him in a death grip and forces him to retreat.

In the above examination of pathological phenomena in economic systems, it was continually implied that we knew what a normally functioning economic system was. At the same time, basic difficulties arise in defining normal econology. They stem principally from the fact that in economic reality, where unique new systems are created and generally few systems of any one type are encountered, there may be no models of normally functioning systems of a particular kind. The situation in biology is much simpler, since there are many analogous normally functioning models produced by nature. This is why, in the rigorous study of econological problems, it is essential to resort to the construction of normal models at the modeling level or to seek other methods of experimentation. Naturally, this sharply reduces the potential of econology compared with, for example, physiology.

What is more, for the time being, internally coordinated models in economics can be built for only limited parts of a system and methods found for experimentally testing proposals to improve these individual parts.

In the present work emphasis will be placed on the study of a normal econology within the framework of mathematical models. Problems of pathological econology can be examined accordingly.

On the Relationship between Economics and Mathematics

Out of the multitude of definitions of mathematics, we will use the following: "Mathematics is the language of logic." We construe logic to mean a science that ascertains the rules for selecting premises and arriving at conclusions from them (including the very procedure for selecting premises and arriving at conclusions as well). Logic in this sense is the most universal science.

Now for the use of a mathematical language to describe various systems (we will not go into the problem of a metalanguage). Generally speaking, a given system can be expressed in its own language. But this type of description would acutely impoverish the possibilities for investigating the given system. The point is that other systems have features in common with the system under investigation, and therefore the experience amassed in them can be used in analyzing this system. To identify isomorphisms in the systems, linguistic correspondence must be established.

Here one can proceed in two ways, as is customary in translating from one language into another. A direct correspondence can be established between all languages. Such a technique has sometimes been used in economic research when mechanical analogue devices are created to solve so-called economic transport problems. Such a method of establishing linguistic correspondence is not effective enough, however, and greatly complicates the possibility for generalizing the results in various systems.

The second method of translating from one language into another entails the introduction of an intermediary language to which various languages are correspondingly related. Mathematics is such an intermediary language. Accordingly, mathematics makes it possible to describe phenomena of various systems in a single language. This makes it much easier to discover the isomorphism of systems.

Like any language, the language of logic has its own semantics and semiotics, which allow one in a very general form to express the diversity of processes taking place in the universe.

The language of mathematics has its own semantics, words that very strictly express the most common properties of various types of phenomena and the relationships between them (the concepts of variables, operations on elements of sets, etc.). Because of this, the language of mathematics makes it possible to describe rather complex properties of the systems being investigated. The universality of the language makes it possible to see to which class of structures the object under study belongs.

The semiotic properties of language exert a very substantial influence on our perception of reality. Thus the language of traffic signs permits us to react quickly to an existing situation that consists of a comparatively small number of elements. The laconic form of notation achieved by means of mathematical symbols makes it possible to obtain in <u>visible</u> form a <u>complete</u> clear picture of a depicted object that consists of quite a large number of elements.

The very fact that an economic problem can be expressed in mathematical language would be a strong enough reason to apply mathematics in economic research. Naturally, the basic role of mathematics is not limited to providing the rigorous notation for an economic problem. The use of general mathematical methods to solve a problem when it is expressed in mathematical form is trivial.

It is also known, for example, that the interaction of physics and mathematics is not limited to the one-sided use of mathematics to describe and solve physical problems by known methods. Penetration of the physical essence of the processes under investigation has made it possible to equip mathematics with new models and has enabled mathematics to produce new problem-solving methods. Thus by means of mathematics not only the premises of the problem but also the course of its solution are translated from the language of a given concrete system into the language of logic.

I should like to dwell in somewhat greater detail on the role of mathematics in investigating economic processes, a role not so characteristic for the study of other systems.

More refined is the reciprocal process of that described above as translating from the language of a particular system into the language of mathematics. Mathematics has amassed many images engendered in its course of development. It uses these images to create effective new problem-solving methods. If solving a problem is sometimes understood as outlining the alternative paths of a process and the mechanism of functioning of a system, then the translation of a method of problem solving from the language of mathematics into the language of a given system would make it possible to discover the hitherto unknown course of the process.

There have been a number of such cases in physics and chemistry.9 However, in these sciences the use of mathematical methods to discover the course of unknown processes has a very limited potential. The point is that the mechanism of functioning of a system is already defined for the researcher by that system. The mathematician, on the other hand, may use to solve a problem generated by a certain system a method that in no way repeats the mechanism of functioning of the system. Moreover, the actual course of natural processes must always satisfy the law of conservation of matter and energy. But, a mathematician may propose an algorithm based on virtual foundations, and thus the aforementioned laws are not observed in the course of solving the problem — only the solved problem satisfies them.

Something similar happens when mathematics is used to analyze existing economic mechanisms. Even though many of them have been created artificially, their creators do not know in a rigorous, formal way how they operate. Here mathematical methods can be found that imitate the basic features of the processes at play. Such a mathematical construction may make it easier to understand the action of the mechanisms under investigation.

This is especially important in studying the process of functioning of complex economic objects. For example, certain Soviet economists and mathematicians have wanted to understand the work of USSR Gosplan through direct study of the process of its functioning. However, they quickly became bogged down in its very informal planning technology. It would be more expedient to have hypothetical pictures of the processes going on and on their basis to try to make out the actual planning technology in Gosplan.

Investigators who attempted to study directly the mechanism of functioning of the brain experienced similar methodological difficulties. To some extent the development of cybernetics advanced the study of the mechanism of functioning of the brain, since it offered a number of hypotheses in this regard.

We might note that from this point of view, a broader palette of mathematical methods can be applied in the study of existing economic objects than in the natural sciences. The reason is that in an economic system there is an explicitly expressed system of anticipation — contracts, plans. In the process of compiling contract-plans, the laws of conservation of matter and energy need not necessarily be observed: the equilibrium (optimal) system of contract-plans must necessarily satisfy them. Because of this, virtual mathematical methods of problem solving can in principle imitate the process of compiling contract-plans. Imitation of the process of realizing contract-plans requires a narrower set of algorithms, since the laws of conservation of matter and energy must be observed here.

Economic science is concerned not only with the study of existing mechanisms but also with the construction of new ones. In constructing new mechanisms a variety of new types of algorithms can be used as prototypes.

Thus in economic science there is an enormous potential for using all kinds of algorithms as prototypes of mechanisms of functioning. Considering the myriad areas of application of these algorithms (both to study the functioning of objects, including their system of anticipation and to create new mechanisms), it is safe to say that an economic interpretation can be given to any algorithm used in economics. In other words, any such algorithm can be translated from the language of mathematics into the language of economics.

Mathematical constructions used in an algorithm may be interpreted as corresponding economic categories (for example, Lagrange multipliers may be interpreted as prices). Every step in such an algorithm can be expressed as a link in the technological process of functioning of the system.

All the foregoing remarks concerning the role of mathematics in the formation of economic mechanisms apply not only to algorithms as constructive devices but also to the theorems that prove the existence of a solution. Proving such a theorem can itself be considered the precursor of a more developed mechanism of functioning of a system given in the algorithm.

The theorem of the existence of economic equilibrium is an example of this type of theorem. Brauer's fixed point theorem, later generalized by J. von Neumann and Kakutani, is usually used to prove it. If the proof for the theorem of the existence of equilibria is interpreted by means of Brauer's theorem, then one can see that the idea of the change in prices depending on the difference between supply and demand is used here. For a long time the course of this proof was not considered to be constructive, that is, it was impossible to construct an algorithm of the search for equilibrium on the basis of it. It was quite obvious, however, that the construction of the proof could be interpreted naturally in economic terms, so that it should have been possible to construct an algorithm. And indeed, the American economist and mathematician H. Scarf succeeded in constructing an algorithm of the search for economic equilibrium, the precursor of which was the proof of the theorem of the existence of equilibrium by means of Brauer's theorem. [10]

The striving of certain Soviet scholars to call attention to the multifaceted role of mathematics in economic research encountered decisive resistance from a great many Soviet economists of the older generation, who are unable to use mathematical methods. Under pressure from the authorities, who were attempting to use mathematics and computers for their own purposes, these economists were compelled to admit that mathematical methods must be employed in Soviet economics as well. But they tried in every way to demonstrate that mathematics as a science operates only with numbers and geometric forms, that mathematical methods are merely convenient technical means for making calculations, and that computers are nothing more than high-speed adding machines.

These remarks concerning the relationship between mathematics and economics and the existing bilateral relationship between mathematics and the processes occurring in the simulated object describe very complex interactions between economists and mathematicians. The role of the economist does not simply amount to the formulation of the problem, nor does the role of the mathematician amount to its formalization and solution. As with the physicist and the mathematician, the economist and the mathematician jointly formulate the problem and seek ways to solve it. If a problem is found to enter into a class of problems that is already known and for which methods of analysis have been developed, then one can proceed directly to the solution of the mathematical problem arising in the study of the given object. As the development of science shows, however, situations frequently arise in which the model of the object has a structure for which analyses there are still no mathematical methods. In such a case an extremely important question arises: can the premises of the model be simplified in such a way that the model does not lose the important specific features of the object under study and at the same time can be included in a class of already known structures that are amenable to mathematical analysis? The decisive role of economists, who must single out the most important aspects of the object under investigation and reflect them in an appropriate mathematical model, makes itself known precisely here. In turn the mathematical models with previously unknown structures that are created during the investigation of new objects stimulate the development of mathematics and lead to the emergence of new schools of mathematics. New branches of mathematics such as linear and nonlinear programming and so on have come into being as a result of the study of planned production processes.

The experience of the economist may also suggest to the mathematician new constructions that are expedient to use in algorithms. A mathematician armed with the power of the apparatus and the ability to reason deductively can construct a formal procedure to analyze economic problems that incorporates constructions proposed by the economist. Together with the mathematician the economist can also offer an interpretation of the derived algorithm as a possible process in the functioning of the object under investigation.

Consistent implementation of the methods of mathematical model building, which entails a large volume of calculations, is unthinkable without the use of the latest computers. Where production processes can be formalized completely, computers can lead to the creation of automated optimal control systems. This can be done for individual enterprises, power systems, and so on. Given our present level of knowledge of economics and of the factors and conditions determining its development, however, there is no way in which the processes taking place within the discipline can be formalized fully. Hence man plays an enormous role in the system for management of the economy. Insufficient consideration of this role can lead to the view that management of the economy can be fully automated through the use of modern mathematical methods and computers. Under the influence of powerful modern methods of management, some Soviet economists and engineers did indeed arrive at the idea of something close to "pushbutton automation" that would exclude man from the management of economic life. But this is already in the past. The present system of management is usually conceived as a man-machine system.

The overall role of man in this system is assured by the fact that his intuition and experience frequently offer greater opportunity for formulating and solving problems than the existing formalized methods. Man has knowledge of the object, can single out its most important features in order to construct a formal model, and is able to use heuristic problem-solving methods.

In principle we should recognize the possibility that all the experience amassed by mankind might be formalized. As science develops, man's intuition is won from him piece by piece, and the corresponding processes are transferred to control by an automaton. In turn intuition, enriched by the formal apparatus, becomes richer and richer, and the decisions based on it become increasingly substantiated. Such a process can continue for a very long time. For this reason, in the foreseeable future man will continue to be the leading agent in the system of management.

To a great degree man's control of a not entirely formalized system is similar to the activity of a designer who is creating a new object. In principle the manager and the designer are confronted by one and the same problem — finding the most effective solution given the available possibilities and modes of action.

We know the role played by the relevant theory (for example, the theory of mechanisms and machines) in the designer's activity. But the mastery of theory does not negate intuition — "engineering art" — but rather enriches it and makes it possible to create more sophisticated equipment. Just as it is impossible to create an original new design solely on the basis of theory, without "engineering art," so it is impossible to create such a design without a knowledge of theory, solely on the basis of "engineering art." Control theory plays a similar role in the activity of the economic manager. Under modern conditions, at a time when complex objects must be controlled in the face of rapid technical progress and more sophisticated personnel, the economic manager must have special knowledge of the management of production; intuition not enriched by theory proves to be insufficient.

Unfortunately, this is not yet entirely understood in the USSR. Today there are few who will deny, for example, the enormous role played by the theory of optimal functioning of a socialist economy in the further improvement of management methods. But it is still widely held that one can speak of the value of this theory only after an optimal plan has been compiled and concrete numerical values have been obtained for the economic quantities sought. Meanwhile, methods of economic management must be improved on the basis of existing conceptions.

If, however, one understands that the role of theory consists primarily in enriching man's intuition and engaging his creative potential for producing numbers, then the practical evaluation of theory changes radically. Training cadres enriched with new ideas about the mechanism of functioning of the economy is of no less practical importance than solving specific problems by computer.

2

The Role of Marxism in the Formation and Development of the Soviet Economic System

To reveal the influence of Marxism on the formation and development of the Soviet economic system, we will try to single out what would be adopted from Marxism regardless of the level of economic development of a given country. We will thus try to separate the influence of the Marxist tenet of the need for the simultaneous victory of socialism in developed countries[1] — which was rejected by the Bolsheviks — from the general Marxist principles on which the Soviet economic system is based.

Of course, the degree to which Marxism influences the development of the Soviet economic system has changed. Initially, the revolutionaries who effected socialist reforms in Russia for the most part sincerely believed in Marxism. Later, Marxism ceased to be the only real ideology in the eyes of the powers that be. A characteristic feature of the Stalinist period was the mixture of Marxism with old Russian ideology — with faith in the tsar-father, motherland, and God.

In the years following the death of Stalin, Marxism simply became the ideological cover for the various government measures and party decisions. But this cover is not entirely innocuous; often a dear price has to be paid for it. Of course, if one or another Marxist tenet must be sacrificed in the interests of current practical goals, Soviet leaders will in principle do so.

Nonetheless, for all the cynicism the ruling powers entertain toward Marxism, it does to a large degree influence them substantively as well. This can be seen at least in the following. First, the Marxist principles on which the economy is based are extremely difficult to change, since this would require radical reforms. Second, while much of the common sense of the leaders is naïve, at the same time it does agree with Marxism. Lacking knowledge of other theories, the leaders sincerely believe their opinion is correct;

Marxism thus supports their delusions. Third, even if the leaders were to agree to the practical revision of Marxism, such a move would be hindered by the caste of priests that has arisen in the Marxist cult. Moreover, outwardly new views must be given a Marxist appearance in any case, and economists exert great efforts to do so.

Many tenets of Marxist economic theory — first and foremost the economic theory of value — support and agree entirely with common sense. Largely ignorant of other theories, the overwhelming majority of economists believe in these Marxist tenets and shape the opinion of the leadership accordingly.

Finally, let us note the nihilistic attitude toward Marxism on the part of individual groups within the Soviet intelligentsia which ignore even some valuable aspects of Marxist theory. Such nihilism is primarily the result of and a reaction to the transformation of Marxism into a religious dogma in the USSR.

It will take a very long time and drastic changes in the political climate in the USSR before the attitude toward Marxism becomes an element in the framework of pluralistic thought.

In this and the other chapters the types of Marxist influence on the functioning of the Soviet economic system mentioned above will be examined in greater detail.*

Communist Society and the Perpetual Motion Machine

In my view the basic factors that determine the influence exerted by Marxism on the formation of the Soviet economic system have been the demand to build a new, ideal, controlled society without any blueprints whatever. In this regard let us briefly remind the reader of the ideas of so-called dual control, which were developed in connection with technical systems in the works of the well-known Soviet scientist Fel'dbaum,[2] and summarize them to some degree.

---

*The Marxist views presented below, which have influenced the development of the Soviet economic mechanism, have not always belonged to Marx alone. In this sense it would have been somewhat more accurate to speak of the influence of various theories. But Marxism integrated these theories into a single system of views. Thus we will speak of the influence of Marxism on the development of the Soviet economic mechanism without going into the genealogy of individual ideas.

According to the idea of a dual control, first a model of the process is built. Naturally, this model reflects a process only to a first approximation. In implementing the model not only are products required in other spheres produced, but information required for updating the initial model is also accumulated. In connection with this, the following problem arises in the control process: under what conditions can the initial information required for building the model of a process be considered sufficient to begin using this model in the production process? Alternative possibilities here are dictated by the following circumstances:

1) to continue research and experimentation, and only after a certain level of knowledge has been reached to produce a model that is sufficient to begin introducing the process in production;

2) to begin implementation of the process having attained the possibility of more rapidly using its direct results in the fields in which they are applicable and to amass additional information needed to improve the initial model.

In principle the optimal problem arises of searching for the "switching point," that is, the state in which it becomes advantageous to accompany the further development of the model by its practical implementation. The answer to this question depends on many circumstances: on the degree of elaboration of the model; on expenditures to develop the model further outside of production; on the possibilities for initiating production using the process described in the model; on losses in production resulting from the use of a half-finished model; on the value that information derived in actual operation of the production process holds for further improvement of the model.

Naturally, other things being equal, the greater the loss in production from the use of the unfinished model, the more time and effort will have to be spent on further improving the model outside of production.

Applying the theory of dual control, one can interpret the Marxist approach to the construction of communist society in the following way.

The development of a fruitful idea evidently passes through three basic stages: (1) the dream — construction of the outline of the model; (2) doing experiments based on the dream under earthly conditions; (3) the creation of a developed theory and its correction on the basis of practical implementation.

Among many peoples the dream finds its embodiment in tales. Tales preserve in the memory of a country's people its age-old aspirations. In this lies the great part tales have played in human history. At the same time, tales have always been distinguished by the fact that they attempt to resolve these age-old problems in one fell swoop — with the aid of magical devices. In this lay their limitation.

The tales were exciting. From time to time there appeared people who tried to use real, earthly means to immediately transform a dream into reality. Since these methods were naïve, their inventors were unsuccessful. But the people preserved the memory of them in legends. The value of many legends is that they remind people of unsuccessful experiments on realizing their fabulous dreams — for example, the legend of Icarus and Daedalus.

Finally, there were two outcomes in the third stage. In the first people appeared who found effective earthly means to make the legend come true. The more ingenious the dream, the more complex the means required for its realization and the more painstaking the preliminary work to create a developed theory of the process and experimental methods for testing the effectiveness of these means. In other cases people appeared who determined that the dream was unrealizable, since its fulfillment contradicted the nature of things. This had enormous practical significance, since it shifted the orientation toward a search for ways to improve the situation slowly within the limits of possibility.

For a long time the dream of building a perpetual motion machine excited the minds of men who sincerely believed that it was possible. The great role played by the laws of thermodynamics, which were discovered in the early part of the nineteenth century, was that they revealed the prohibitions inherent in the nature of things and therefore demonstrated that the perpetual motion machine is an impossibility. Awareness of the impossibility of building a perpetual motion machine had a profound influence on the psychology of inventors. After the discovery of the laws of thermodynamics, it became clear to the talented inventor that he had to strive laboriously for a gradual increase in the efficiency of machines; the attempt to find an immediate, absolute solution to the problem doomed him to fruitlessness.[3]

A prominent Soviet mathematician once observed that scholars in the social sciences unfortunately have not yet worked out such a rule of prohibition, and some of them still want to build a society according to the principle of the perpetual motion machine.

People in many countries have dreamed of building a <u>heavenly</u> society, a society of universal abundance and prosperity on earth.

These dreams can be considered as a model for a future society if, for the time being, we do not investigate whether its construction is possible in principle.

Marxism also promised the construction of communist society. The basic principle of this society was proclaimed to be "from each according to his abilities, to each according to his needs." The illusion was created that it was possible in principle to build a society in which all the needs of the people could be satisfied.[4] Such a society cannot be built, however, for in principle all the needs of the people cannot be satisfied.

The rational element in the idea of communism is believed to be the possibility of building a society in which people will be freed from heavy, monotonous labor, in which they will have the opportunity to develop their natural potential and realize their creative abilities, and most importantly, in which the production of basic essentials will reach such a level that every member of society will be independent of the chance "whims of nature." But man cannot become entirely independent of nature, because the boundless world threatens him with cosmic catastrophes. Hence in the struggle with nature the resources available to man will always be limited.

It goes without saying that in principle, as long as dynamic society exists, the needs of people generated by their social life cannot be satisfied. The thirst for power, for example, is evidently a nonconvex function — the more power one has, the greater the thirst for power.[5]

Thus the Marxist theory of the possibility of building future society as a heaven on earth is unfounded. The dream of this society is reminiscent of the striving of people to build a perpetual motion machine. Essentially both communism and the perpetual motion machine are the same kind of phenomenon: they are systems that lack retardant forces on motion.

The sincere belief of Marxists in the possibility of building communist society makes them fanatics. The belief that communism can be attained by eliminating certain details gives them the strength to perpetrate follies aimed at destroying people who resist this idea.[6]

As regards the Soviet Union, V. I. Lenin promised his generation that communism could be built on earth. This idea influenced people's minds and helped them to reconcile themselves to existing difficulties. But this promise was forgotten. In the early 1960s N. S. Khrushchev promised anew that "the present generation" would live under communism. By then, however, the promise evoked only a smile. The point is that — unlike that other phenomenon, heaven — communism was promised here on earth. And earthly promises can be tested. For a long time it was possible to "feed" the Soviet people with promises of communism, to explain its absence as due to capitalist encirclement, to the war and its aftermath. By the 1960s, however, when the USSR had healed the wounds of the war, declared a policy of peaceful coexistence, and so on, it became more difficult to attribute the low growth rates of the standard of living to the actions of external and internal enemies. People cannot live very long on earthly ideals that remain unfulfilled. Thus the ideas of communism no longer have the power to attract the overwhelming majority of Soviet people.

Nonetheless, as an ideology communism exerts a certain practical influence on the program for shaping the future.

Thus in the late 1950s China announced its program of "great leaps forward," which were to lead to the rapid building of communism. A parallel propaganda action was undertaken in the USSR. Essentially, a program of "great leaps forward" was also proclaimed there. According to the party program, the building of communism was slated for the year 1980. To this end, starting in 1960 it was planned to overtake the developed countries in level of production within the space of several years and then in a short time to overtake them in per capita production as well.

In the late 1950s work began on compilation of the twenty-year plan for 1960-80, which was to be the concrete embodiment of the projected economic program. This plan was never compiled. But by way of developing the ideas of the plan, campaigns were organized to increase the production of individual agricultural products in comparison with the United States. As is widely known, these campaigns had a ruinous impact on agriculture.

The idea that it is possible to build communist society as a society of universal satisfaction of needs also exerts a negative influence on the development of economic science, hinders comprehension of the mechanism of functioning of a planned economy, and thus hampers its improvement. This question will be examined in detail in Chapter 5. Here we will only note that in the USSR there is still a strong belief that prices, money, and similar parameters in the price mechanism are transitory phenomena, or even the legacy of the past. This mechanism will become extinct in the future. From such a base of departure, it is difficult to reveal the features of the price mechanism that are invariant for various types of economic systems and on this basis to seek ways to improve it.

After drawing the outline of future society as a society of universal prosperity, Marx failed to examine the mechanism of its functioning: he postponed this examination to the future, to the postrevolutionary era. One can assume that such postponement was dictated chiefly by the opinion that the planned, purposeful development of communist society in itself would make everything clear and understandable, in contrast to the spontaneously developing market mechanism of capitalist society. It was senseless to waste effort on examing the details of the society of the future. Since Marx believed that communist society was ideal, he did not even pose the question of a mechanism for improving the initial model of this society.

This is the basic limitation of Marxism; it is associated with a lack of understanding of the role played by control in large dynamic systems, such as even communist society must be in the event of its realization.

An awareness of the uncertainty and diversity of types of people as basic facts[7] should have compelled Marx to seriously ponder the role of the decision-making mechanism under these conditions. Strictly speaking, democracy is such a decision-making mechanism. Developed society requires a mechanism for elaborating, selecting, and changing programs, since it is impossible to say beforehand which program is best. If one takes into account human nature, particularly the striving for monopoly, then special independent organizations — parties and an independent information service (press, radio, etc.) — are required to develop programs and to criticize the programs that are adopted.

The adoption of a certain strategy of actions on the basis of the program requires the separation of legislative power from executive power, which is concerned with the solution of tactical problems. An independent court monitors the actions of the legislative and executive powers.

To Marx, however, a democratic mechanism was only a reflection of the power of the bourgeoisie. Focusing attention on the class nature of the state, he was unable to see the general principles of functioning of the system of government in developed dynamic societies, principles realized by the state.

Marx saw future society as a system without a state, since it would be classless and there would be no one to oppress. As al-

ready noted, all other functions were considered to be so simple
that it was not worth spending time analyzing who would perform
them and how.

In the absence of even theoretical clarity with regard to the
mechanism of functioning of the proposed system, the simplest
thing for Marxists to do after they seize power is to introduce a
totalitarian regime. Relatively speaking, this government regime
is very simple. It is based on the <u>unified</u> hierarchical principle of
government and does not permit significant diversity in modes of
functioning, especially with respect to political institutions.

Such was and is the situation in Russia following the seizure of
power by the Bolsheviks — proponents of the Marxist revolutionary
doctrine governing the construction of communist society. There
is such a vast body of literature on this point that these problems
will not be examined in the present work.

Thus the Marxist theory of a future society has been based on a
false ideal — the possibility of creating heaven on earth.

The Marxists' Rejection of Experimentation
in the Social Sciences

The false goal set by Marx for the development of mankind would
not be so dangerous if he used scientific methods to verify its practicability.

The great utopian socialists also tried to build heaven on earth
and to find earthly means to realize this dream. They acted in
rather strict accordance with the principles of dual control, although they did not even claim to have scientific substantiation for
their proposals. The utopians tried to work out a model of ideal
society in the greatest possible detail so that initially people would
have at least some sense of the practicability of the idea. They
understood how great would be the losses sustained by mankind
if these untested models of the ideal society were implemented by
force. For this reason they suggested that people voluntarily organize their lives on the basis of the new principles. In their opinion the positive experiment of volunteers should demonstrate to
others the possibility of organizing their lives along new lines.
And then all people would undertake to organize their lives according to the utopian plans.

Attempts to implement these plans proved unsuccessful, however.
And even if there were positive results in the work of individual

communes, this was still not sufficient reason to conclude that organizing society as a whole along these lines would prove effective. The point is that the value orientation of people plays an essential part in the selection of one or another form of organization of human society. There may be a group of people for whom collective forms of organization of life, including production, are the most desirable. They may achieve a high level of satisfaction of their needs under such collective living. But it by no means follows from this fact that other people will also be satisfied by collective living, for they may have a different value orientation. [8] Thus, for example, in Israel there are kibbutzim based on the principles of collective organization. People in them have attained a high level of satisfaction of their needs. But this does not mean that the entire population would agree to live on kibbutzim; the overwhelming majority of the population is building its life on the principle of individualism. Thus when new forms of society are introduced on earth, one must be extremely cautious even if individual experiments have proven successful.

The experiment of the utopians that history records has become a legend of sorts. Marx did not heed the utopian experiment, however. He criticized the utopians for their "naïve" ways of creating a new society. As already noted, unlike the utopians Marx and Engels failed to examine plans for a future society in greater detail. They scoffed at attempts "to fantasize ... on the topic of the organization of the society of the future."[9]

Marx rejected the need for experimentation in the social sciences and basically emphasized demonstrating the inevitability of future society and the forces that would destroy the old world. He contrasted analytical methods in the natural and social sciences, commenting that "one does not use a microscope or chemical reagents in the analysis of economic forms. Both of them must be replaced by the power of abstraction."[10]

The point, however, is that in principle abstract thought frequently cannot grasp all the premises that are necessary to confirm the picture of a process or to find strictly indicated procedures for analyzing them. This is why experimentation is needed. The works of Claude Bernard, who argued the necessity of the experimental method in science, were already known in Marx's day at the time Capital was written. But these works, like many other outstanding accomplishments of human genius in the nineteenth century, remained outside Marx's field of vision. Thus, for example, as his mathematical manuscripts indicate, Marx tried to rediscover the foundation of differential and integral calculus, knowing nothing about the outstanding works in this field by the great French mathematician Cauchy.

Naturally, the problem of experimentation in the social sciences, as in other areas dealing with man or other types of unique objects, is extremely complex. Past experience can serve as a basis for testing a hypothesis as to the practicability of a process. But this is permissible only if analogies of the proposed design have been encountered in the past.

Communism did not exist in the past, however. Primitive societies cannot be considered communistic, since they were small tribes with a characteristically stationary life process (without the introduction of new technology) and quite a low level of consumption.

For systems with unique objects, which primarily include human society made up of individuals, it is especially necessary to find methods of indirect experimentation, that is, experimentation that is not performed on the object itself. Evidently, the degree of maturity of many sciences is determined precisely by whether they have succeeded in finding an object for experimentation that is not one of the objects being studied.

Thus in medicine, which deals with man, it is forbidden to experiment on even a single person; indirect experimental verification must be performed beforehand. Marxism, on the other hand, has consecrated its experiment on millions of people.

Even if no possibility for a preliminary experimental verification of results exists, improvement is still possible. It can be made on the principle of "reversibility" — when we are sufficiently certain that the changes made have proven unsuccessful, we can come back (as close as possible) to the starting point.

Had Marx and Engels been aware of the impossibility of experimental verification of the concept of communism, they would not have spoken of any kind of scientific socialism. But their belief in the power of logic and in the objective laws of development found through logic was too great for them to turn their attention to the need for experimentation.

Naturally, a person may be a proponent of one model of social organization or another. But if he understands its limitations, then within the framework of the democratic mechanism he can try to bring about slow, evolutionary changes by inclining the majority of society to make a change while preserving the right of the minority to disagree. This applies equally to models of socialism. In the northern European countries in which social democrats have come to power, they have tried to influence the course of development in just this way. Of course, such a mechanism is also a compromise, since it does experiment on people. But such experimentation produces relatively small changes in the system and takes place within the framework of a democratic decision-making mechanism — we can say that it rests on the principle of "reversibility."

The awareness of this compromise makes more and more urgent a program to develop indirect methods of experimentation to pretest proposals for improving the socioeconomic mechanism. Advances in model building by computer and progress in the science of ethology in the works of Nobel laureates K. Lorenz and J. Tinbergen (these studies make it possible to portray the behavior of animals in groups from the standpoint of human behavior) hold great promise for the development of an experimental base in the socioeconomic sciences.

Summing up what has been said, we can suggest that the possibility of constructing an entirely rationalized economic system in which everything is simple because the goal and potentials are clear is the realization of the Marxist method of modeling systems as applied to communist society.

This kind of clarity in the approach to the analysis of a system has many consequences.

First among these consequences are a simplistic interpretation of reality and the reluctance to deal with many real constraints.

It seems that the striving to see the world clearly, without religion, should have resulted in a profound analysis of the constraints inherent in it. But such is the paradoxical nature of the situation. The illusion of having found total clarity has discouraged a deeper study of the world and has not stimulated a more complete examination of the constraints in the world. It turned out that it was possible to be satisfied with all kinds of speculative ideas concerning the nature of the world that were not confirmed by any experiments.

All that has been said about Marxism's attitude toward the formation of future society was accepted by Lenin and the Bolsheviks and was reflected in the course of preparations for the revolution. Lenin considered the seizure of power to be the basic issue; what happened afterward was secondary.

The October Revolution in Russia was an attempt to create a new type of system without a preliminary test of the efficiency of the proposed model and the mechanism for improving it. Under these conditions the attempt to find an effective mechanism while the system functioned proves extremely costly. At the same time, it must be taken into account that the issue here is the creation of a mechanism that is rationalized to a considerably greater extent than the market mechanism, which has considerable elements of automatism and the action of "the invisible hand."

In the Soviet literature it is not yet customary to discuss the Soviet economic system as a whole in terms of a model and its experimental verification. Moreover, the created rigid system of control exerts an enormous influence on opportunities to improve the Soviet economy. Major decisions on the reorganization of socioeconomic life are usually made without preliminary experimentation. Since these decisions have a political orientation, appropriate quotations from the classics of Marxism-Leninism and speculative, disjointed arguments in favor of innovation often replace experimentation.

This happened, for example, in the creation of the regional economic councils [sovnarkhozy] by Khrushchev. No doubt, the question of how to improve territorial planning is very important. However, it is essential to find a very refined procedure to link it to the branch principle of planning.

In September 1953 Krushchev received the post of first secretary of the Central Committee of the Communist Party of the Soviet Union. Within a few years he managed to appoint "his" people to the party apparatus, primarily at the level of regional committee secretaries. Many of them were promised considerable career advancement in the event of the defeat of Khrushchev's opponents.

The strength of Khrushchev's opponents lay in the economic apparatus. Khrushchev then proposed the creation of the regional economic councils.[11] Through these councils Khrushchev attempted to disperse his opponents and deprive them of the old economic apparatus. Upon being appointed to the regional economic councils, not all of the executives from the old apparatus got new good jobs. Moreover, the supervision of the economic councils passed into the hands of the provincial [oblastnye] party apparatus. And as already noted, Khrushchev had "his people" in the regional party apparatus.

After Khrushchev became the de facto one-man ruler, combining the duties of first secretary of the Central Committee of the CPSU and chairman of the USSR Council of Ministers, he began spending a considerable amount of time on foreign policy (including travel outside the country) and on resolving other general problems. He had to transfer a considerable amount of the routine work concerning the party to F. R. Kozlov, second secretary of the Central Committee of the CPSU. The second secretary of the Central Committee of the CPSU is a rather dangerous figure. He decides many routine matters and, in practice, possesses enormous power. Secretaries of regional committees must turn to him for their daily needs and hence are largely dependent on him.

As shown by the experience of Stalin, who under Lenin actually performed the role of second secretary, such a person can be the first claimant to the post of first secretary of the Central Committee of the CPSU.

I cannot guarantee the accuracy of what is stated below, but supposedly at a session of the Politburo in 1962 Kozlov (with the support of Politburo member M. A. Suslov) demanded that Khrushchev share power, i.e., cease holding the two leading posts; he hoped to win the post of first secretary of the Central Committee of the CPSU.

The stormy Politburo session ended with Khrushchev's victory. Kozlov was removed from the party leadership and soon died of a stroke.

Meanwhile, it became clear to Khrushchev that the party apparatus lay largely outside his control. It would have been difficult to replace the many regional committee secretaries. At this point Khrushchev carried out the well-known reorganization of the party apparatus and the regional economic councils. After dividing the regional party committees into industrial and agricultural, he reappointed the secretaries of the regional committees. But the main thing he achieved in so doing was that, while essentially retaining the officials from the old apparatus, he divided them and set them against each other. Thus, for example, what kind of friendship between secretaries of the industrial and agricultural regional party committees could there be when only one of them could be the first to greet Cuba's chief Fidel Castro when he visited the region?

As regards the regional economic councils, Khrushchev hastened to remove them from the power of the regional committees. The number of economic councils was sharply reduced. The economic councils became zonal. They were subordinated to the secretaries of regional committees only as organizations situated on their territory.

The current reorganization of industry in the USSR and the introduction of associations [ob''edineniia] are also, evidently, largely of a political nature. Yet I do not want to belittle the role of associations, which in principle may prove to be effective organizations of decentralized management. But in any case there remains the serious suspicion that associations are also intended to destroy the old central

economic apparatus and subordinate the management of industry
to the local party apparatus. It is enough to recall that the apparatus of ministerial chief departments [glavki], which the
associations are meant to replace, includes approximately two
thirds of the apparatus of the ministries. We also know that the
associations can be interbranch and distributed throughout the entire USSR. From what has been said one can try to derive a hypothesis about who among the country's collective leadership finds
this reorganization advantageous and who so resolutely resists it.

And so an economic system has been created on the basis of
Marx's approach to the formation of future society that is doomed
to an agonizing search for ways to improve.

Which economic factors actually hinder such improvement and
the performance of more effective experiments during the formation of the system that has been created?

The Demand for the Destruction of Old Institutions: A Highly Important Trait of Marxism

The increased dynamism of the world's leading countries during
the nineteenth and twentieth centuries once again posed the question of ways to achieve social equilibrium. Social equilibrium
means attaining a balance of forces between the rulers and the
ruled. During this period many new ideas aimed at solving this
problem were born. Let us briefly examine only four of those
that have exerted a decisive influence on the development of the
world's leading countries.

The first belongs to the leaders of the American labor movement. They proposed balancing the interests of the rulers and
the ruled on the basis of their countervailing powers, with minimum intervention by third forces in the person of the state. This
scheme was realized through the creation of powerful labor unions
that could countervail the rulers. Equilibrium was attained in the
struggle between the rulers and the labor unions. The participation of the state in the resolution of conflicts was minimized. Such
a system also satisfied the traditions of the United States, which
were grounded in the Protestant ethic.

The second way to attain social equilibrium was proposed by
social democratic leaders. Their basic idea is that a social democratic party, which expresses primarily the interests of the ruled,
comes to power within the framework of a democratic mechanism.

In its policies it sets the task of thoroughly constraining the power of the rulers. This is achieved primarily on the basis of sharply reducing the disparity between the incomes of all strata of society through high taxes on the rulers, an increase in the role of social services (free education, medical care, etc.), etc. This mode of development has been adopted for a certain time in some Scandinavian countries and to an appreciable degree in Great Britain.

The third idea for attaining social equilibrium was born in Germany in the nineteenth century (Schaeffle and others) and was quite completely developed principally in the activity of Mussolini. According to this idea the rulers and representatives of the ruled, in the person of trade unions, should sit down at the same negotiating table. But since there may be irresolvable conflicts between them, the introduction of a third force to balance them is necessary. The state is this force. The state has a leader who expresses the interests of the nation as a whole and thereby provides the country with criteria for resolving the conflicts that arise. A bundle of forces of this type is the essence of fascist theory. It should not be confused with nazism even though fascism essentially stimulates nazi ideology.[12] Fascist regimes have emerged in countries that have a tradition of hierarchical power: Germany, Italy, Spain.

And finally, with respect to Marxism. The Marxist theory of social equilibrium presupposes that in accordance with laws predetermined by history, the ruled will destroy the ruling exploiters and will themselves in fact become the rulers. This does not contradict the idea in Marxism that future society will be classless. Since the existence of classes is determined by property relations, given the existence of only social ownership, the future society will have no classes. At the same time, as a planned society it requires control.

Marxist theory of social development required the elimination of the ruling exploiters through the most thorough destruction of old economic institutions, and first among them the basic evil of mankind: private ownership.

In this connection the inspiration of Marxism bore a religious character of universal purification from the foulness of the old world. To destroy as much of the old as possible and to begin to live in an entirely new way — this was largely the ideal of Marxism.[13] In the first years following the October Revolution in Russia there were even people who proposed destroying all the old implements of production and in their place building sunny factories and plants with new machines, delicate bridges, etc.[14]

However, given the gradual development of society, the old institutions are usually not destroyed but are only restricted in their action.[15] Continuity is thereby maintained in the use of old institutions, since the latter have also performed positive functions.

One can understand Marx's criticism of private ownership, which does have quite a few negative features. Among them are such features as: following selfish interests in the development of production to the detriment of social interests, the hypertrophied role of property owners' greed and material interests, the possibility of a high degree of personal consumption at the expense of accumulation, the threat of the advent of the rentier, etc.

At the same time, private ownership has many positive aspects in that it creates powerful incentives for man to perform active work and a sense of responsibility for the work, especially if it entails risk, independence, etc. From the political point of view all these positive aspects of private ownership predetermine its role as a powerful means for the support of democracy. Naturally, private ownership is not a sufficient condition for democracy: private ownership persists under fascist regimes. But in any event, it is an empirical fact that developed private ownership exists in all democratic countries.

The elimination of the institution of private ownership and its replacement by essentially state ownership under the banner of public ownership led to very complex problems in the management of the USSR economy. In this connection we need mention only the following three consequences.

Managers at all levels of the economic hierarchy are appointed by the appropriate higher-echelon agencies. In the appointment system at least the following two principles are taken into account: the professional qualities of the appointee and his loyalty to the appointer. The latter principle is dominant.

As a rule a manager's good professional qualities entail his initiative, his desire "to grow," which is dangerous to the higher-level executive. A professional manager who does not strive for a career is a rare exception. Executives on the higher level dream about such managers.[16]

Thus since the appointer does not want to have managers who are more competent than himself, in the appointment system the level of competence of the appointees is lowered. This principle of appointment is especially characteristic of the highest level of the Soviet economic hierarchy. At the same time, it should be noted that a manager at any level in the hierarchy (all the way down to shop chief) appoints cadres to approximately three levels below him. He does so to ensure stability of the managers and to prevent leaders at the lower levels from creating their own staff. An indirect result of this is the potential weakening of cadre loyalty through two or three levels of the hierarchy to the benefit of their professional qualifications.

All the foregoing is quite normal for any bureaucratic system. The peculiarity of the Soviet economic system is that the principle of appointment is universal.

Another negative manifestation of the elimination of private ownership is the absence of a sufficient degree of responsibility on the part of executives, which is particularly evident in the introduction of new technology.

Indeed, on the one hand the introduction of many new technical processes into industrial production may require considerable time, their success is open to question, and it is difficult to monitor interim results.

On the other hand, the state cannot, generally speaking, trust a manager who, with a certain degree of probability, promises a result in several years, especially when it is difficult to monitor his interim results. The state prefers to encourage relatively short-term investments in the creation of new technology — investments, moreover, that assure positive results.

To a certain degree one exception is new military technology, the development of which is directly monitored by the heads of state.

Finally, let us see how the abolition of private ownership influences the variety of directions in the development of science and technology. In every society there is the problem of producing consumer goods and works of art, of developing science and accumulating means for the expansion of production. Socioeconomic mechanisms differ in the way they solve this problem. One can solve this problem through the institution of private ownership. This mechanism has its own dark sides, since the private owner may spend more on personal consumption at the expense of the development of art, science, and accumulation. However, this mechanism also has its positive aspects, since it principally provides the best opportunities for pluralistic development of science and the arts and for the introduction of new technical ideas.

Given the variety in the sources for financing science and the arts, and hence the diversity in the views of their patrons, it is much simpler to develop variety in scientific and artistic trends.

Private funds largely perform this function.

If the means are concentrated in the hands of one owner, it is considerably easier for him to monopolize the development of science and the arts and to prevent diversity whatever kinds of control there are over this owner.

In its own self-interest the Soviet state sometimes promotes divergent trends; however, they are extremely unstable. Thus we know that under Stalin several design offices were created to design one type of aircraft. However, each of them could be closed at any time.

In subsequent years, following the ouster of Khrushchev, the diversity of trends in science expanded somewhat and became a bit more stable, since the top rung of the political ladder resembled an oligarchy. Oligarchs, in accord with their views on the development of a country, specifically support appropriate trends in the development of economic science. However, this diversity is also unstable, since there is the threat of a return to one-man rule (see Chapter 3 for greater detail).

Thus state ownership, which replaced liquidated private ownership, formed the basis for the totalitarian regime created in the USSR (and in the other so-called socialist countries) as the type of ownership most appropriate to this system.

In no sense does all the foregoing mean that private ownership is the sole effective form of ownership. One must carefully study the functioning of systems in which some positive economic results were achieved under similar conditions with either state or other nonprivate forms of ownership.

The experience of the USSR during the NEP period is instructive in this connection. During the NEP period the USSR had an interesting combination of state ownership in large-scale industry and private ownership in small-scale industry.[17] Of course, it must not be forgotten that this was under the conditions of a totalitarian political regime. At the same time, the level of production was low, the structure of industry was simple, and technical progress was weak.

The development experience of Yugoslavia, which introduced cooperative ownership, bears considerable interest. However, it must not be forgotten that Yugoslavia is not a democratic country. And it is difficult to define the influence of the economic mechanism proper, since a large part is played by external factors: one million of the approximate ten million members of the gainfully employed Yugoslavs go to work outside the country each year. For the twenty million people in the country's population there are approximately

40

twelve million foreign tourists a year. The country receives substantial loans from foreign countries, etc.

Still, man's accumulated experience suggests that for the present the basic way for large dynamic systems to develop property relations is evidently to surmount their negative aspects through gradual deconcentration, the banning of the rentier, etc.

His Majesty the Working Class

Finally, let us note the enormous influence exerted on the functioning of the Soviet economic mechanism by Marxist tenets on the revolutionary forces that must destroy the old society and build the new one. This influence will be examined from the standpoint of the formation in the USSR of the decisive productive force — skilled labor.

In Marx's opinion the working class is the class capable of destroying the old society and building a bright classless society. This is determined by the fact that, on the one hand, the working class is the most organized class owing to its concentration in large-scale industry. On the other hand, the working class lacks property and "it has nothing to lose but its chains and a whole world to win."

It must be said from the outset that Marx had no strict definition of the working class. From Marxist tenets it follows that the working class is a class devoid of property. In this sense the proletariat and the working class are synonyms. However, Marx and his followers tried in every way to restrict the concept of the working class, removing from it the intelligentsia as a force that serves the ruling class and receives a large income, etc. In practice the concept of the working class boiled down to people doing physical labor, lacking property, and employed in industry, construction, transport, agriculture, i.e., in the so-called material production sphere.

Marx's admiration for the working class as a revolutionary force made sense if the goal was a radical remaking of the world. It is extremely difficult to involve the developed intellectual forces of society in this process, since they perceive the impossibility of immediately building heaven on earth by destroying the old world. And they are more responsible for their actions, since they have something to lose. Of course, a certain segment of the intelligentsia will believe in this idea and will lead the masses to the revolutionary act. But nonetheless, it will be a small segment of

41

the intelligentsia, for the most part of the insufficiently educated first generation.

It was comparatively easy to incline the working class to revolution, especially in the early part of the nineteenth century in the West and in the early twentieth century in Russia, at a time when the workers' living and cultural standard was very low. Owing to its lack of education, the working class is ready to believe that it can win happiness at a single blow by taking wealth from the capitalists.

Marxist doctrine did not strictly distinguish between the influence of the production and distribution factor on society's wealth. In a number of works Marx and Engels noted the decisive role of the level of production in the workers' attainment of a high standard of living. At the same time, the theory of surplus value focused attention on the causes of the poverty of the workers, which were rooted in distribution of the product. Hence the workers got the idea that if the capitalists were destroyed in the revolution and all their wealth was given to the workers, it would be possible to build the good life through redistribution.[18]

To be sure, in his Critique of the Gotha Program Marx wrote that in future society as well, resources would be required for accumulation and for various types of social expenditures. Focusing attention on the point that everything in future society would belong to the workers themselves, he did nothing to dispel the illusion he created that the rapid enrichment of the workers could result from eliminating their exploitation.

And here we cannot say that this is a Marxist invention to take advantage of the feelings of the masses by arousing in them the illusion of possible enrichment through seizing others' wealth supposedly amassed from the exploitation of the workers. This is an old device in the hands of experienced demagogues. It is based on a law I would call "the law of psychological aberration." The essence of this law is: sharp deviations from the normal create the illusion that their elimination can resolve a corresponding burning problem man faces.[19]

This phenomenon is based on the highly efficient principle of man's perception of the surrounding world, which has a corresponding physiological basis. Experiments on the cerebral cortex of animals show that in a state of rest the motion of the biological current on an oscillograph is characterized by an almost straight line. One need only stimulate the cortex with a pulse of electrical current to produce an oscillation. If the magnitude of the charge is not changed, the functioning of the cortex will again gradually return to a line that is close to straight. These experiments at the physiological level show that in its perception an animal reacts to deviations. And indeed this is very efficient: why expend the activity of the brain on a stable situation?

A similar situation also holds true for man. (If a person looks at the same point for a long time, he ceases to notice it.) This is why it is extremely important for man's intellectual powers to correlate the action of the perception system.

Many people react quite sharply to deviations. Other things being equal, this reaction may reach a rather high level: an emotional surge. It may be negative — anger, indignation.

Social demagogues, many traits of whom existed in Marx, have used this law in their attempts to arouse the ire of the masses. The lower the cultural level of the masses, the more they believe that universal happiness can be achieved by eliminating sharp deviations from the norm in social life. In certain cases these deviations may be the more prosperous national minorities: Jews, Armenians, and so on. Fanning anger at them to the point of starting pogroms promotes an increase in the stability of the powers that be.

Thus intellectuals who sincerely wanted to build happiness on earth for the people aroused the people's passions by playing on their envy of the wealth of capitalists.

After winning power in Russia the Bolsheviks began to implement Marx's demands. Reliance on the working class was in large measure forced, since it was necessary to quickly form from its strata an intelligentsia loyal to the regime to replace the one destroyed or emigrated.

At the same time, in the interests of demagogy it was convenient to proclaim his majesty the working class the leader.[20] As before, the low cultural level of this stratum of the population was exploited. To be sure, this also had its reverse side, since Soviet workers were also dissatisfied with certain actions by the government.[21]

After Stalin determined in the 1930s that there were two classes in the USSR — workers and peasants and the stratum between them, the intelligentsia — for many years discussions ceased on who the workers were.

In the early 1960s, evidently at the initiative of the western communist parties, there was a lengthy discussion in the journal Problems of Peace and Socialism [Problemy mira i sotsializma] concerning the definition of the "working class." The implications were as follows.

Technical progress leads to sharp growth in the number of engineering and technical personnel creating new technology and in the management of more complex production. At the same time, under the influence of total mechanization and automation there is a pronounced absolute and relative drop in the number of workers. This creates the prospect of a threat to the existence of the working class in its classical interpretation as a social force that is appreciable both in importance and in size.

In the communist movement the existing concept of the working class had very substantial practical importance: in accordance with the notion of who the workers were, party cadres were formed with preference given to various groups in the party. This is why technical progress engendered the need to amend the definition of the working class in order to save communist parties as parties of the working class.

The international discussion during those years did not deeply touch internal life in the USSR and did not spread to the pages of the Soviet party press. Conservative circles in the Soviet party leadership preferred the old, customary definition of the working class. The growth of the intelligentsia in western communist parties threatened to intensify critical attitudes toward the Soviet Union. The Soviet party press returned to this discussion only later, when it became relevant to internal life in the USSR as well.

At the end of the 1960s there evidently arose major differences in the Soviet party leadership about ways to further develop the USSR. The extraordinarily high rates of production attained by Japan and West Germany, U.S. successes in space, and difficulties in internal economic development as a result of prolonged extensive expansion of production had to rouse the passions of the powers that be about the problem of the fate of Russia. This struggle of passions can be schematically pictured as follows. Among the leadership there were people prepared to place more reliance on the intelligentsia as a force that could help increase the efficiency of the Soviet economic system. They realized that the intelligentsia had to be given more freedom (as a Soviet mathematician once put it, slightly lengthen the chain on which it was tethered) and that there had to be some liberalization in the country. [22] Of course, this was merely a question of certain concessions to the intelligentsia, and not a radical reform like the abolition of serfdom in 1861. Another group of leaders insisted on a return to

44

Stalinist methods of governing (but preferably without the mass destruction of people).

The demagogy adopted by Stalin about the support of the working masses, especially of a working class understood to be made up of people doing physical labor in the so-called sphere of material production, was also normal for these leaders. They believed that it was relatively simpler to rule the working class since its desires are known: to obtain more material goods. It could easily be deceived by all sorts of promises. The working class in the USSR has no need for any freedoms that encroach on the interests of the ruling circles. Accordingly, for the stability of power it is best to rely on these strata.

Internal disputes among the leaders concerning the role of the working class somehow came to the surface. Thus in the early 1970s there was actually a debate about the concept of the working class on the pages of Communist [Kommunist], the leading theoretical journal of the party. This debate concerned both the international and the internal aspect of the problem for the USSR.[23]

Thus theoretical disputes concerning the definition of the concept of the working class have very real significance. Behind them in fact lies the selection of forces on which the given political organization will rely in its struggle for power.

In this instance Marxist doctrine is used only to conceal very specific political tasks.

On the basis of one example let us see how the debates in the late 1960s concerning the role of the working class were reflected in Soviet life.

After the 1917 October Revolution the capitalists and their "attendant" intelligentsia were for the most part annihilated or they emigrated. Thus Russia lost enormous wealth in the person of the highly cultured stratum of population that had emerged in it. Work immediately began on the creation of a new worker intelligentsia.

The first-generation intellectual was usually semiliterate. He received a formal education but did not acquire culture. The family in which he was reared did not instill in him a high level of culture. In totalitarian systems such a semicultured person is usually the best object for manipulation. He is easily convinced that he must serve the state devotedly, since it has been his benefactor, has given him a higher education, and has raised him "from rags to riches."

The issue is considerably more complex with respect to the second-generation intelligentsia. It is largely educated within its own families; the priceless capital of the nation — the knowledge and experience the intelligentsia has at its disposal — is transmitted as a legacy to the children. The second-generation intellectual receives an enormous segment of his education thanks to the persistence and help of his parents, who rear their children in their own image. For this reason the children of intellectuals do not have the same dependence on the state as intellectuals of the first generation.

While after the October Revolution the regime's reliance on first-generation intelligentsia was strictly determined by the loss of the former intelligentsia, in subsequent years it was dictated by some degree of fear of the obvious independence of the second-generation intellectuals, even though this independence was also created under Soviet power.

The immediate results of this fear were quite odd. For example, fear of the student movement in the West during the second half of the 1960s led to a sharp increase in the number of children of workers and peasants in Soviet higher educational institutions. For this purpose special workers' faculties [rabfaki] were opened under the schools. If a graduate of this faculty passed his examinations, he was admitted without competition to a higher educational institution. Graduates of these faculties and intellectuals' children entering higher educational institutions study in the same groups.

According to the idea of the authors of the workers' faculties, in each group the workers' faculty students, who are grateful to the state, would be a reliable defense against the rowdies from intelligentsia families. Since the graduates of workers' faculties have substantially less knowledge, the educational level of the students drops as a result of such "mixing of blood."[24] But these losses are compensated by a temporary increase in the political stability of the regime!

Naturally, propaganda presents this entire campaign to organize workers' faculties as a measure aimed at the social leveling of the ranks of students, thereby assuring all strata of the population equal representation in the student body.

Unquestionably, the humanization of society will inevitably be accompanied by ever greater social mobility, by the accelerated renewal of the elite, etc., which in turn will require the greater enrollment of children from various strata of society in higher educational institutions. However, if society lacks the opportunity to give all children a higher education, it should be selective and should try to attract the most capable children to higher educational institutions. It is understandably more difficult for children from less cultured and less affluent strata of society to gain admittance to higher educational institutions. For this reason, even during the highschool years it is essential to select capable children and to promote their best education. A great deal of work has been done in this regard, for example, by Academicians A. N. Kolmogorov and M. A. Lavrent'ev, who have created special boarding schools for children gifted in mathematics. Gifted children from low-income families should be given special scholarships to higher educational institutions, as is done in the United States and other Western countries. But solving the problem of the social leveling of the student body by sharply increasing the percentage of less educated children from the families of workers and peasants, as is the case in the USSR, not only results in reducing the skill level of cadres and the economic might of the nation but also corrupts people.

Thus Marxist doctrine inevitably requires the creation of a new intelligentsia from among the workers, since in one way or another a considerable portion of the old intelligentsia is lost in the process of the proletarian revolution. But subsequent reliance on the first-generation intelligentsia is by no means a direct demand of Marxism. However, a totalitarian regime created on the basis of Marxist doctrine inevitably relies on subsequently using first-generation intelligentsia. Naturally, there may be different specific reasons for this.

What has been said permits one to formulate the following law of the functioning of systems with a totalitarian regime: the totalitarian regime strives to rely on first-generation intellectuals.

3

Conflicting Trends
in Soviet Economic Science

Economic science is in essence the first of the humanities in the USSR in which a rather broad diversity of views has been permitted. This fact is all the more important because Soviet economic science is not only rigorously linked to ideology but has in its arsenal the most developed part of Marxist doctrine — the economic element reflected in Capital.

As we know, in the USSR the variety of trends in history, law, and philosophy is not yet as developed as in economics. The reasons why economic science broke the "blockade of unification," a characterization of the variety of schools existing in it, and the conditions for their stability are the subject of the subsequent exposition.

The Status of Soviet Economic Science

We know that the development of economic science was largely halted under Stalin. There existed a uniform, monolithic view of the mechanism of functioning of the Soviet economy. Such a situation in economic science was in significant measure due to the following factors.

First, no economic mechanisms existed to promote the creation of a high level of military power in a short span of time. These goals could be attained primarily by means of the noneconomic devices of coercion and a system of forced labor. The degree to which the goals were justified is, of course, another matter. As demonstrated by the experience of World War II, it is entirely conceivable that victory could have been won with significantly smaller capacities than those that existed before the war.

Second, the economic development rates proposed by some

48

economists, based on the smoothed curves of development of Western countries, did not satisfy a Stalinist political leadership striving to force the development of military might.

Third, during this period economic science could not provide sufficiently serious constructive proposals to improve the mechanism of functioning in accordance with the goals set by the dictator even within the limits in which the economic mechanism was permitted to operate (evaluation of the performance of enterprises, selection of new technologies, etc.). Since the economic theories elaborated then were chiefly based on some interpretation of the Marxist theory of price formation, the mechanism of compiling the plan in physical values became totally divorced from the price mechanism. Quite often the demands of the price mechanism would have necessitated making decisions divorced from major goals. In addition it must be kept in mind that many proposals made by economists not only did not help the dictator solve the problems he posed but could even have led to criticism of the mechanism he created. In such a situation, if sensible proposals were made even from the viewpoint of the dictator, they were crushed by the general atmosphere.

Thus during the Stalin period the major task of economic theorists was to sanctify the latest decisions of the party and its great leader as the pinnacles of wisdom. The economists were to bring to the people the supreme Marxist-Leninist teaching, particularly the works of Stalin, and to instill in the broad masses a belief in the advantages of socialism. Political economy was a very important component of ideology, and those who did it were essentially required to perform priestly functions. It was no accident that teachers of ideological disciplines in the USSR were called "priests."

The management of economic science was organized in accordance with the function it performed. Just as the system of government of Soviet society, headed by a tyrant, was organized hierarchically, so were individual domains of social life. They were also headed by petty leader-dictators responsible for the development of the field entrusted to them. The power of such a leader-dictator was further determined by the degree to which he combined theoretical and practical work. Lysenko was powerful because he simultaneously moved theory in the requisite ideological direction and at the same time constantly offered practical advice that promised rapid and decisive progress in agriculture, frequently without substantial capital investments.

Economic science was fortunate in this respect. Stalin himself was its first leader and the first economist. In the mid-1940s P. A. Voznesenskii, a member of the Politburo and deputy chairman of the USSR Council of Ministers, also tried to lay claim to the role of being at least leader number two in economic science. But this attempt was short-lived. Moreover, it was later explained, he published a "fallacious" theoretical work on the USSR wartime economy.[1]

When I wrote that economic science was fortunate in having Stalin as its leader, this was not entirely in jest. Indeed, following the death of Stalin there was no leader to direct its development: economic science became "an orphan."

Since Stalin himself was the leader in economic science, it was only provided with a "fuehrer-curator." K. V. Ostrovitianov was installed as the curator of economic science in the 1940s. He spent his time annotating Stalin, had no opinions of his own, and made no practical recommendations. For this reason Ostrovitianov could not acquire as much power as Lysenko had.

As already noted, in Stalin's time there was no diversity of views in economic science: the unified position on all substantitive questions was dominant. One and only one point of view was possible in any area. This point of view was the Marxist one. All other views were anti-Marxist.

Such a situation generated a fierce struggle for survival and correspondingly gave birth to a special type of creator-economist on the human level. Naturally, in economic science there remained some areas as yet untouched by Stalin's hand, areas on which a final opinion had not yet been expressed. The first one to seize such an area, to trumpet the claim that his position was Marxist, and to support this in print was in the saddle. An opponent would not only be disgraced but might even be sent to "not so very remote places." For this reason a "genuine" economist had to use any means to pin an opponent of his views to the mat.

This is why even today many of the economists of the older generation are so aggressive: they are accustomed to the fiercest mortal competition. It never occurs to them that today there is no mortal threat for heterodoxy within legitimate limits. All moral constraints are incomprehensible to these people, since they are accustomed to think in situations in which one would stop at nothing for survival. If one also keeps in mind that they are unable to master new ideas, that is, they cannot work more actively within new schools or occupy the same high positions they held in their own schools, their aggressiveness becomes even more comprehensible.

Of course, the extremely dark picture that I have painted of Stalin's dominance in economic science is somewhat oversimplified. There were people who attempted to develop economic science, including economic-mathematical methods. There were economists whose moral qualities remained very high despite the reigning moral dissolution. There were few such people and they had a very trying time. Nonetheless, their existence is very important, since they played the role of "mutants" that assure development in the face of changing conditions.

Thus in its structure the variety of "mutants" in the economic-mathematical school has proved quite successful. Among the surviving representatives of this trend was a man who could head it organizationally under new conditions — V. S. Nemchinov. There was a man who provided a new scientific foundation for this school — L. V. Kantorovich. There was a man who was able to expound the scientific ideas of this school with sufficient precision and clarity — A. L. Lur'e.

Academician L. V. Kantorovich, a Nobel Prize laureate, is a true innovator in the realm of economic science who has blazed new trails in its development. He is an exceptionally talented man. He graduated from Leningrad University at the age of eighteen and was already a professor of mathematics at twenty-two. He published brilliant works on set theory at sixteen. Subtly combining knowledge of functional analysis, an area new to Soviet mathematicians at that time, with the solution of practical problems, in 1938 he succeeded in solving the famous "plywood trust" problem. For this purpose he used methods that were subsequently known as linear programming.

To a mathematician this method of solving the problem and its comprehension from the standpoint of a strictly mathematical angle — the solution of the Monge problem — might have been sufficient. But the exceptional talent of Kantorovich lay in the fact that having solved this problem and having found a number of other similar practical problems, he reached the general conclusion that the national economy as a whole could also be described as an optimization problem. He further realized that the Lagrange multipliers used by him in the course of solving the problem were not simply a kind of mathematical parameter but were very profound economic categories — prices. The role of prices as a tool in the compilation and implementation of the plan, perceived by Kantorovich, is even today unclear to the majority of Soviet economists.

Of course, from the positions of the present level of development of economic science, the strengths and limitations of Kantorovich's work are obvious. But it must be remembered that these scientific generalizations were made and presented in the manuscript of a 1942 book by a thirty-year-old mathematics teacher totally cut off from Western economic thought.

For seventeen years Kantorovich tried to have his book published, and he finally succeeded. Unfortunately, it proved to be his swan song in the field of mathematical economics.

A notable group of economists who respected new ideas and disliked conservatism also survived the Stalin regime. These people promoted the development of new trends in science by being the first reviewers of new works at publishing houses, the first opponents for candidate and doctoral dissertations by scholars from new schools (and new trends cannot develop without degree-holding scholars), etc. Among them one can mention such names as Berri, Breev, Fel'd, Cheinman, Klimenko, Lukomskii, and so on.

The rejuvenation of economic science in the USSR in the mid-1950s was promoted by a general change in the country's political course. In the Report at the Nineteenth Congress of the Communist Party, G. M. Malenkov stated that Russia departed from the capitalist world after World War I, China and the other people's democracies departed from the capitalist world after World War II, and if there were a World War III, it would be followed by the final death of capitalism. In a short speech at this congress, Stalin declared that the bourgeoisie had thrown down the banners of liberty and that it was our business to pick them up. All this was evidence of direct ideological preparation for a new world war.

Soon after the death of Stalin the principles advocated in Malenkov's report were retracted. The opinion from the West that there would be no victors in the event of a new world war was gradually accepted in the USSR. The new Soviet government renounced the policy of world domination. There began a gradual transition to the old Russian policy under which Russia tried to be a world power. Having withdrawn the extraordinary goals, a new policy had to replace them. The growth of military might had to be supplemented by a rise in the people's standard of living. At the same time, the idea of achieving the goal by any means had to be abandoned. In particular, it was no longer possible to make labor camps one of the basic suppliers of labor power.

In order to attain new goals under the new conditions, it was necessary to better improve the economic mechanism. Here it is important to note that the postwar crisis-free development of the Western economic system had to affect the views of certain Soviet leaders about the need to improve the Soviet economy in the direction of strengthening market mechanisms. No matter how much Soviet propaganda praises the socialist system and no matter how fiercely it reviles the capitalist, Soviet leaders nonetheless recognize the unquestionable successes of capitalism.

It is also necessary to note that in the late 1940s and early 1950s in the West there appeared new means of economic management that were entirely suitable for the Soviet planning system, particularly for military purposes. We have in mind the input-output tables and operations research that widely employ mathematical methods and computers.

Thus in the post-Stalin period there was a practical need to develop new directions in economics and there were new opportunities to do so.

In this connection I should like to make several general comments about Soviet pragmatism which will help us understand better why economic science gained the right to a variety of views.[2]

The introduction of something new is associated in all systems with appreciable difficulties. First, there is the risk of failure. Second, the new devalues the old: not only existing technologies but people's knowledge as well. It encroaches on the interests of those people who have adapted themselves to the old and who, moreover, can no longer master the new if only by virtue of their age.

However, in Western countries the structure of society generally promotes the introduction of the new and the overcoming of conflicts that arise here, albeit also with great difficulty. If there are signs that an idea is practicable, there are usually forces in Western countries that will begin to develop it.

Soviet pragmatism is of a different type. Using the existing ideological monopoly, the people who are accustomed to the old hasten to crush the new idea and, if possible, the people behind it. But when the new idea has been implemented in practice in the West and when it has been used for military purposes, they gradually begin to beat a retreat in the Soviet Union. As one of my acquaintances put it, the USSR has a "Western complex," i.e., they believe that the capitalists do not throw money away and hence they have done a useful thing. Spurred on by fear of lagging behind the West, especially in military power, the Soviet leaders then feverishly begin making up for lost time. Here a weighty word belongs to the military.

So it was at one time <u>with atomic energy</u>. As we know, many physicists working on the atomic problems were annihilated in 1937 (the Kharkov group in particular). In 1948 the rout of physics was being prepared under the guise of a battle against idealism (like the rout in biology).

But it seems to me that physics was primarily saved by the military significance of atomic problems. Still some devastation of physics, naturally not as great as had been slated, nonetheless occurred. Thus in the physics department at Moscow State University many professors, especially Jews, were ousted, and courses in quantum mechanics and the theory of relativity were curtailed because they were imbued with idealism.

In the mid-1940s a rout was also being prepared in <u>mathematics</u>, in those branches called "pure mathematics." This impinged on the interests of a large number of famous mathematicians working in "pure mathematics." The organizer of this rout was a Leningrad mathematician (ironically with a typical Jewish name which I do not remember). Preparations were already underway for an all-union conference at which many mathematicians were to be accused of not making a contribution to socialist construction and of devoting themselves to useless abstract problems. But a handful of mathematicians somehow managed to forestall the events by showing that mathematicians were helping the military. I was told that certain works by Academician A. N. Kolmogorov figured among the arguments for usefulness of pure mathematics. We know that Kolmogorov worked in pure mathematics; but at the same time, he was also interested in applied military problems. Thus he was the author of the idea that antiaircraft guns should not be mounted rigidly but should be given free play. Free mounting promotes firing performance. This idea was supposedly adopted. At any rate, dissertations (it seems even doctoral) were written about it.

In the post-Stalin period <u>cybernetics</u>, previously persecuted, was developed. By that time it had been practically implemented in the West. The application of cybernetics for military purposes is common knowledge.

While I am not sure of the accuracy of the information, the military supposedly played a decisive role in Lysenko's ultimate fall, since they called attention to the fact that Lysenko was hindering the development of genetics and thereby the creation of new types of bacteriological weapons that the West already possessed.

Conflicting Trends in Soviet Economics

The methods of systems research, which began developing in the 1960s, are highly irritating to official philosophers, since they realize that these methods weaken their positions. Attacks on these methods were undertaken several times, particularly by the Department of Philosophy of the USSR Academy of Sciences. But these attacks were blocked by a powerful defensive screen. As in other sciences the day was saved by the use of systems research for practical purposes in the West. In particular, some years ago the status of systems research in the West was discussed by the Presidium of the USSR Academy of Sciences. The Institute of the USA presented a lengthy report portraying the development of this trend in the United States and ways to practically apply these ideas in the most important areas of government activity, the elaboration of space programs, and other major military projects.

If we also bear in mind the fact that systems research is performed by a small group of philosophers rather than an individual institute (such as the Central Economic Mathematical Institute [TSEMI], for the time being the "diamatchiki" (exponents of dialectical materialism) have evidently reconciled themselves to the existence of the "sistemniki" (exponents of systems research).

However, when the issue is new trends in science that do not promise practical utilization and that encroach upon the interests of the ruling group, these trends are still subjected to ostracism today.

The situation in biology is interesting in this respect. The dominant view is that evolution is a random mutation process and that the fittest survive in the course of natural selection. However, such an approach makes it difficult to directly answer a number of questions pertaining to the development of life, and particularly to the formation of such complex organs as the brain. The view exists that there are internal patterns in the development of life. I shall not present this point of view now; I shall only note that it is extremely difficult for the proponents of this view to develop their position. Even many geneticists who were themselves persecuted in the not so distant past are up in arms against them. Proponents of the nondominant theory of evolution are sometimes forced to work in applied areas in order to be protected from attacks by the ruling group of biologists who control the press, the awarding of postgraduate degrees, etc.

The development of the science of law is frozen.

There is no need to mention the fact that a series of sciences known in the West as the <u>humanities</u> has not yet undergone serious development in the USSR. The attempt by a group of young <u>historians</u> to use the structural method of analysis has been thwarted. An expository article against this group appeared in the journal <u>Communist</u> in the late 1960s. A. Ia. Gurevich, one of the leaders of this group of historians, was expelled from the Institute of Philosophy, where he worked on the methodological problems of history. It is true that Gurevich was later summoned to the editorial office of the journal <u>Communist</u> and told that there had been a misunderstanding, etc.; but naturally, no article of retraction was published. Gurevich was hired by a history institute. But the new school is not developing.

For a long time in the USSR <u>sociology</u> was not recognized as a science. But the significant results obtained by sociologists from the West in the investigation of specific areas of life stimulated the creation of a school of sociology in the USSR. This is evident from quite numerous surveys of newspaper readers and public opinion, the formation of plans for the social development of enterprises, etc. I do not want to assess the practical value of this here. In any case it can be said that the difficulties entailed in using it are very great.

In parallel with the development of applied sociological research there has also been development in theory. Theoretical sociological research has been motivated by the need to create intermediary sciences between applied sociological research and the foundation of Marxist sociology: historical materialism. In the mid-1960s the Institute of Applied Social Research was created, with Academician A. M. Rumiantsev as its head. Almost all of the nation's best personnel concerned with sociology were gathered at the institute. But experienced philosopher-<u>istmatchiki</u> (exponents of historical materialism) realized that they were threatened by sociological science and directed all their vast experience in ideological struggle toward its eradication. Among these fighters were Academicians Konstantinov and Mitin, renowned veterans of the ideological battles of the 1930s. They have skillfully exploited the weakness of sociological science and the fact that in the USSR developed Western sociological theory cannot be applied directly at the level of the nation as a whole (compare this with the situation in economics). Lacking such a base and clearly encroaching on ideological principles and "stable" ideological cadres, sociology has doomed itself as a science.

56

What is more, the existence of an academic institute of sociology created yet another channel of information on social processes taking place in the nation. Unlike party agencies and the KGB, i.e., closed "sociological" institutions supplying materials in closed forms, this institute was open in principle. (It is no accident that there were all sorts of rumors concerning the transfer of the institute to the charge of the Central Committee of the CPSU, which would have made it closed.)

And in the early part of the 1970s the Institute of Applied Social Research was crushed. The overwhelming majority of the institute's leading associates were fired from the institute for one reason or another. The "istmatchiki" celebrated their victory. Henceforth the basic task of the institute amounts to illustrating the principles of historical materialism.

The Structure of Soviet Economic Science and Relations between Economists of Various Schools

We can conditionally divide economists in the USSR into three major classes from the standpoint of their attitude toward the existing economic system: conservatives, guardians, and modernizers. The conservatives include economists who favor a return to the old strict Stalinist system of government in which administrative methods predominated. We should note that these economists reflect the views of a large number of practical workers who also dream of returning to the "blessed" Stalinist times, when there was rigid discipline in the country, when there were no difficulties, for example, with labor power — strict assignments to enterprises and camps with millions of prisoners provided enterprises and construction sites with cheap labor power.

The guardians are economists who are prepared to do everything in their power to protect the existing economic system. Such economists are in the overwhelming majority.

The modernizers are economists who want to improve the existing economic mechanism.

But in order to better understand the proposals of the economists in the various groups, we must also provide some classification of Soviet economic science proper. Using the Soviet terminology, we can conditionally divide economic science in the USSR into two large parts: political economy and applied economics. Applied economics includes functional problems (finances and credit, labor, etc.), branch-territorial problems, and national economic planning. In what follows we shall examine mainly political economy, which we can conditionally divide into three parts: engineering, social, and philosophical. The engineering part of political economy is concerned with a range of questions for which precise answers can be obtained from mathematical models and experiments. This range of problems includes the mechanisms of functioning of hierarchical systems that use all kinds of economic parameters, including prices, money, etc.

The social part of political economy includes such problems as selecting classes of a system's mechanisms of functioning (market and centralized), forming sources of monetary resources for enterprises (credit, own resources, subsidies, etc.), and associated methods of forming agencies of management (appointment, election, "self-appointment," etc.).

The philosophical part of political economy works on questions entailed in defining socialism, communism, etc.

Each of these parts of political economy directly affects ideology to a greater or lesser degree. Every economist or economic institute has his or its view of all the parts of political economy. If these views are not expressed directly or indirectly, we will consider them guardians, since official opinion is tacitly supported.

I would like to focus greatest attention on the modernizers. All modernizers have in common that they are against the existing order and thereby conflict with the interests of the people who stand for this order and who are its guardians. However, there are differences between modernizers.

Various groups should also be noted among the modernizers. The criterion for classifying modernizers will be the relationship of their proposals to political power, in other words, the influence of their economic proposals on restricting political power.

We emphasize such a criterion because political power is the last thing the powers that be are willing to relinquish in any way. To strengthen their political power they are even willing to surrender a substantial portion of their great achievement — Marxist ideology. It is extremely important to bear this in mind in order to understand the nature of various groups of modernizers. The stability of certain groups of modernizers that revise Marxist ideology stems in considerable measure precisely from the fact that in so doing they actually strengthen the political might of very conservative circles. And conversely, the attempt to be Marxist sometimes characterizes modernizers of quite leftist persuasion who want to greatly weaken the political power of the powers that be. These modernizers are subjected to more intense persecution and are less protected.

Thus, using the criterion mentioned above, we can distinguish three groups of modernizers. The first is the most radical: it wants to organize a free economy within the framework of a democratic system. Soviet dissidents advocating the democratization of Russia usually make radical demands of this type. Such demands were most completely reflected in the program developed by Czechoslovak economists in the mid-1960s for building "socialism with a human face."

We can call the second group of modernizers oppositionists. They try to make proposals for improving the mechanism of functioning of the socialist economy which, although not directed at eliminating the existing political system, nonetheless require limitations on political power.

Two subgroups can be delineated within this group of modernizers. The first tries to modernize the economy from below on the basis of experiments they perform. These experiments have demonstrated the possibility of new forms for organizing production that promise a significant economic effect. Since under these new forms of organizing production collectives of personnel become largely independent, the party apparatus is left with significantly fewer functions, with all the ensuing consequences.[3] We should note that this group of oppositionists has not impinged on the existing political economy. The explanation here is primarily that the experiments performed by them have been confined to relatively small collectives in which the organization of production does not require economic theory. Moreover, these reformers have not yet reached the level of possible changes in the management of the national economy as a whole that require a developed economic science.

The second subgroup of oppositionists has attempted to effect reforms from above within the entire national economy. We have in mind the well-known economic reform proclaimed in 1965 by A. N. Kosygin, a member of the Politburo and chairman of the USSR Council of Ministers. As we know, this reform was stopped largely because it called for limiting the role of the Communist Party. We should also note that in an economic sense as well, the reform was poorly prepared, since it was based on the dominant economic theory. As we have already stated above, in the 1930s this theory could not ensure the introduction of a developed economic management mechanism. For the same reasons it would have been unable to ensure the functioning of the Soviet economy on the basis of developed economic principles in the 1960s as well.

If we study the works of economists who participated in the economic substantiation of the reform (for example, those of E. G. Liberman), it is evident that along with a few interesting comments, on the whole the conception once more amounts to the accepted interpretation of Marxist doctrine.

I should like to dwell in somewhat greater detail on the third group of modernizers, whom we shall call reformers. They have attempted to effect changes in the existing economic mechanism while keeping political power basically inviolable.

In some sense we can say that the group represented by mathematician N. N. Moiseev, corresponding member of the USSR Academy of Science, was at one time the most radical among the reformers. In one of his articles published in the newspaper Izvestia in the late 1960s, he boldly wrote that it was necessary to create a scientifically substantiated decision-making mechanism and to include scientists in it.

The development of this trend is associated with hypermodernistic views on the functioning of systems under conditions of uncertainty.[4]

The second subgroup of reformers wanted to change the technology of planning quite radically and proposed ideas on the optimal functioning of an economy. Representatives of this school left all power to existing authority and, moreover, provided it with new planning tools. Among these reformers is the group of Soviet economists represented by such administrative figures as Academicians A. G. Aganbegian and N. P. Fedorenko. One can assume that this group of reformers exerts the strongest pressure on the development of Soviet economic science, particularly on the engineering part of political economy. Yet it is precisely the development of this school that quite starkly raises the question of the validity of the Marxist labor theory of value.

For now we will not pursue a discussion of this theory. We will only note that the theory of optimal functioning of an economy dispenses with the labor theory of value and advances another interpretation of the nature of the price formation process to replace it. According to this theory the need for prices stems from the nature of any economic system in which individual participants have an option in making decisions on input-output proportions.

From such an interpretation of the nature of prices it follows that they are not a rudiment of capitalism and that they are not a temporary phenomenon. Prices must exist in the most distant future as well, even under communism, since there options will continue to exist for participants in the optimal decision-making process. Naturally, such an approach contradicts the assertions of Marxist theory, which considers the price mechanism the result of a spontaneous market economy.

The third subgroup of reformers is primarily concerned with improving the existing mechanism of functioning of the economic system. Roughly speaking, two types of such economists can be delineated: some of them try to improve this mechanism on the basis of the "manual" technology of planning and management, while the others try to improve it by using the mathematical methods of input-output tables and the computer technology they entail.

A large number of economists fall under the first heading. It is sometimes difficult to distinguish them from the guardians, since it is hard to find guardians in pure form: they all have to admit certain inadequacies in the economy. But all representatives of this type of reform are somewhat more radical than the guardians. They make more substantive proposals for improving the planning and management system, e.g., such national economic proposals as a shift to building the price formation system on the formula which involves interest on capital.

Quite a notable group of economists belongs to the second variety of reformers. Administratively speaking, the economic wing of this type is represented by V. V. Kossov, deputy chief of the Summary Department of USSR Gosplan, and Academician A. N. Efimov, director of the Scientific Research Economics Institute of USSR Gosplan, who advocate introducing input-output tables, and so on. We shall subsequently touch on some aspects of the activity of the representatives of this type. Let us note here that Academician Glushkov, one of the leaders of the economic-mathematical school, is an extreme spokesman for this type of reform. Even though he is vice-president of the Ukrainian Academy of Sciences and the director of the Kiev Institute of Cybernetics, he still plays a very prominent role in the all-union effort to introduce computers in the national economy.

Glushkov does not know economic science and has no desire to know it. Like every type of "repudiator," he does not realize that he is using the most primitive economic conceptions that are the result of his "common sense." He simply tries to create a rigidly centralized system and to shift the entire burden onto computers, even to the point of organizing a system to combat theft through the payment of wages and the purchase of commodities by computer.

As follows from the nature of the universe, there must be a struggle between various trends in economic science. And this struggle is going on. The guardians are struggling against both the conservatives and the modernizers. The conservatives and the modernizers are fighting among themselves. A struggle also is in progress within various groups.

First, let us discuss the struggle of the "dissidents" with the "oppositionists" and "reformers." It is hard to achieve unity between these groups because they have opposing methods of influencing the political system. The dissidents would like to see a radical change in the political structure, while the oppositionists and reformers want to see only its restriction or preservation. While the dissidents tend to unite the powers that be, the latter two groups try to split them and to gain the support of the authorities for the introduction of new ideas.

Among the radical, dissident, and oppositionist economists in the USSR there are in fact no specialists who have mastered the modern methods of economic analysis. While I have enormous respect for the courage of the radicalists who are attempting to bring about socioeconomic reform, at the same time I would like to note that many of them, while quite progressive in the social part of political economy, adhere to guardian and even conservative ideas in its engineering part. They defend Marx's labor theory of value and try within its framework to make recommendations on improving the mechanism of functioning of the socialist economy. Thus one of the active radicalists gives lectures like "K. Marx's Labor Theory of Value and Improving the Mechanism of the Socialist Economy."

The paradox of the situation lies in the fact that in the USSR the attitude toward the law of value is frequently the litmus paper that reveals one's affiliation with the proponents of decentralization and the strengthening of market relations. This is because the law of value is the personification of the market; it is synonymous with the market. At the same time, for the majority of economists the Marxist theory of value is the truth. They believe that this theory correctly explains the market mechanism. This is why economists who reject the law of value are classified as centralizers despite the fact that they contrast to it the conservative Marxist view that under socialism the law of value will not operate and everything will be strictly planned, or they adopt Western theories of values and associated ideas on the construction of flexible mechanisms for the economy's functioning.

Here we face some significant negative aspects of the activity of the radicalists.

A large industrial society like the USSR cannot be governed on the basis of a primitive conception of the market economy. Yet a considerable segment of the intelligentsia in the USSR, including a number of economists, seeing the successes of Western countries but not being familiar with their economic mechanism, believe it would be best to shift to the system of free enterprise and the free play of competitive forces, which they picture very primitively. They view this mechanism as an auction, a bazaar, i.e., as a system in which a producer offers his commodity and sells it depending on the demand for it. There is usually no awareness that the market is a developed mechanism of horizontal relations directed toward anticipation, with a complex structure of institutions: banks, stock exchanges, etc. Moreover, under the conditions of dynamic, large-scale production, market mechanisms must be coordinated with vertical mechanisms. The history of Western economics provides evidence for this: the development of vertical mechanisms moved both from bottom to top (the formation of multilevel hierarchical complexes in the course of competition) and from top to bottom (awareness of the need to strengthen the role of the state in the economic mechanism). Everything hinged on the strength of the relationships between the vertical and horizontal mechanisms. In measuring this strength an enormous role in economics is played by the humanities, which help shape institutions; at the same time, on many issues mathematical methods can help as they win this right from the humanities. Such a consideration is not common among radical Soviet economists. Although they perceive the advantages of a market economy, they do not sufficiently consider the question of how the market relates to the state. It strikes them as all very simple and a matter of common sense.

The role of the humanities in the development of economic theory is determined principally by the fact that every country has its own particular features which must be considered in the process of forming an economic mechanism. Failure to understand the peculiarities of the influence exerted by a country's culture on the development of its economic mechanisms encourages attempts to blindly imitate, to mechanically transfer to the USSR the experience of various Western countries, with all the ensuing negative consequences.

A struggle is also going on between the oppositionists and the reformers, even though they are apparently united by the great similarity of their political positions. The main reason for the incompatibility of these groups is that each has tried to guarantee the victory of its views. The oppositionists believe, and not without foundation, that if the ideas of the reformers were adopted, this would create among the rulers the notion that a way of "saving Russia" had been found, and oppositionist views would be rejected.

A rather fierce struggle is also in progress within the reformers' camp. Its causes are the same as in the relations between the oppositionists and reformers. The various groups of reformers actually intend only to replace one monopoly in the economic realm with another, to replace one technology of management with another, albeit a more sophisticated one.[5]

These are some aspects of the relations between various groups of Soviet economists.

An extremely characteristic feature of the status quo in Soviet economic science is that it is frequently impossible to say whether a given economist or economic institute is progressive or conservative as a whole. The point is that only a few economists are conservative or progressive in all parts of political economy. An economist is usually progressive in one direction but conservative in another. The terms progressive and conservative can only be used relative to the existing conditions. As regards an absolute evaluation of the schools themselves, all trends are necessary. The only exceptions are those trends whose examination as a whole is amenable to the action of the law of the excluded middle (this applies primarily to the engineering part of political economy).

The following general conclusion can be drawn: relative to the existing conditions, the majority of the leading young Soviet economists and economic institutes are progressive in their works on the engineering segment of political economy, and they are conservative in the social and philosophical portions. Conversely,

some leading Soviet economists of the older generation are conservative in their works on the engineering and philosophical parts
of political economy, and they are progressive in the social segment.

From the standpoint of a possible preservation of the diversity
of views in economic science depending on relations between
economists, the following can be posited. The severest critics of
pluralism in economic science are economists of the older generation who inherited the Stalinist style of scientific work (this style
has already been described above). Among the young economists
and the economists of the middle generation, who for the most
part were reared in the post-Stalin period, thugs are now quite
rarely found: the influence of the external environment makes itself felt. But if the environment changes, quite a few thugs will
presumably be found among the new generation of economists as
well, if only because the majority of them do not have and are not
now getting appropriate knowledge about new trends in economic
science.

The Relations of Soviet Economists
with the Party Leadership

We will now examine the attitude of the authorities, i.e., the
Politburo, toward various trends in economic science during the
post-Stalin era.

The spirit of reform dominated during Khrushchev's time. It is
even possible that Khrushchev was prepared to support the oppositionists: for various reasons he was sometimes inclined to limit
the power of the party. The post-Khrushchev era has been a time
of equilibrium between conservative forces and the modernizers.
Evidently, the overwhelming majority of representatives of various
groupings in the Politburo were particularly opposed to dissident
economists — the left wing is always the most dangerous for
authoritative systems, since it calls for creating a society with a
division of powers and their restriction, compulsory change in accordance with the law, and an economic mechanism suitable to this
society. The right, conservative wing is also unacceptable to many
of the authorities. But they are more tolerant of it because it does
not object in principle to the foundations of the existing social
mechanism and its economic system but only demands that they be
made much more rigid.

We assume that modernizers in the Politburo were represented primarily by oppositionists, who by that time were able to offer an alternative program of development, the so-called economic reform. The reactionaries evidently adhered to the view that it was necessary to return to Stalinist methods, and they did not combine this notion with any serious proposals to somehow improve those methods.

For a long time, until the end of the 1960s, Brezhnev's role was probably to balance these two opposing groups in the Politburo. The oppositionists in the Politburo could not win, since party functionaries guarding the inviolability of party privileges had a great deal of power. Despite the many maneuvers by the opposition,[6] it was nonetheless in fact forced to halt the economic reform and even to turn back in some respects: the role of physical indicators in the enterprise plans was again intensified. Opposition economists proposing that the economy be improved from above were criticized.

As for opposition economists who proposed improving the economy from below, the Politburo members supporting them were evidently forced to curtail their activity as well. The existence of this support can be judged from such facts as speeches by G. I. Voronov, a former member of the Politburo, in defense of the integrated links in agriculture which embodied the new forms of organization of production. A number of Politburo members were opposed to these links. It is obvious that a successful experiment with integrated links on the "Akchi" State Farm in Kazakhstan was thwarted in 1971 through the direct connivance of certain Politburo members. I. Khudenko, the organizer of the experiment, was imprisoned on trumped-up charges, and he died in jail in November 1974.

Evidently, it was the inability of any one group to win that led to the increased activity of Brezhnev. He proposed a guardian policy. Under this policy urgent problems in the country's development were to be solved at the expense of external forces — the Western world. A significant improvement in relations with the West made it possible to hope for a strengthened position in the Far East in the struggle with China, enemy number one, largely through the transfer of troops, the withdrawal of some armed forces from Eastern Europe, to say nothing of the direct disruption of a closer alliance between the West and China. Moreover, credits might be received from the West for the expansion of industrial production, especially in the Soviet East; the West might supply new technology, particularly military technology, etc.

Improved relations between the USSR and the West over a long period of time are hampered, however, by the incompatibility of democratic and autocratic systems and the lack of guarantees by the Soviet Union that it will fulfill its long-term agreements. Hence the West is very cautious in offering credits and other aid. Thus the guardian policy, like the centrist, is relatively unstable.[7]

In order to grasp possible ways to further develop economic life in the USSR, one must examine more carefully the present structure of the reactionary forces, since they are rarely found in pure form. We can assume that among the reactionaries who dream of a return to Stalinist times there are also those willing to somehow modernize Stalinism. It is likely that the most extreme Stalinists are in the minority. The program of such extreme forces — the program of Russian national socialism — is reflected in I. Shevtsov's book In the Name of the Father and the Son. (There were persistent rumors that Politburo member Polianskii supported the publication of Shevtsov's book.)

Many Stalinists want to return to the "bright times" with a certain degree of modernization. Naturally, reactionaries of this type must close ranks with such modernizers as the reformers, since the latter do not urge limitations on political power. Certainly there are also serious problems of compatibility in this "union," but they are far easier to resolve.

What then brings the reactionaries close to the reformers? It is not only the need for the reactionaries to present their opponents with a more refined program: the demand for a simple return to the past is not sufficiently persuasive. Reactionaries also need a growth in military power and therefore are prepared to use new means if those means do not contradict their political power. Thus reaction does not contradict the possibility of introducing new means if they make it possible to strengthen the regime. However, the introduction of such new means sometimes entails the need to forego to some degree ideological principles, or more precisely, the interpretation of them that has become dominant and that is preserved by tens of thousands of their priests. Thus, as experience shows, these reactionary forces are willing to pay for the possibility of strengthening the regime by making ideological concessions.

In order to gain a better understanding of the attitude of reactionary circles toward reformers, let us examine this question on a more differentiated basis, using attitude toward the economic-mathematical school as an example. As we have seen above, the economic-mathematical school is reformist. But it irritates the authorities because it is linked to the direct rationalization of their own work. Since the authorities are directly involved in the planning mechanism, lack of knowledge of the new methods interferes with their work. This emerged quite starkly with respect to the reformist subgroup that proposed improving the economic mechanism on the basis of decision-making theory and including scientists in this mechanism.

It should be noted that the direct inclusion of scientists in the decision-making mechanism is by no means necessary and, generally speaking, is not a new phenomenon. Experience has shown that the participation of major scientists in the nation's government has produced varying results. Such major economists as Turgot and Schumpeter proved ineffective as ministers. Yet Böhm-Bawerk, Wieser, and Keynes exerted an immense positive influence on the economic development of their countries when they were drawn into government.

I do not know of any cases in which the involvement of major mathematicians in the government of a nation produced good results. Napoleon, who was a rather well-educated person himself, tried to involve a large group of scientists in the government. At one time a mathematician of Laplace's stature was appointed minister of internal affairs. However, it quickly became apparent that Laplace was not coping with his duties, since he overlooked a major conspiracy. It is said that Napoleon removed Laplace from his ministerial post for applying the ideas of infinitely small magnitudes to infinitely large affairs of state.

At any rate, the idea of drawing scientists into the highest agencies of government is evidently foreign to all present rulers who are afraid that scientists will be an alien element in their milieu: after all, in nature there are also limitations on cultural compatibility. For example, the call by N. N. Moiseev, mentioned above, for involving scholars in the decision-making mechanism did not find support among the rulers. Indeed, in the early 1970s Moiseev was not even invited to the All-Union Conference on the Application of Mathematical Methods and Computers in the National Economy, which was very representative and was attended by several members of the Politburo.

A trend toward improving the economic mechanism through automation of the existing planning technology is much closer to the position of the authorities. Yet it is possible that even reactionaries in the Politburo fear Academician Glushkov, the leader of this school, since he wants to automate everything under the sun. Given such a "comprehensive" approach to automation and his enormous thirst for power, Glushkov is somewhat dangerous. But he is needed for the "cause." Judging by the way Khrushchev removed Marshall Zhukov, we can assume that the autocrats will be able to get rid of the technocrat if he oversteps his mark.

The reformist trend evidently most acceptable to conservative forces in the Politburo is optimal planning of the national economy, since it promises to increase production effectiveness and does not entail including scientists in the country's political leadership.

Moreover, while Glushkov and Moiseev are genuine doctors of mathematics (their academic titles were not awarded for scientific services), Academician N. P. Fedorenko is by comparison not a scientist at all. He is, however, a gifted person in his way and is quite skilled in getting power. And this makes it easier for him to maintain contact with the powers that be. He is one of the few reformist leaders who is culturally quite compatible with the ruling clique.

Finally, a central question is entirely natural: What are the political premises for the stability of this diversity?

Diversity of opinion and competition were also allowed during Stalin's times in specific fields of technology that were of decisive importance. Thus in the aircraft industry parallel offices headed by Tupolev and Miasishchev were created to design heavy bombers. Fighter plans were designed in offices headed by Iakovlev and Mikoian-Gurevich. But this was artificial competition, fostered and controlled, subject at any moment to elimination from above. Miasishchev was removed from his job several times then rehired.

It is also known that during the Khrushchev era competition was permitted in rocket design organizations. One such organization was headed by Chalomei, who sometimes beat his competitors not so much with the quality of his output as by the fact that he had Khrushchev's son working for him. He and the son would carry petitions to the Central Committee of the CPSU (soon after Khrushchev's removal his son went to work at the Institute of Electronic Control Machines).

During the Khrushchev era the revivification of economic science began. It was accompanied by the creation of new structural formations, in short, new economic institutes (laboratories), with new views on the development of the economy. As before, however, scientists could not be certain of their future, since their views usually could only be criticized or ignored by the leadership. All

positive proposals by economists used by the leaders were presented in the name of the leader. In 1958, before the reorganization of the machine and tractor stations (MTSs) and the sale of
machinery to the collective farms, Khrushchev decided to "con-
sult" the experts. He invited agrarian economists, personnel
from the Ministry of Agriculture, collective farm chairmen, and
so on, to a conference. Among those present was V. Venzher, a
doctor of economic sciences and a well-known Soviet economist.
In his day Stalin had used his work Economic Problems of Socialism in the USSR to severely criticize Venzher and his wife Sanina
for their proposal to reorganize the MTSs and to sell the machinery to the collective farms. Khrushchev had known Venzher for
a long time, almost since the 1920s. Venzher had been a Red
Guard in the Khamovnichesk District in Moscow during the revolution and later was involved in party work, which is how he met
Khrushchev. Thus Khrushchev was virtually on a first name basis
with him. Before the conference Khrushchev said roughly the following to Venzher: "Don't think that this is your proposal: your
proposal was different and erroneous." Such an attitude toward
the proposals of economists stemmed, on the one hand, from the
fact that the head of state, by virtue of his functional role as the
head of government, tried to show the people that he was the cre-
ator of new ideas and, on the other hand, from the fact that these
proposals themselves were of a comparatively specific nature,
were the fruit of the individual activity of individual economists.

The only exception to this attitude toward the opinions of economists during Khrushchev's time may have been the case of doctor
of economic science E. G. Liberman. His proposals to improve
the economic mechanism, which revolved around the intensification of the role of profit, were advertised — they were published
in the central party press. But later, when the economic reform
was begun after Khrushchev's removal, Liberman was forgotten.
Yet none of the party leaders had been officially named as author
of the reform. Thus even though variant views on economics were
allowed, there nonetheless remained the same atmosphere of ano-
nymity for economists when government decision-making was
involved.

At the same time, the post-Khrushchev era saw both the old
economic institutes and the new ones created under Khrushchev,
with their new trends in the development of economics, flourish
and develop. Since the mid-1960s the diversity of points of view
on the development of economic science has been represented not

only by individual economists — this was characteristic of scientists at the Institute of Economics, for example — but by organizations as well. Now the government frequently examines proposals by heads of large collectives rather than by individual scientists. Among these collectives one can single out at least the Central Institute for Mathematical Economics (TSEMI) and the Institute of Cybernetics of the Ukrainian Academy of Sciences.

The diversity of schools evident in economic science also has a firmer political basis today. Competition between these institutes is no longer organized by one person; it is based on oligarchic, or so-called collective, leadership. This situation evidently emerged because after the ouster of Khrushchev there was no single dominant group in the Politburo. There might be several powerful groups in the Politburo, not fully formed or stable. Each of them needs proposals to set against competing groups. Hence they strongly support the institutes that elaborate the proposals for them. The equilibrium between powerful opposing groups in the Politburo assures the existence of these organizations.

I shall use the following example to try to prove this hypothesis about how the nature of the diversity of views on improving the economic mechanism has changed since the mid-1960s.

Three issues of the journal Planned Economy [Planovoe khoziaistvo] for 1972 carried three articles by doctor of economic sciences A. Kats under the single, rather pretentious title "Belated Admissions and Fruitless Borrowings." They exposed the bourgeois essence of econometric research in the West and were directed against Soviet scientists conducting economic-mathematical and econometric research on the development of the Soviet economy based on the use of the production function. The very fact that there were three articles in one journal by the same author in the same year is an unusual phenomenon for the Soviet press. A journal usually prints one or, very rarely, two articles by the same author in a single year. The length of each article was also unusual for Planned Economy: the first article in issue no. 7 ran eighteen pages (91-108), the second in no. 9 occupied twenty-one pages (107-27), and finally, the third in no. 10 ran nineteen pages (103-21). An article devoted to an important theoretical problem usually does not take up more than fourteen pages in a journal. In addition to all this, in order to increase the length of Kats's articles, a large part of the text was set in brevier. Moreover, if one considers the pretentious style of the articles and the procedures in Soviet journals, it becomes obvious that the authorization to print these articles could have been given only at a very high level (as high as a secretary of the Central Committee of the CPSU or member of the Politburo).

Later, issue no. 5 of Planned Economy for 1973 carried both an article by Iu. Belik, "Scientific Forecasting in Long-term Planning" (pp. 24-35), which was directed against mathematical methods used to forecast economic development, and an article by Ia. Kronrod, "Theoretical Problems in the Optimal Development of the National Economy" (pp. 80-92), aimed at the concepts of optimal functioning of the socialist economy elaborated at TSEMI. All three authors thundered against the new trends in economic science from the lofty positions of Marxism-Leninism and the decisions of the Communist Party.

In the early part of June 1973, Pravda unexpectedly published a paragraph signed by an unknown economist named Solov'ev which criticized the articles by the authors mentioned above. They were accused of writing against the decisions of the Twenty-fourth Party Congress that fostered developing the economic-mathematical trend. The criticism was also in the best tone of the party press. When my friends and I discussed this paragraph in Pravda, we were extremely upset by the tone of the criticism. The most reactionary means had been chosen to defend progress.

The matter also had its amusing side. The last names of two of the authors — Kats and Kronrod — were Jewish, and the name of the third — Belik — resembled a Jewish name (in fact Belik is pure gentile; he works at the Central Committee of the CPSU, which precludes his Jewish nationality). During those days many of my acquaintances who had nothing to do with economics called me and asked: "Is this the start of another anti-Semitic campaign?" The tone of the articles and the Jewish names of the authors prompted the view that progressive Jews were being maligned for criticizing the Party's decisions. And it seems quite evident that only a member of the Politburo could sanction the publication of such an article in Pravda.

In the latter part of June 1973 Planned Economy, of course, organized a discussion, or more precisely a condemnation, of the article in Pravda. Therefore the rather lengthy account of this conference carried in Planned Economy (no. 10, 1973, pp. 152-57) of course made no mention of the article in Pravda, claiming that this was only a session of the editorial collegium of the journal, organized with the participation of scientists, practical planners, and representatives of the press solely to "continue the discussion of problems in the theory and practice of national economic planning."

This very representative assemblage was attended by approximately 200 persons from various scientific and nonscientific Moscow institutions, including the Academy of Social Sciences attached to the Central Committee of the CPSU. There were forty speakers. Thirty-eight of them, including all the authors of the articles in Planned Economy, condemned the article in Pravda. Nor should it be forgotten that Belik works in the apparatus of the Central Committee (he holds the position of consultant, which is somewhat higher than an instructor) and he too spoke against the central organ of the Central Committee of the CPSU.

Some of the speakers scoffingly demanded that the author of the article in Pravda attend the meeting, realizing that the economist Solov'ev did not exist. Only two persons — E. I. Kapustin, director of the Institute of Economics of the Academy of Sciences, and V. V. Kossov, deputy chief of the Summary Department of Gosplan — mildly supported the article in Pravda.

The collegium of USSR Gosplan also discussed the article in Pravda. Even though a resolution on the "anti-Marxist character of many branches of the economic-mathematical trend" had already been prepared and the speakers attacked TSEMI, the first session of the collegium ended in failure for its organizers. Academician Nekrasov, chairman of the Council for the Study of the Productive Forces — an organization that is subordinate to Gosplan — addressed the collegium and declared his disagreement with the criticism of TSEMI. He added roughly the following words to his declaration: "Science can get along without Gosplan, but not Gosplan without science." Nekrasov was supported by several other people.

When he saw what was happening, N. K. Baibakov, chairman of USSR Gosplan, who headed the collegium, interrupted the meeting and said that it would be necessary to return to this question. And indeed, in September 1973 the collegium reexamined this issue and adopted the prepared resolution.

But in October 1973 there was a conference of economists organized by the Science Department of the Central Committee of the CPSU. (Previously there had been a similar conference of philosophers. The Science Department observed the state of affairs in ideological disciplines.) At this conference at the Central Committee of the CPSU, all the leading reports were presented by reformers working on the new trends. Among those taking part in the discussions, the majority either belonged to the new schools or supported them. We can assume that both the articles in Planned Economy and in Pravda and the reports at the Central Committee conference were sanctioned by various members of the Politburo.

Various reasons might have prompted certain members of the Politburo to criticize the application of mathematical methods in economics. The simplest is conservatism, the preservation of the existing economic mechanism. But it may also be assumed that there were other reasons for such action, including the following. For some members of the Politburo sympathetic to the idea of economic decentralization, the application of mathematical methods and computers is a symbol of political conservatism and the strengthening of the centralized political system. On the other hand, for the politically reactionary members of the Politburo, mathematical methods in economics are at times very attractive, since they promise to increase the effectiveness of the operation of the economic system while preserving intact their political power. And hang ideology in the meanwhile. In any event, support for applying mathematical methods and computers in economics also comes from members of the Politburo who cannot be accused of aspiring to political liberalization.

At present it is difficult to say what the future holds for economic science in the USSR. Will it be able in the future to preserve its diversity, will it again be taken over by a single doctrine, perhaps even by the theory of optimal functioning of a socialist economy? It is hard to answer this question. The answer depends on the nature of the future political structure of power in the USSR. But in any case the struggle in economic science continues.[8]

II

Economic invariants and their use in the Soviet planning system

4

Methods of Describing Economic Systems and Representation of the Soviet Economy

Every system can be described by different methods while preserving the invariance of quantitative characteristics of the variables sought. At the same time, the various methods of representing a system, first, make it possible to link its modeling with opportunities to obtain the necessary information; second, stimulate the use of the corresponding images to investigate certain mechanisms of the functioning of the system; third, as a result of the transformation of one method of description into another, make it possible to reveal new properties of the system and to use them in the search for new methods of problem solving — the construction of mechanisms of functioning of the system.[1]

We can assume that using a variety of methods to describe systems will also prove very useful in analyzing economic systems. Here it is important to bear in mind that the description of an economic system may be invariant relative to the economic principles and the class of mechanisms by which it functions. Which method of description proves preferable for one or another economic type of system and mechanism of functioning of the system is another matter.

The economic system will be described in two stages. In the first we will examine macroeconomic methods of description; in the second — microeconomic methods of description. And in all cases we will greatly simplify the methods of description. We will assume the existence of complete information on systems, "good" properties of functional dependences between parameters (convexity, differentiability, etc.), etc.

Macrodescription of Economic Systems

Production Functions

Among the macroeconomic methods of description, we shall differentiate between two: the phenomenological and structural methods.

The phenomenological method characterizes the description of a system as a black box in which one can see only exits and entrances. Production functions,[2] which express the relationship between national income and inputs of labor and capital, are the classical means of such description of a system.

Production functions indicate a knowledge of the law that links national income to inputs of labor and capital. At the same time, in the absence of an extended history of economic development and with significant changes in the economic structure of the system, using production functions to predict the future is very risky. Let us recall once more that a production function claims to play a role analogous to a law in physics. However, physical laws reflect stable relationships between parameters. As the history of discovery of physical laws shows, these discoveries are preceded by a major effort to reveal the deep-seated parameters in the dynamics of the development of a system. It is relatively unproductive to reveal the relationships between parameters of direct interest in the system on the basis of a set of statistical data. Thus, for example, the discovery of the law of universal gravitation was preceded by the discovery of such deep-seated parameters as mass and acceleration. Only on their basis was it possible to establish the law that linked the parameters of direct interest: the weight of a body and the time it takes to fall to earth.

We can assume that economic science as well will have to determine which deep-seated parameters characterize the dynamics of development of an economic system. It is likely that on this basis stable relationships can be more extensively revealed that the dynamics of the development of a system should satisfy.

Thus the construction of production functions is of general economic significance. They can be used in any economic system to reveal relationships between the adopted global output parameter and the inputs of resources.

Naturally, they can be used in various ways in different economic systems. In market economies the production function is used primarily for forecasting and, on its basis, to devise mea-

sures for regulating economic dynamics, i.e., here the normative
character of these functions emerges indirectly. In planned systems the production function can be used directly to form the initial data of long-term plans as well as to analyze the future (e.g.,
to ascertain the permissibility of an extensive mode of development, etc.).

Of course, owing to the absence of long statistical series, the
production function may not always prove to be a sufficient means
to reveal future development. Nonetheless, if one bears in mind
the possibility of iterative hierarchical analysis of the future, use
of the production function may greatly improve the analytical process. Indeed, on its basis initial generalized characteristics of
development may be given in the first step at the highest level of
the hierarchy. After disaggregating these data, one can begin
using a multisector model. Then one can specify the type of production function, obtain new generalized characteristics of development, etc.

As we know, production functions have been widely applied in the
West. They have recently been supplemented by studies at the
interbranch level.

In the USSR the application of the production function method
has long proved unsuitable for the Soviet planned economy. This
was primarily because, as is usually the case in the USSR, there
was no acute utilitarian need to use the apparatus of production
functions. The ideological rejection of this apparatus, it seems
to me, only aggravated the situation: when there is an urgent practical need for some method of management, Soviet leaders are in
fact willing to sacrifice ideology.

Indeed, the process of industrialization in the USSR began under
conditions in which not enough experience had been amassed to
make it possible to construct production functions. On the other
hand, the planning agencies were assigned specific economic development goals for the five-year plans, and there was no need to
use production functions. Moreover, it must be kept in mind that
the first experiments with using the production function in the
United States in the 1920s were unsuccessful: the failures in applying Mitchell's economic barometer were well known.

Nor were production functions used in national economic planning in subsequent years in the USSR. The common sense of the
economic leaders who defined the basic directions of development
of the Soviet economy, primarily by establishing physical indicators of production development for the next five to seven years,

freed them from the need to adopt production functions.

Moreover, we should also consider the ideological aspect of using production functions. First, these functions create the impression that they can be used only for forecasting, for predicting the future based on extrapolation of the past; hence they are naturally applied in spontaneous market economies. Describing planned economies would evidently require using models that explicitly express the goals of the executive agencies and compiling plans that are law. Second, production functions are studied on the basis of the theory of marginal utility, which has a clearly pronounced anti-Marxist bent. If we also recall that in the early 1930s in the USSR mathematical methods in economics were generally outlawed as bourgeois, we can understand how fundamental were the reasons that for a long time prompted a negative attitude toward the apparatus of production functions.

The application of mathematical methods in economic research, legalized in the USSR in the mid-1950s, opened up opportunities to develop the apparatus of production functions as well. However, the basic path that the Soviet science of mathematical economics followed was the study of input-output tables and optimal planning. Comparatively little attention was devoted to the apparatus of production functions. Perhaps the only strong group that studied production functions at the national economic level was created under the guidance of A. I. Anchishkin at the Scientific Research Economics Institute of USSR Gosplan.[3] (Subsequently, the leading members of this group were transferred to TSEMI, where a group headed by B. N. Mikhalevskii studied such problems.)

In the 1970s considerable opportunities were created to construct production functions based on experience amassed by the USSR in the realm of industrial development. These functions may prove to be very useful for long-term planning. They may serve as the basis for the iterative compilation of the plan which, as already noted above, is construed to mean the multistage process of interconversion of macro- and microeconomic indicators, as well as for analysis of ways to develop the Soviet economy (further possibilities for the extensive expansion of production).

The decision of party agencies to work out a fifteen-year plan for the development of the Soviet economy for 1976-90 prompted the search for new methods of long-term planning. In this connection great attention was focused on the apparatus of production functions. TSEMI began an intensive elaboration of long-term planning methodology based on the use of production functions.

At the same time, the apparatus of production functions was used in long-term planning rather one-sidedly, primarily to analyze and forecast development in the future. Emphasis on such use of production functions evoked the corresponding political passions. The impression was created that development in the future must be based on forecasts rather than on strict directive plans.[4] The functioning of the economic system on the basis of forecasts is associated by Soviet politicians with indicative planning, which was either rejected in the late 1920s by the then Soviet political leadership or which is now used in some capitalist countries.

Structural Models

We will now examine the relationship between the phenomenological method of description based on the production function and the structural principle.

The structural principle presupposes that relationships will be ascertained between individual macroeconomic parameters of the process that determine the dynamics of development, i.e., its driving forces and technical potentials.

The internal life of the system was captured by using the production function. The causes producing some relationships between input and output parameters of the system were left aside. Since production functions are used to analyze the future, it was as though the system was assumed to have functioned sensibly in the past. In other words, when production functions were used it was assumed that people had sufficiently sensible aspirations and had been sufficiently sensible in realizing them within the bounds of limited technological potentials and available resources. And these sensible actions were repeated many times, thereby providing an accurate statistical picture.

The structural method of describing macroeconomic processes presupposes the explicit determination of the aspirations of people and their potentials so as to subsequently select an effective trajectory of development on this basis.

We can distinguish between the differential and integral mode of expressing the aspirations of people. The potentials of the system under each mode of description can be given in the form of technological constraints on permissible volumes of production.

With the differential mode of expressing people's aspirations, one can in turn single out a direct and indirect form. Under the direct form people's aspirations are expressed through differential utility, i.e., through the function that links the magnitude of marginal utilities of products with the volume of their consumption. This function forms the basis of the well-known Walras-Wald economic model. Under the indirect form people's aspirations are represented through the function of demand. The demand function links demand for consumer goods with the prices on these goods and the income of the consumers.

With the integral mode people's aspirations are expressed through the criterion of optimality. The works of E. Slutskii show the possibility, under certain conditions, of transforming the indicated function of demand into the criterion of optimality (and all the more so into the differential function of utility).[5]

The integral mode of description has a number of advantages. They concern primarily the formulation of the problem, since the assumption of the existence of the optimality criterion sometimes provides greater heuristic possibilities for expressing people's aspirations than does the differential mode. The integral mode of description also facilitates solving the problem because it presupposes a greater degree of order in the structure of the problem (the existence of potential). Finally, this mode of description provides great opportunities to find new methods of solution, since it is not rigidly bound to the use of the dual variables inherent in the differential mode of description.

Let us now see how structural models are used to describe the Soviet economic system. We shall first examine the kinds of models that practical personnel work with even though they themselves may not clearly perceive this.

It is natural for the personnel of planning agencies to think that the planned system has a goal for its development. This goal is formulated by the executive agencies. During Stalin's time, when the emphasis in developing the economy was placed only on the creation of military might, the shortest time to attain the corresponding potential was the criterion for optimality of economic development. Thus, for example, following World War II, when Stalin set himself the task of attaining world dominance, the simplest formulation of the economic problem for him was (as he expressed it in his speech to the voters in February 1946) to produce 50 million tons of pig iron, 60 million tons of steel, 500 million tons of coal, and 60 million tons of oil, i.e., to attain the corresponding economic potential in a minimum span.

In the years since Stalin's death, Soviet leaders have begun focusing more attention on improving the well-being of the people, naturally, with a parallel increase in military power. Planners attempt to take satisfaction of the needs of people as the basis of long-term planning. Since planners are people who are quite realistic in their thinking, they confine these needs only to the top priority, most urgent ones. To be sure, under these needs they group not only food, clothing, and housing but also "entertainment." It is quite natural for such planners to ascertain the people's needs by establishing corresponding scientifically substantiated norms. In the USSR this mode of determining needs has undergone appreciable development. The USSR Academy of Medical Sciences and other scientific institutions have been asked to compile rational norms for nutrition, clothing, housing, and other goods forming the basis of long-term planning. The value of the results of this research is largely dubious, since science is not yet sufficiently developed to formally consider the variety of human needs. It goes without saying that the results of the work of scientists in this area are subjected to "political correction."

It is an even more complex matter to set out the paths of movement toward the established norms, i.e., to determine how much the production of various types of products must be increased to lessen the degree of people's dissatisfaction. I do not know of any research on this question.

We should also note that the use of so-called scientific norms of consumption for the planning of production entails certain inherent dangers. The existence of rational norms in itself does not in any way suggest man's obligation to use them. If these norms are actually justified, their purpose can be explained to people. Only in an act of free choice can man define the structure of his consumption. And production should follow this structure.

If such scientifically substantiated norms are adopted for planning, they will serve as the basis of production. For the time being we will ignore the fact that people's needs for certain products may be oversaturated from the standpoint of their usual desires. We will even consider that the distribution of the goods produced will be realized not gratis but through a price mechanism. And in this case, generally speaking, prices will be found that will clear the market. However, people's needs will then be satisfied to a lesser degree: the production of goods may be dictated to some degree by the falsely understood needs of people.

Another avenue open to the planner for determining the needs of people might lie in building a function of utility on the basis of the transformation of the demand function, which is already based on statistical information about people's real behavior.

However, considerable difficulties are entailed in constructing a function of demand in the USSR that would reflect the real needs of people. Among these difficulties we should first mention the absence of a flexible system of retail prices in the USSR. As we know, there are a certain number of so-called scarce products, i.e., products for which demand exceeds supply at the given level of prices and incomes. Nonetheless, prices on these products do not change toward establishing equilibrium prices. This situation has its own political causes (see Chapter 7 for greater detail).

Thus the Soviet planning system lacks reliable guideposts to establish goals for the system. Hence the choice of goals for five-year and one-year plans is a result of compromise between the extrapolation of previous trends of development and political considerations linked with the level of the arms race and the ascertainment of the population's standard of living. Available resources and input-output coefficients are taken as constraints in the problem. Planners do not formulate the general goal of compiling the national economic plan in terms of any formal, strict models.

We shall now examine macroeconomic description of the national economy on a theoretical plane.

Soviet economists are in the habit of using the reproduction models developed by K. Marx and subsequently augmented by V. I. Lenin to describe the national economy. There is a considerable amount of literature on this question in the USSR and in the West, so I will not explore this mode of description. I will only note that it belongs among the structural modes in which people's intentions are latent. These models are essentially reminiscent of production functions, i.e., they also attempt only to disclose the laws governing the growth of the social product, the laws linking the production of consumer goods with the necessary inputs of the means of production. The Marxist-Leninist mode of description has had direct practical significance as a means of ideologically supporting demands by the executive agencies for the preferential development of the means of production compared with the production of consumer goods. For political purposes, however, the authorities sometimes have to proclaim the preferential development of consumer goods (as was the case during the short-lived reign of G. M. Malenkov in the mid-1950s or under the present Soviet leaders). Then an attempt is made to ignore consequences stemming from the models of Marx and Lenin.

A number of Soviet economists have also proposed other methods for the macroeconomic description of economic systems which are based on the explicit determination of the aspirations of the planning agencies. Here the methods of description are given in integral form. Such a method of describing the economy has struck Soviet economists as most natural for a socialist economy that explicitly develops in accordance with a set goal. It also made it easier to visualize possible practical ways to saturate these models with statistics.

And finally, the ideological aspect of the problem has been a circumstance of no little importance in shaping the use of this descriptive approach. We will try to show below how Soviet economists who are proponents of the optimality approach have had to resort to mimicking dominant Marxist ideology in order to ensure their "survival." Here it should first be borne in mind that, given this mode of describing the system, it has become necessary to somehow respond to the question of the comparability of goods. As we know, the Marxist labor theory of value rejects the possibility of directly comparing consumer goods to one another. It admits comparison of goods only through inputs of abstract labor. Second, if dual models are used to describe the economy, it also becomes necessary to interpret prices and their relationship to inputs.

I above all would like to show how such distinguished scholars as L. V. Kantorovich, V. V. Novozhilov, and A. L. Lur'e — the founders of the theory of optimal planning in the USSR — have been compelled to mimic Marxism. Mimicry has helped these scholars survive because their research on the optimal distribution of resources and the associated shadow prices has generated ideas on value parameters that cannot in fact be reconciled with Marxist economic theory. Unfortunately, the problem of bringing the ideas of optimal planning "into correspondence" with Marxism has not yet been entirely farmed out to history: it is still a current issue in Soviet economic science.[6]

I shall begin with V. V. Novozhilov who has permitted in his works the greatest degree of "Marxoidness."[7] It stems not from his genuine ignorance of world economic thought (as was the case at one time with Kantorovich) but only from political mimicry. While the method of mimicry he adopted was largely justified between the 1930s and 1950s, in the sixties, when broader development of economic science became possible, its negative aspects emerged quite starkly.

The mode of mimicry proposed by Novozhilov was created in the 1930s and was based on the following considerations.[8] After the stormy debates of the 1920s and early 1930s, it became clear to economists that the question of determining which final products to produce and their quantities was the purview of the party and its leader. For this reason economists turned their efforts to answering the question of how to produce and how to better fulfill the party's targets. Therefore in the mathematical models of Novozhilov (as well as of many other creative economists at that time) knowing the volume of the final product to be produced was taken as an axiom. Since it is known what and how much must be produced and one need only ask how to produce it, the optimal solution amounts to cost minimization. Inputs are to be measured in terms of labor. Available resources are introduced as constraints. But here the question immediately arises of the comparability of various types of labor, i.e., the well-known problem of the reduction of labor. Novozhilov passed over it in silence.

On the whole, Novozhilov's model has the following appearance:

$$\sum_{ij} a_{ij} x_{ij} \rightarrow \min. \quad \sum_{ij} b_{ij}^k x_{ij} \leq \beta^k \quad \sum_j x_{ij} \geq \alpha_i \quad x_{ij} \geq 0,$$

where a_{ij} are known labor inputs for the production of a unit of product i according to method j; x_{ij} is the desired volume of production of product i according to method j; b_{ij}^k are known coefficients of inputs of resource k for the production of a unit of product i according to method j; and α_i is the given volume of production of product i.

Analyzing the dual relationships in the given model of the type

$$y_i = a_{ij} + \sum_k b_{ij}^k p^k,$$

Novozhilov concluded that the price of the product — y_i — is measured in labor units and is equal to labor inputs — a_{ij} — plus feedback inputs $\sum_k b_{ij}^k p^k$ expressed in terms of shadow prices of limited resources p^k (the term feedback is taken from cybernetics; it became fashionable in the USSR starting in the mid-1950s).

Thus it seemed that on the theoretical level the model should satisfy many people: first, everything is measured in terms of labor, and thus the transformed formula of value under socialism is found; second, what is to be produced is given, and the notorious problem of utility does not exist; and third, both mathematics and cybernetics are used. The model was also appealing from a practical point of view, since it seemed that it could be saturated with statistical data.

But such a model had substantial theoretical gaps. First, it separated the questions of what to produce and how to produce it; and this cannot be done, since the volume of production of various products also depends on the production methods used. Novozhilov and his followers have tried to avoid this fault of the model by changing constraints on given volumes of production. But how to change these volumes remains unclear. Second, this model posed the false problem of labor reduction, which within its framework basically required external solution.

Thus on a theoretical level Novozhilov's model was based on two unresolved economic problems. What is more, one of them, associated with the reduction of labor, does not in principle have an external solution.

Such a model is also extremely limited on the practical level. Assume that today it is possible in some way to find palliative data for the practical application of a given model. But the practical role of the model does not amount merely to serving the system of planning today. More sophisticated models can also be used practically, e.g., to organize statistical material that can be incorporated in planning practice "the day after tomorrow." The same can be said, for example, about building a model with an optimality criterion that expresses the striving of people for greater well-being.

Moreover, if false problems are set up in the model, they can distract scientists from the solution of real scientific problems. Thus the discussion of the problem of reduction within the framework of the traditional ideas has attracted an appreciable number of scientists who have even organized conferences on this topic. But the problem cannot be solved within this framework. Seeing the reduction question as deriving from more refined models could thus have saved a great deal of the effort people expended in vain.

Kantorovich's method of mimicry was somewhat different from that of Novozhilov.[9] Kantorovich had in mind as his initial problem the "model of the plywood trust," where the product mix and resources were given, and the goal was to maximize a single variable representing the intensity of operation of a vector that specifies the proportions in which certain end products are to be delivered. This model has the same vulnerable point as Novozhilov's: what is to be produced is known. To be sure, this constraint is weakened by the fact that only the structure of output is fixed; the volume of production is sought.

The problem of reduction of labor in Kantorovich's model is solved simultaneously with the problem itself by the search for the shadow prices of various types of labor. Further, Kantorovich studied problems in which the minimization of the expenditure of resources or time on the attainment of the goal was the criterion. In these problems not only the structure of final demand but even its volume were given.

Thus Kantorovich analyzed problems in which either the maximization of output in a given assortment or cost minimization was the criterion. Hence the shadow price of the product, as well as of resources, was obtained from the plan as a dual variable of the corresponding constraint on the fixed proportions of output or the minimum volume of production. Comparison of Kantorovich's model with models in which an optimality criterion explicitly expresses the degree of satisfaction of people's needs makes it obvious why it is hard to understand the economic nature of shadow prices of final products in the Kantorovich model. Kantorovich avoided the problem of the preference of goods, replacing it with a priori partial criteria and constraints which in one way or another presupposed that the preference of goods was already predetermined.

Since in Kantorovich's models shadow prices are not explicitly measured in terms of labor inputs, he showed through a number of transformations of dual relationships that shadow prices can be expressed in average socially necessary expenditures of labor. I refer readers interested in greater detail on this question to appendices in Kantorovich's work The Best Use of Economic Resources.

Now a word on the method of mimicry proposed by A. L. Lur'e.[10] Passages have been found in Marx and Engels from which it follows that labor value will not exist in future society, that products will be compared in terms of utility, that the plan will aim at distributing resources to satisfy people's needs, etc. These passages, which are entirely in keeping with the spirit of Marxism, have created a definite barrier to criticism in forming models in which the optimality criterion was already expressed in terms of the function of satisfying people's needs.[11] Technological potentials and available reserves of all kinds of resources were constraints in such models.

Unfortunately, as a man of the older generation, A. L. Lur'e still tried to somehow "flirt with labor." Imitating Novozhilov in his model he called shadow prices "differential expenditures."

Likewise, he performed the following operation with a model in

which the optimality criterion was given in the form of a function
of utility. From this model he found the volumes of output. Then
he transformed this model by taking the volumes of output found
as a constraint and advancing the minimization of the expenditures
of a given factor as the criterion. The results of problem solving
based on the new model, i.e., the intensity of production methods
and shadow prices, will remain the same. As an example, Lur'e
cited a model in which the criterion was the minimum of labor
inputs, even though it could equally have been the minimum of any
other resource. Lur'e's work subsequently generated all sorts of
speculation in the Soviet literature.

A number of middle-aged Soviet economists who were brought
up under conditions of relatively greater freedom and who have
already set out on the paths conquered by the older generation have
developed another mode of mimicking Marxism. A scientific work
must rest on an exposition of the material that <u>sincerely</u> expresses
the scholar's view. Then citations from the classics that the author deems correct are added to it. In principle the latter requirement can be satisfied even though it requires special work on the
study of "canonical texts." (After all, in the works of a classic
one can find a positive answer to any question bearing on one's
work.) It is certainly desirable that citations be few and without
corresponding epithets. Through such a mode of mimicry the definition of price is given without references to labor inputs but, for
example, as the contribution made by a variation of a given resource to the goal posed by society.

It stands to reason that this mode of mimicry also has its negative aspects because, even though the passages from Marx cited
in works by these authors may not contradict their convictions,
the writers provide only positive references to Marx. They do not
cite appropriate general economic remarks from the works of the
Austrian or other Western schools. Hence a distorted picture of
Marx is created, and his role is exaggerated.

A Microdescription of an Economic System

A microeconomic description is characterized principally by
the fact that it explicitly represents the <u>individual</u> aspirations of
participants in an economic system and their potential. Major
difficulties under this mode of description arise with the transition
from individual independent participants to their system, i.e.,
when participants are connected with one another in acts of ex-

changing the results of their activity. These difficulties depend on solving the problem of the interaction between the production capacity of every participant and the volume of consumption. In other words, one must determine the degree to which the participant with more favorable production potential can obtain a greater quantity of consumer products. Within the framework of the premises introduced, it is impossible to write a model of the economy without clarifying the distribution problem.

The distribution of income among participants may be given parametrically, using for this purpose, e.g., a given system of tax withholdings, or may be obtained deductively, based on introducing the appropriate premises into the model. Among these premises we should at least list the characterization of dependences between the quantity of goods received by the individual by a certain point in time and his potential in subsequent time, the influence of the quantity of goods obtained by other individuals on the activity of a participant (the effect of envy, of altruism).

There are many methods for the microdescription of economic systems: game, equilibrium, optimality, etc.[12] Before examining them briefly, let us note that the very division of the mode of describing a system and the mechanism of its functioning is rather arbitrary. It is possible to differentiate a hierarchy in the methods of describing a system from the standpoint of the degree of reflection of the mechanism of functioning of a system in the description.

In its most complete form the model of the description of the system will include:

a) describing individual participants and the nature of the demands on their interaction (e.g., the exchange of commodities while preserving for each participant the right to ownership of the product);

b) establishing the parameters by means of which the interaction of participants will be organized (e.g., price);

c) determining the class of the mechanism on the basis of which the system will function (vertical or horizontal classes of mechanisms).

The game model of the economy can in some sense be considered the basic model of the economy. Its merit lies in the fact that it explicitly reveals the interests of each participant in the economic system and the area of his individual potential. At the same time, this model is nonconstructive, since it does not reveal the way in which the choice of strategy by some players will influence the

90

choice of strategy by others, nor does it establish the parameters that link the actions of the participants.

In this connection one can view microeconomic models of equilibrium as a method of presenting the game in a more constructive form. In these models it is demonstrated how the choice of strategy by one player is linked to the choice of strategy by other players so that the players ultimately attain equilibrium throughout the system. It is assumed at the same time that the mechanism is one in which each participant himself seeks his optimal strategy and receives from the system, i.e., from other participants, information in concise form about their potentials and demands, i.e., the parameters linking the actions of the participants are already evident. We should also note that the models of equilibrium do not analyze classes of mechanisms for elaborating these parameters. It is assumed that they exist and that prices are such parameters. Thus price is the parameter of the functioning of a system that makes possible autonomous decision-making by a participant and very economical transmission to every participant of information about the system as a whole that assures him the possibility of moving independently in an optimal direction. Prices may be established by various classes of mechanisms: either through a central agency or through the local interactions of participants. This is a matter of indifference where this model is concerned.

There are many models of equilibrium, each of which focuses attention on some aspect of the functioning of an economic system. Given the existence of a Pareto optimum, the model of equilibrium can be transformed into a model of scalar optimization.[13] In this transformation particular interest attaches to the parameter that performs the role of a system participant's weight in the global criterion of optimality. This weight depends on the marginal utility of a unit of income for the participant. The less this utility, the greater is his participation in the system.

We also note that prices do not figure directly in models of scalar optimization. Nonetheless, as usual, in such a model partial derivatives arise that characterize the influence of the variation of each individual constraint on the magnitude of the national economic criterion of optimality. These derivatives are nothing other than the prices used in the model of equilibrium.

The reason why prices assure the optimal solution of the system in models of equilibrium is evident from the analysis of the model of scalar optimization. Indeed, in models of scalar optimization prices are directly shown as global parameters that carry infor-

mation concerning the state of the entire system. As partial derivatives of the global criterion with respect to a given constraint,
they depend on all parameters adopted in the model — here, on all
individual objective functions of participants, areas of their potential, and distribution relationships. If small changes take place in
the system, thanks to the stability of prices all participants can as
before follow the existing prices and can be confident that an optimal state of the economy will be attained.[14]

Transforming a microeconomic model of equilibrium into an
optimal model is useful for the same reasons as transforming
macroeconomic differential models into optimal (integral) models.
Some of these reasons have already been noted above. We shall
make only one additional general comment in this connection.

In the process of selecting the global criterion of optimality, an
important question arises: Is the optimality criterion taken from
the system itself, or is it brought in from outside? The teleological
approach to the analysis of systems presupposes that the global
criterion is brought in from outside, while the causal approach assumes that the criterion exists in the system itself. In addition
there are points of view that reject in general the global criterion
in the system. The transformation of the equilibrium model into a
model of scalar optimization shows that the construction of a global
criterion of optimality in the system entirely corresponds to the
causal approach.

Indeed, models of equilibrium do not presuppose the existence
in the system of a general goal. Therefore they create the impression that they are not teleological. But these models are also
based on the external principle, which concerns the character of
the distribution of incomes. This principle is based on moral and
ethical norms and is not properly economic. As is evident from
the transformation of the model of equilibrium into the model of
scalar optimization, it is specifically the principle of the distribution of income that determines the weights of participants in the
global criterion of optimality. Thus, specifying the principle of
distribution of income and expressing the interests of participants
independently are essentially equivalent to finding the global criterion of optimality with the corresponding weights of the participants.

Thus even if the model of equilibrium is considered natural in
the sense that it is not associated with any general goals of the
system, this does not contradict the existence of a global criterion.
However, the latter must be understood as the heuristic principle

of integrating the value parameters of the system, as a means of expressing the striving of individual participants along with the relations between them given from without.

The need for such heuristic integration of value parameters may be due to the following considerations. It is not always possible to formally express the entire expanded set of premises that must be taken into account in building a model. Genetically and in the learning process, some of the premises take shape in people's intuition, which they cannot formally express. In such a case the description of the system is mixed: some of the premises are given formally, and some are given intuitively. Man performs the synthesis. Since it is sometimes convenient for man to express value characteristics in integral form, this type of representation of the system appears in some sense to be teleological. Indeed, if the system is reduced solely to the formalized part, the impression may be created that the global criterion is introduced from outside by some rational being. In actuality we are using the causal approach, but only with regard to the system that includes man, with his capacity for intuitive thinking and manipulating integral value characteristics. And if it is at all legitimate to speak of a teleological approach to defining the criterion, that is so only when we intend to isolate specific features in the representation of the system and it is useful to thus combine formalized information with intuition.

Given existing management practices, the microeconomic description of the Soviet economy by means of an optimal model strikes Soviet economists as entirely natural. Game models and models of equilibrium seemed natural as ways to describe a capitalist economy in which there is a play of free forces through the price mechanism.

However, the preference for the model of scalar optimization in the USSR stems not only from the fact that it seems natural from the standpoint of the existing mechanism of functioning. This method of describing the economy is also very convenient from a political point of view, since it masks the relations between participants in the economic system behind the so-called general global interest of developing socialist society.

Quite well known is the view that the national economic criterion of optimality, in accordance with the basic economic law of socialism, must express the maximization of the level of satisfaction of the needs of all members of society. Nonetheless, the question of the weights ascribed to various members of society remains open. In models of scalar optimization, where the global criterion is based on the individual objective functions of the participants, this issue has frequently been bypassed; in particular, it has been assumed that the weights of the participants are uniform. Since it was shown that the structure of the national economic criterion of optimality also ultimately depends on an accepted principle of distribution expressed in the weights of the participants, in its formulation it is essential to consider not only the individual objective functions of members of society but also certain relations between them.

Let us examine this question in greater detail. Since an economic system is a large system, its control requires that it be broken down into parts — the formation of an appropriate structure for the system. In forming the economic structure it is necessary to consider at least two aspects: technological and territorial. The technological aspect entails the formation of a departmental hierarchical structure of management. The territorial aspect entails the formation of the corresponding hierarchy of territorial agencies.

When describing the system by means of a model of scalar optimization, both of these aspects can be considered in the model only as means of resolving a problem of greater dimensionality appropriate to a large economic system. Here basic attention is focused on the formulation of local criteria for economic cells; for example, profit may be such a criterion. Further, beyond the framework of the model it is assumed that the interest of the workers is directly aimed at improving the significance of these criteria.

The description of the economic system in the form of a model of equilibrium is another matter. Even though it is formally possible to avoid many political difficulties with this method of describing the system (they will be discussed below), nonetheless here it is naturally necessary to explicitly establish the interests of various participants. The question of the representation of the interests of participants when departments are the basic cell at the national economic level remains completely untouched. The question of the formation of the interests of participants when the territorial unit is the basic cell at the national economic level has been discussed to a great degree in Soviet economic literature. [15]

The point is that the solution of very serious political problems depends on the method used in shaping the basic territorial unit. As we know, either economic regions or national republics can be such units. One can cite well-known arguments that artificially

formed economic regions should be such economic units. These
arguments are associated with the technical expedience of formulating the planning problem. In this problem it is important to
divide the system into blocks so that each concentrates the greatest
possible number of internal relations.

One can cite well-known arguments that national republics
should be the basic economic units. These arguments are associated with a number of important aspects of management from the
standpoint of the existing community of groups of people, their traditions, customs, etc.

Political considerations are also of decisive importance in
choosing the economic unit.

The territorial distribution of income may be based on the
postulate that the resources within a given region belong to the entire population of a given country or community. This postulate is
accepted most painlessly by the population of countries that are
ethnically homogeneous (such as China, for example) or countries
in which various nationalities are mixed (as in the United States,
for example).

In countries with a multitude of nationalities that are by their
historical tradition territorially separate from one another, the
redistribution of income between individual territories provokes
quite a painful reaction on the part of the population in the regions
with better resources. One of the reasons for the emergence of
centrifugal forces in such multinational empires is the feeling of
the population from some territory that it is being exploited by the
center, that the center is extracting income from its rich resources.

What then should be the relationships between the center and
such national formations? In principle associations of nations can
be based on quite diverse principles, including those like the Brit-
ish Commonwealth of Nations, the Common Market, COMECON,
etc.; there is a rich spectrum of relations here.

We should note that within the framework of COMECON, relations between the USSR and Eastern European socialist countries
are based on the principle that each country receives the full income from the resources that it has at its disposal.[16] This gives
rise to a very real question: Why must relations between socialist
republics within the framework of the USSR be based on the redistribution of incomes between republics? The answer to this
question is skirted in Soviet literature.

Returning to the role of the method of describing the system,
we note that when the national republic is selected as an economic

unit, the problem of income distribution emerges immediately and sharply, and the issue arises of what portion of the income from the existing resources of the republics is taken from them. As we know, this question is one of the most important sources that feeds nationalism, since, with the exception of Belorussia, other republics are rich in natural resources or skilled personnel. Thus, for example, in Uzbekistan it is quite widely believed that Russia is robbing the republic, since for very low prices it takes from the republic its white gold — cotton, gas, and gold itself (the extraction of gold in Uzbekistan accounts for roughly thirty to forty percent of all gold mined in the Soviet Union. New gold-mining towns — Zeravshan and Navoi — have been built in the republic).

The growth of nationalism in the USSR [17] clearly threatens the stability of the Soviet empire. A solution to this problem can be sought in various directions. It is possible to continue the policy of emphasizing the national qualities of individual peoples. Then, as shown by Stalin's experience, in order to preserve the empire it is necessary to develop Great Russian chauvinism and at the same time to severely suppress the national movements of other peoples.

One can attempt to emphasize the role of the shared purposes of all nationalities and to speak of the Soviet people as a unified whole. In this case the political division of the country, which can be based principally on the principles of economic zoning and not on national republics, can also be used to combat nationalism. [18]

Thus the question of the preferred, and perhaps also permitted, method of describing the Soviet economic system will ultimately be resolved depending on the political situation.

5

Value Parameters and Their Use
in the Soviet Economic Mechanism

This chapter has three unequal parts. In the first we will examine the diversity of value parameters as production invariants, i.e., as usable in any production system irrespective of whether man is a participant in this system or whether it functions without man's direct participation.

In the second part we will examine only those value invariants generated by the nature of man's participation in the system. Analysis of value invariants of this type appears in the last two chapters, which examine work incentive methods, inflation, and the spectrum of markets.

And finally, in the third part we will investigate some theoretical and practical aspects of the use of value invariants in the Soviet planned economy.

Value Invariants in Production Systems

In any economic system there are constraints. These constraints may limit both used or produced resources and products, natural and labor resources, means of production, technologies, permissible volumes of consumption of certain products, as well as institutions engendered by the system — contracts, plans, etc. Each of the constraints in the system receives a valuation that characterizes the degree of its importance in the mechanism of the system's functioning.[1] Let us first examine these valuations relative to an economic model in which the existence of complete information is presupposed, the production of collective goods is absent, etc.

Price and Profit

In the model of a rather developed economic system, one can see subsystems — economic cells — whose internal structure permits them to organize their external and internal behavior in various ways. Given the corresponding changes in demands on input-output vectors for external products, these cells can reorganize their internal structure. The existence of options for the economic cell is based on technical and organizational flexibility expressed in the possibility of using existing means of production and personnel to produce different products or, at any rate, in the possibility of varying the intensity of the activity of personnel or the operating conditions of the equipment.

If for the sake of simplicity we assume that every such economic cell strives for equilibrium throughout the system as a whole, it must have information on the status of other cells. Only with this information can the given cell organize a state of its outputs and inputs that guarantees equilibrium throughout the system as a whole. In the limiting case such information will be expressed in the form of a full characterization of all remaining cells, including their internal potential. However, if the economic system is quite large, it is extremely difficult to supply the information and then to process it in the given cell.

For this reason developed economic systems function under conditions in which individual cells receive information in condensed form on the status of all other cells. The forms of obtaining this information may vary. One such form is prices — the global parameters of the economic field. They are magnitudes applied to every external parameter of the cell. In other words, prices are introduced for all products and resources in the system. It is not significant whether a given product is a result of production in the system, whether it is obtained from outside as a product of nature, or whether it is a final or intermediate product.

Prices "draw" every parameter included in input-output vectors in the appropriate direction, assuring the cell reaches a state of equilibrium. Prices appear in the form of global parameters that carry information in condensed form to the subsystems about all conditions of the system's development (both about the aspirations of its participants and about their potential).

Thus the functional role of prices is to assure the autonomous decision-making of economic cells, i.e., to provide them with the opportunity to independently organize their internal structure and to find their own input-output vector when each such cell does not possess all specific information on the system as a whole.

In order to perform this function, prices must have certain <u>properties</u>. Indeed, for the price on a certain final or intermediate product to perform its directing role, it must reflect a marginal benefit from the product not lower than the marginal cost. Otherwise there will be a nonequilibrium state. If for some product the difference between its marginal benefit and price or between its price and marginal cost is positive, this indicates underproduction of the commodity. On the other hand, a negative difference means the production of a surplus of commodities less beneficial for the system. Thus the equilibrium price of the product reflects both its benefits and the cost of its production.

What has been said about the relationship between the utility of the product and the cost of its production is expressed in a criterion of the cell's activity like profit. <u>As the criterion of the effectiveness of the development of a cell, profit is an invariant of production systems.</u> In any economic system the local object in an equilibrium situation must assure equality between the value of inputs and outputs.

Finally, let us see how the incomes of participants in the economic system are coordinated with the value of the consumer goods produced.

First, we shall examine the simplest case, in which the production of consumer goods is immediate. Their value is equal to the value of the available resources. Since the income of the participants is equal to the value of the resources, there is no problem in coordinating the value of consumers goods and available incomes. The situation is somewhat more complicated for an expanding economy with collective goods, and so on. In such a case, in one way or another — through savings, taxes, etc. — the sums necessary for accumulation, collective goods, and so on, are deducted from the incomes of the members of society. Such coordination of the value of the mass of consumer goods produced with the incomes of society's members that go to purchase these goods is above all effected specifically through withholdings from income. This is due to the fact that given such a mode of coordination, equilibrium prices are automatically preserved on consumer goods, and on all resources in general.

Thus the above solution of the price problem makes it possible to coordinate a large number of aspects of the functioning of the system and, at least,

1) assure autonomous decision-making by the cell in the direction of equilibrium throughout the system;

2) compensate expenditures through the sale of products for the given price; and

3) coordinate prices on consumer goods with overall expenditures of the expanding system (capital investments, defense, etc.), and so on.

We note further that the aforementioned functions of price and its properties are not tied to the social character of the system and the type of mechanism underlying its functioning. These functions of price are an invariant of economic systems. They are equally valid for capitalist, socialist, and any other social systems. They are valid both for centralized systems and for systems with a free, totally unconstrained market economy. Differences here lie in the fact that prices are established by the center or in the free play of market forces. Thus such differences can be quite substantial.

On the basis of all the foregoing, let us analyze some theoretical concepts concerning planned systems. The basic idea behind the mechanism of the functioning of economic systems is the balancing of its local objects and the system as a whole. In the simplest case the situation of Robinson Crusoe is relevant. For him the local object could be various production methods and products. Since the resources he has at his disposal are to a greater or lesser degree universal, he must choose methods of production and products that will generally assure his greatest satisfaction.

The matter is more complex in production systems with a large number of heterogeneous resources, production methods, and final products. The controlling agency cannot encompass the total set of elements in the system. All its power lies in the fact that it can create methods for the mediated control of this set of elements. These methods are expressed in the organization of a hierarchy of objects. Since formations that have an internal structure take shape in the hierarchies, in the general case degrees of freedom emerge in these formations thanks to the possibility of varying the intensity of the use of the substructures forming them.

Then a rather complex problem arises. The center attempts to reach an optimal global solution. At the same time, owing to the aforementioned factors, it does not know the internal potential of the cells. The cells therefore must themselves find the optimal internal structure. But for the following reasons they do not know what their optimal structure means from the standpoint of the system as a whole. The goals of the center may not be directly tied to the output of a given cell; the possibility of obtaining resources for a given cell also depends on the needs of other cells for them.

Under these conditions it becomes necessary: (1) to communicate to the cell in concise form information about the system as a whole that is directly linked to the cell's potential to make its own decisions in the best direction; (2) to obtain from the cell concise information about its internal potential.

Thus the existence of choice in production systems requires the creation of appropriate effective methods of functioning that coordinate the actions of local objects and the center. In comparatively simple situations characterized by the determinacy of information or by its probability representation and moderate dimensionality, mathematical procedures already exist that are analogues of possible mechanisms of functioning of such systems. They are the various methods of mathematical and dynamic programming.

In essence these methods solve one problem: how to secure the ordered, <u>consistent</u> selection of production methods. Given such a process, at every step it is necessary to select methods that are tested for the admissibility of their inclusion in an optimal program. For such a selection there must be pertinent, concise generalized information about the system as a whole. The variety of methods of mathematical and dynamic programming is characterized by the modes of forming this information.

Two basic varieties can be distinguished among these programming methods. The first variety stems from the fact that the controlling agency only formulates the general goal of development (the attainment of equilibrium or of a global optimum equivalent to it) and sets the rules of functioning. In accordance with these goals and rules, cells that directly interact with one another reach a state of equilibrium.

The rules of functioning may be based on various principles, many of which do not require the use of prices. Thus if exchange between cells were based solely on random collisions of pairs (groups) without involving prices, in principle it would still be possible to attain equilibrium throughout the system. This is shown by the corresponding theorems whose proof is presented in the works of O. Guseva and V. Polterovich.[2]

However, the introduction of prices facilitates the solution of the problem. Prices reflect accumulated experience in finding the optimal relationships for participants in exchange. But if a random act of exchange is locally effective, this does not mean that there are no other possibilities for exchange that might produce a greater effect. It is prices that provide the guidepost for clarifying this question and that eliminate losses which might arise from random, less effective acts of exchange. Accordingly, prices provide the given participant with the opportunity to more quickly find an exchange that guarantees his reaching a state of equilibrium.

Mathematical methods simulating the search for equilibrium on the basis of local interactions by means of prices are least developed. I know of an attempt by the Soviet scholar V. M. Polterovich to create such methods. Even though it has not been theoretically possible to prove the convergence of the proposed algorithm, experimental calculations have proven its workability.[3]

The second variety of mathematical methods for solving problems presupposes a vertical mechanism in which there is a central agency that processes information about the system and that provides local objects with guideposts for their activity.

Let us examine the foregoing through the example of one variety of mathematical programming that simulates the mechanism of optimal functioning of a production system in which there is already a hierarchy of cells.

The problem to be solved here will look like this:

$$F(x) = F(x_1, \ldots, x_k, \ldots, x_K) \to \max.$$

$k = 1, 2, \ldots K$ is the index of the cell;
$\quad\quad x_k$ is the input-output vector for cell k;
$\quad\quad x \in Q$, where Q is the set of all general constraints
$\quad\quad\quad\quad$ in the system (technologies and resources);
$\quad\quad x_k \in q_k$, where q_k is the set of local constraints of the
$\quad\quad\quad\quad$ object (technologies and resources).

The decomposition procedures may be used on the most varied principles for coordinating the activity of the cells and the system. In one form or another some of these methods use value parameters, and others are confined to physical characteristics. Thus there is one known decomposition procedure[4] in which the central agency gives a lower echelon cell in step σ a variant of the plan that is optimal and feasible from the standpoint of center $\bar{x}_k^\sigma$. The cell is to ascertain the measure of its feasibility from the point of view of its internal potential q_k and, taking this into account, to propose its own variant of the optimal plan $\dot{x}_K$ which deviates minimally from the plan proposed by the center.

$$| \mathring{x}_k^\sigma - \overline{x}_k^\sigma |^2 \to \max.$$

$$\mathring{x}_k^\sigma \in q_k .$$

On the basis of optimal plans of cells accumulated by step σ (let us denote the set of these plans as G^σ) and in keeping with its optimality criterion, the center will seek the optimal plan for system $\overline{x}^\sigma$. To this end it solves the following problem

$$F(x^\sigma) \to \max.$$

$$x^\sigma \in Q$$

$$x^\sigma \in G^\sigma, G^\sigma = \{\mathring{x}_1^1, \ldots, \mathring{x}_1^{\sigma-1}; \ldots; \mathring{x}_k^1, \ldots, \mathring{x}_K^{\sigma-1}\}.$$

In the course of the iterative process of exchange of information between the center and the cells, an optimal state for the system as a whole is ultimately achieved.

There are decomposition procedures, for example the Dantzig-Wolf algorithm,[5] in which prices are used. We will designate their vector as p. The center develops prices as guideposts for the cells to select the best input-output plan considering their internal potential. The maximum possible profit serves as the criterion of effectiveness of such a plan. The problem of the cell appears as: $px^k \to \max. x_k \in q_k$. The center, after accumulating locally optimal plans of this type — we will designate their set by G — coordinates them with its potential and solves the following problem $F(x) \to \max. x \in Q, x \in G$. In the course of the iterative process, a global optimal plan is found.

Unfortunately, there is no possibility of ascertaining the effectiveness of various decomposition procedures that utilize or ignore value parameters.

I will now attempt to state some considerations supporting the fact that in certain situations and in the case of vertical mechanisms, the use of the price mechanism is evidently most preferable.

We can assume that the use of the price mechanism is most preferable in the process of underlining{implementing the plan}. The point is that after the plan is compiled, new technological opportunities, for example, might arise for the cell. Strictly speaking, in the absence of reserves the cell cannot itself resolve the question of the expedience of implementing a new proposal, since under the new conditions its actions must be coordinated with the supply and demand of other cells. But in any case, the cell itself can resolve the question of the expedience of submitting a new proposal to the coordinating agency. It can do this best by using prices.

Indeed, if in this case we were to use the aforementioned algorithm in which the cell receives the plans, it would be necessary to do a considerable amount of computational work. It would be necessary once again to resolve the optimal problem, including the new potentials of the cell, and then to compare the magnitude of the resulting deviation from the plan with the magnitude of the previous deviation. If this magnitude favors the new plan, the new proposal can be used.

In the event that prices are used, the situation is greatly simplified. One need only appraise the new input-output vector. If it has a positive profit, it can be used.

The use of prices in implementing the plan does not in any sense mean that it is also essential to use prices in compiling the plan. But in any event, when comparing the effectiveness of algorithms used in the planning process, one should bear in mind the kind of information that can be obtained from them for the implementation of the plan. Thus production systems can use algorithms that organize their activity with the use of prices. Such algorithms are already being used to create control systems for automated oil refineries. Computers control the activities of a hierarchically organized factory, using concepts of price that are customary for economists.[6]

Let us now examine a similar hierarchically organized production system that incorporates man as the controller of the corresponding cell (in this sense the worker controls an elementary cell — the production process). Control of this process could be based on the use of the same decomposition procedures, particularly the Dantzig-Wolf procedure.

What would be the difference between production systems incorporating man and fully automated systems? In the latter instance the prices transmitted to the cell would be used by it without any counteraction to obtain an optimal plan. In the first instance man can in principle counteract the intentions of the center to obtain an optimal plan from him. He may try to conceal information concerning his true potential, thereby attempting to obtain unduly high prices on individual types of products. In this connection special problems arise in creating an incentive system that minimizes the efforts of workers to conceal their production potential (see Chapter 6).

Subsidies and Superprofits

Under certain conditions the economic parameters examined

above, such as price and profit, proved adequate for the search for equilibrium (the optimum). These conditions principally presupposed the existence of convex functions characterizing the dependence between a cell's inputs and outputs. But given nonconvex functional dependences characterizing cells, these economic parameters are adequate for attaining equilibrium throughout the system.

As applied to the description of a system by means of equilibrium models in which a Pareto optimum is sought, this principle is demonstrated in a work by S. Smale.[7] In a work by A. Lur'e[8] a similar phenomenon was demonstrated under the same conditions as applied to the problem of searching for the scalar optimum throughout a system. It was shown that some cells need a subsidy in order to reach the optimum; other cells, on the contrary, will have a superprofit.

Just as prices and penalties are insufficient for reaching equilibrium (the optimum) in the case of the nonconvex functions that characterize cells, so they are also inadequate given the discontinuous (integer) character of these functions.

Based on the example of the description of a system by means of the model of optimal allocation of resources, let us see which additional economic parameters must be included in the process of optimal functioning with integer variables.

$f(x) \rightarrow$ max. (optimality criterion)

$g(x) \leq b$ (constraints on resources)

$x \in (0; 1)$ (constraints of the integer character of variables).

We will understand x to be the vector of intensity of the use of methods of production; x_{ν} is the intensity of the use of an arbitrary method ν.[9]

Let there be an optimal solution to the above problem in which the ν-th method is used with an intensity equal to unity. In this case we can find a system of valuations for the constraints in the problem.

Integer constraints will naturally also receive corresponding valuations. But what is the economic meaning of these valuations? Since the ν-th production process is part of the optimal solution, its application is useful from the standpoint of the function $f(x)$. Nonetheless, the requirement that the intensity of the process be integer, generally speaking, reduces the value of the objective function. If it were not for this requirement, quantity x_{ν} could be greater than unity or less than unity. (If the intensity x_ν were equal to unity even without the integer condition, the requirement of this condition would prove to be nonessential, and the study of the input and output of this production process would add nothing new to the analysis.) We will examine each case separately.

1. If the requirement to be integer of x_ν is eliminated, in the optimal solution it will be found that

$$0 < x_\nu < 1.$$

Accordingly, by virtue of the requirement to be integer, the most effective volume of output of a given product is exceeded, and an excessively large quantity of resources is diverted for its production. In such a case the sum of production costs in process ν will exceed the value of the output. Here the above constraint determines the lower limit of intensity x_ν.

Hence the meaning of the valuation of this constraint is clear. It determines the effect that could be obtained if it were possible to diminish the intensity of process ν somewhat and to direct the liberated resources into more effective channels. In this case subsidies are used to secure the balance of cost and benefit. The value of the available resources and superprofits, which we will discuss below, serves as the source of these subsidies.

2. If the requirement to be integer of x_ν is eliminated, then in the optimal solution it will be found that

$$x_\nu > 1.$$

Accordingly, by virtue of the requirement to be integer, the volume of production by method ν in the optimal solution will prove to be less than most effective. In such a case the total production costs will be lower than the value of the output. Accordingly, production method ν will yield additional income. This means that the resources in method ν will be used more effectively than in all other methods, and hence the intensity of its utilization should be increased. However, the condition of discreteness of x_ν, which limits the intensity of method ν from above, hinders such an increase. As can easily be shown, the additional income obtained in this case is used for the same purposes as the value of resources.

Subsidies and superprofits are production invariants and can be used with various mechanisms of the functioning of the system. The method of describing an economy by means of models of scalar optimization only facilitates the understanding of these categories as applied to vertical mechanisms.

It is possible that the interpretation of certain algorithms for the solution of problems of nonconvex, integer programming by means of prices will make it possible to arrive at a constructive procedure for using subsidies and superprofits to find equilibrium throughout the system. It is also important to bear in mind that the subsidy and superprofit categories are engendered by the need to seek equilibrium under conditions of using the price mechanism given the integer and the nonconvex character of functions characterizing the cell, and they are not the result of any malfunction in the system and an associated imbalance of inputs and outputs.

Productivity of the System

Let us first examine this problem in physical terms and then in value terms.

The remarkable capacity of informational means (production methods) to organize existing material and energy ingredients to ultimately obtain certain products is the source of potential growth of the production system. Various types of informational means are expressed in the specific methods of reproducing a greater number of ingredients with the same structure or functions. These methods may be based on the ability of a given formation to divide itself into similar formations or on the ability to form elements through differentiation and integration, with the condition that some of the producing ingredients may participate repeatedly in the production process. (The latter circumstance is characteristic of equipment, for example.)

Naturally, this potential for expanded reproduction does not contradict the law of conservation of matter. Here it is essentially assumed that there are some unlimited nonreproducible resources from which additional matter is drawn for the expansion of production or that waste materials are reduced.

J. von Neumann's model of dynamic equilibrium is a brilliant illustration of a production system's capacity for expansion. [10] If the set of informational resources — production methods — and certain material and energy resources are fixed, the system can be self-expanding; under certain conditions the rate of this self-expansion is constantly repeating. The attained level of production of ingredients will in the future determine the scale of these ingredients. Von Neumann's model can be presented formally as follows:

$$Ax(t) \leq Bx(t - 1)$$

where $A = \{a_{ij}\}$ is the matrix of inputs of i products under production method j;

$B = \{b_{ij}\}$ is the matrix of output of i products according to production method j;

$x = \{x_1, \ldots, x_n\}$ is the intensity of utilization of production methods;

t is time.

The solution of the indicated system of inequalities is associated with the search for maximum growth rate λ

$$x(t) = x(t - 1)\lambda.$$

Since not all nonreproducible resources are unlimited, with the given set of methods of production there arise natural constraints on further expansion. If a system has constraints on inexhaustible nonreproducible resources (such as territory), its expansion factor will equal unity. On the other hand, in the case of exhaustible resources, with the given set of methods of production the system may begin to deteriorate.

At the same time, given the appropriate material and energy ingredients, informational resources can organize new informational resources, and so on. Therefore, in the creation of new methods of production, if available nonreproducible resources are fixed, the system indeed obtains a source for possible further expansion. (This is equivalent to a case in which, within certain limits, the system can expand the set of nonreproducible resources if it has the means to search for them.)

Thus certain principles in the organization of the production process determine the system's capacity for development given specific material and energy ingredients (in their qualitative and quantitative determinacy). Whether these principles are created by nature in the course of evolution, whether they are created by people, or whether they will be created by automatons does not alter the core of the matter.

In accordance with what has been said, we can discuss the productivity of a system. (The mathematical term "productivity of a matrix" essentially expresses a system's capacity for self-expansion.) The marginal productivity of a system is characterized by an increment in the productivity of a system as a result of small changes in the coefficients of production methods. These are some general comments on the physical aspect of the expansion of a system.

The dual, value analogue of this model is associated with the prices of individual ingredients as constraints. Let us designate the vector of prices as p. Proceeding from the requirement that the price of the products not be less than expenditures on their production, let us formulate a dual system of inequalities relative to what was said above,

$$p(t)B \geq p(t-1)A.$$

As we know, in dynamic models of the investigated type, the rate of decline of shadow prices equals the growth rate of the system

$$p(t)\lambda = p(t-1).$$

Such a decline in shadow prices can be comprehended through the following simple considerations. Let there be one unit of resource in the given state. Say that two units can be obtained from it in the subsequent state. Then the existence of one unit at a given point in time is equivalent to two units tomorrow. [11] Thus, as it follows from the investigated model, the decline of shadow prices in the system may depend not on the subjective lesser valuation of the future by man (the discount factor) but on such objective parameters as an increase in the productivity of the system. Since the rate of decline of shadow prices equals the growth rate of the system, in a state of equilibrium the sum of values in it remains invariable $p(t)Bx(t) = p(t-1)Ax(t-1)$. [12]

Von Neumann's model can be expanded, and the production of new production methods can be incorporated in it, i.e., it can be transformed into a model with endogenous technological progress. But there will always remain a constraint in the form of the set of production methods of a certain rank for producing production methods. The rank of a technological set means the measure of its remoteness from the set of production methods by means of which products are directly produced.

The shadow price of the limiting technological set of the highest rank expresses its marginal utility, which is equal to the possible increment in the growth rate of the system or, what is the same thing, the increment of the rate of decline of shadow prices. In other words, the shadow price of the limiting technological set of the highest rank is the shadow price of the productivity of a system.

The productivity of a system and its shadow price are an economic invariant. This shadow price has to be involved in the cost of commodities as the price of all other resources.

Penalties

I will treat penalties, as a production invariant, as the valuation of anticipation.

In the process of its functioning, the local cell can somehow co-ordinate its actions with other participants to secure a balance of inputs and outputs. The opportunity to play out situations be-forehand at the informational level in order to develop such a coordinated program makes it possible to anticipate an im-balance that might arise during the actual exchange of limited resources.

At the same time, the anticipatory program is not given in rigid form. Degrees of freedom are left to the cell. A violation of the anticipatory principle may lead to better results throughout the system as a whole, since it is impossible to foresee everything. The amount of the penalty should reflect a proportion between the unlimited actions of the cells and the strict requirements of ob-serving balance constraints.

Let us examine the foregoing with regard to the vertical mech-anism. The cells' use of prices as parameters to help select their local optimal policy causes significant difficulties in the corresponding situations at every stage of the iterative process. If the prices are constants, i.e., do not correspondingly depend on the volume of inputs and outputs, then they, as is the case, for ex-ample, in the Dantzig-Wolf algorithm, offer too much freedom for decision-making and therefore retard reaching the optimum. It would be possible to try to anticipate the actions of the cell and to limit the possibilities of its activity by establishing strict limits on inputs and outputs (as is done in the Kornai-Liptak algorithm). The limits also block rapid attainment of the optimum, since they may provide too few degrees of freedom.

Naturally, the desire arises to combine the various methods of searching for the optimum and to use prices at every step as a nonlinear function of the input-output volume for the cell. A knowledge of this function would anticipate, for example, the cell's excessive demand for general resources. One constructive way to build this function entails the introduction of penalties for the in-put-output program recommended by the center.[13] This method gives the cell flexibility in optimal decision-making by combining freedom in selecting an optimal action program based on the cor-responding prices with "responsibility" for the expenditure of resources "recommended" by the center.

110

The cell optimizes profit within the limits of its technological constraints and the "recommended" input of global resources. The amount of profit also depends on the penalties that the cell will pay if it exceeds the recommended expenditure of global resources.

$$x_k \overset{\text{opt.}}{\in} Q_k \left[(c_k x_k) - (p^n, b_k^t - A_k x_k) - \frac{K_n}{2} \| b_k^t - A_k x_k \|^2 \right]$$

where c_k is the vector of utility coefficients of goods of cell k; x_k is the volume of production of these goods by cell k; p^n is the price vector for global resources given in iteration n (this iteration is called large because prices change less often than global resources are reallocated); b_k^t is the quantity of global resources allocated by the center to cell k in small iteration t (this iteration is associated only with the reallocation of resources within the limits of prices established in large iteration n); K_n is the rate of the penalty designated in large iteration n; and A_k is the matrix of input-output coefficients by cell k.

In accordance with the optimal program obtained from cell k, in iteration t the center reallocates resources for the following cell $k + 1$.

$$b_{k+1}^{t+1} = b - \sum_{j \neq k+1} A_j x_j^t.$$

After it is determined that the programs recommended by the center are not feasible from the standpoint of the expenditure of global resources, in a certain iteration T the center reviews prices in accordance with the shortage of resources. The size of the shortage is determined by the amount of penalties cells are prepared to pay for the higher expenditure of resources.

$$p^{n+1} = p^n - K_n \left(b - \sum_{k=1}^{N} A_k x_k^T \right).$$

Thus, as is evident from this algorithm, even in vertical mechanisms it is possible to use penalties for violations of anticipatory principles (the use of penalties will be examined in greater detail in Chapter 6).

Money

In economics literature it is commonly believed that money is a means of exchange under conditions in which it is impossible (or inexpedient) for the participants to organize direct barter. Under these conditions money fills the void that opens in such acts of exchange. Money acts as a guarantee to the participant who transferred his commodity to another person whose commodities are not needed by the first participant. While not rejecting this approach to revealing the essence of money, I would only like to note that it restricts the category of money solely to market mechanisms.

The literature also calls attention to a multitude of other functions performed by money, particularly to the role of money as a parameter that restricts the actions of participants. I shall attempt to approach the definition of money as an invariant for the various classes of mechanisms of functioning of production systems. For me such an approach to the definition of money entails understanding money as a universal constraint on the cell's opportunity to obtain the necessary global resources from outside for the appropriate prices.

The overall sum of money in the system reflects the aggregate value of global resources, i.e., resources that can be reallocated among cells. If a cell has resources that cannot be placed in external circulation, they are considered special and are not included in the total sum of values covered by money. The share of money that a given participant has at his disposal enables him to obtain a share of the overall value of global resources for the corresponding prices.

I shall attempt below to demonstrate the constructive sense of this definition of money. The known models of economic equilibrium make it possible to interpret money in this sense. Thus in D. Geil's partial model [14]

$$c^k x^k \to \text{max.}$$

$$px^k \leq d^k$$

$$\sum_k x^k \leq X$$

d^k can be understood as the amount of money in cell k that limits it in obtaining the vector of the necessary products x^k. [15] Here it is a matter of indifference to us how the money is obtained by the cells. We are also indifferent to the mechanism by which prices are set.

This model contains the valuable proof that if a cell has a universal budgeting constraint — a constraint on the possibility of acquiring commodities — a price vector will be found permitting it to make autonomous decisions in the direction of equilibrium throughout the system as a whole. This means that the maximum of utility functions for every cell $c^k x^k$ has been found while observing the balance of commodities $\sum_k x^k \leq X$.

It is further important to note that the analysis of models of economic equilibrium has revealed a parameter like the shadow price of money each cell has. This was represented as a Lagrange multiplier with respect to the budgeting constraint — relationship (2) — that arises in the solution by each cell of the following extremal problem $u^k(x^k) \rightarrow$ max. $px^k \leq d^k$.

These shadow prices are also of great interest from a methodological point of view. They can be regarded as shadow prices of the second rank. I introduce the concept of the rank of shadow prices in order to reflect the number of times previous shadow prices have already been used to form the new parameter subjected to valuation. [16] Thus in this case shadow prices were used only once to define the concept of money. They were used to determine the overall value of universal resources in the system, which in this case was equal to the amount of money. For this reason the shadow price of money a cell has is here of second rank.

I know that these shadow prices of money have been used constructively only in transforming models of economic equilibrium into models with a global optimality criterion (see Chapter 4). The weights of the participants were determined in this criterion by an amount inverse to the marginal utility of money for them. [17] But in general, I know of no works devoted to the use of money in the aforementioned sense of the word and its shadow prices to build constructive procedures to search for equilibrium. The known algorithms used to search for the optimum in a centralized system with autonomous decision-making by individual economic cells, i.e., so-called decomposition procedures, also do not use money. They use only such value parameters as the utility of goods, prices, penalties, and profits.

I have attempted to construct a decomposition procedure that would incorporate a parameter like money. Naturally, an algorithm

113

of this type must also include prices. While algorithms with prices are not necessarily associated with money, algorithms with money necessarily require the introduction of prices that secure optimal decision-making by the cell. Hence I have chosen the well-known Dantzig-Wolf decomposition procedure. This algorithm, based on prices assigned to the cell, forms a <u>linear function</u> of the search for maximum profit within the limits of its production potential and without additional external constraints. We can assume that under these conditions a cell has too many degrees of freedom for developing optimal input-output vectors. This is perhaps the reason for the slow convergence of the Dantzig-Wolf algorithm.

As we already noted above, it is possible to attempt to increase the speed of convergence of this algorithm by introducing flexible additional external constraints in the form of targets for marginal inputs and outputs in physical terms and penalties for their non-fulfillment. However, with this problem-solving method the problem of the cell becomes more complicated owing to the increase in the number of constraints.

In this connection the following compromise solution strikes me as useful: incorporating an additional universal constraint in the form of money in the problem for the cell. In certain cases it may help to improve the convergence of the process.

In accordance with this proposal the Dantzig-Wolf algorithm can be modified in the following way.

The Basic Problem

$$\sum_k c^k x^k \rightarrow \max.$$

$$Ax \leq b$$

$$A^k x^k \leq \beta^k$$

where $k = 1, 2, \ldots, K$ is the number of the cell;

c^k is the vector of the utility of final products of cell k;

x^k is the output vector of final products by cell k;

A is the matrix of inputs — output coefficients;

b is the vector of global resources;

β^k is the vector of local resources belonging to cell k.

114

Value Parameters

The Formation of the Local Problem for Cell

$$c_k x_k^\sigma - p^\sigma A^k x_k^\sigma \to \max.$$

$$A^k x_k^\sigma \le \beta^k$$

$$p^\sigma A^k x_k^\sigma \le d_k^\sigma$$

As in the Dantzig-Wolf algorithm, in every σ step the cell strives for the maximization of profit $c^k x_k^\sigma - p^\sigma A^k x_k^\sigma$ (where
is the vector of prices of global resources) within the limits of its internal production potential $A^k x_k^\sigma \le \beta^k$. The difference lies in the fact that one more constraint — budgeting constraint d_k^σ — is added which limits inputs of the cell — $p^\sigma A^k x_k^\sigma$. The center allocates this money to the cell at every σ-th step.

Relations between the center and the cell become somewhat more complicated. As in the Dantzig-Wolf algorithm, the center must determine the optimal plan that can be proposed by the cell. But in addition to this, the center must determine the amount of money to be allocated to the cell for the "acquisition" of global resources. At the end of the process this sum must be strictly equal to the value of the global resources a cell receives under the optimal plan. Generally speaking, at the beginning of the process the amount of money allocated to the cell may be arbitrary.

In order to obtain information on the necessary amount of money for the cell, the center requires additional information. This information must evidently reflect the marginal utility of money for a given cell at a σ-th step. Let us designate it as λ_k^σ. It is the shadow price of the constraint $p^\sigma A^k x_k^\sigma \le d_k^\sigma$ of the indicated local problem.

Thus in solving the local problem, at the σ-th step the cell finds not only the optimal output vector $\hat{x}_k^\sigma$ but also the marginal utility of money allocated to it λ_k^σ. The cell sends all this information to the center.

The Central Problem

The first stage in the solution of the optimal problem at the center is analogous to the Dantzig-Wolf procedure

$$\sum_k c_k \zeta_k^{\sigma+1} \to \max.$$

$$\sum_k A \zeta_k^{\sigma+1} \le b$$

$$\zeta_k^{\sigma+1} = \alpha_k^0 \hat{x}_k^0 + \alpha_k^1 \hat{x}_k^1 + , \ldots , \alpha_k^\sigma \hat{x}_k^\sigma$$

$$\sum_{\tilde{\sigma}=0}^{\sigma} \alpha_k^{\tilde{\sigma}} = 1$$

The center finds prices on the vector of global resources as dual variables.

In the second stage the center calculates its available money and distributes it among cells. The sum of money, designated as $D^{\sigma+1}$, that the center has at its disposal at $\sigma + 1$-th step is equal to the value of all available global resources measured in prices found at the $\sigma + 1$-th step

$$D^{\sigma+1} = p^{\sigma+1} b$$

Money can be distributed among cells on the basis of the following formula

$$d_k^{\sigma+1} = \frac{D^{\sigma+1}}{D^\sigma}\left(d_k^\sigma + \gamma \left(\frac{1}{m}\sum_k \lambda_k^\sigma - \lambda_k^\sigma \right) \right)$$

Here we are using the structure of the formula common in decomposition procedures like the Kornai-Liptak algorithm for the reallocation of global resources among cells. The difference between the usual formula and the formula from the above algorithm is in the normalization factor $\dfrac{D^{\sigma+1}}{D^\sigma}$. It is necessary in the algorithm in question, since here the sum of money changes from step to step; in well-known decomposition procedures the vector of global resources was fixed.

It is difficult to prove the convergence of this algorithm. It goes without saying that it is impossible to make a theoretical appraisal of the effectiveness of this algorithm.

In this connection an attempt was made to verify the algorithm experimentally by computer. The general problem was solved on the assumption that there were six cells with twenty methods of production each, eight local constraints, and ten global resources.

At the same time, a number of calculations were made corresponding to various values of parameter γ. Its value was taken as equal to 1, 5, 10, and 15. In all calculations the process proved to be monotonically convergent toward the optimum. However, the speed of convergence was lower than in the initial Dantzig-Wolf

Table 1

Results of Experimental Calculations of an Optimal Plan
Based on the Dantzig-Wolf Algorithm and
Its Proposed Modification

	Dantzig-Wolf algorithm	Modified algorithm for values of γ			
		1	5	10	15
Number of iterations	5	10	7	7	6
Time (in seconds)	12.4	17.5	19.8	18.6	18.5

algorithm, i.e., more time and a greater number of steps were required to attain the optimum (see Table 1).

Unfortunately, the experiment to verify the integer algorithm
including money did not show its effectiveness. Yet from all
the foregoing about the role of money, it follows, in our view,
that it would make sense to continue the study of the proposed
algorithm or modifications of it on both a theoretical (proof of
convergence) and experimental level.

Since the speed of convergence of the new algorithm is not sharply reduced compared with the speed of convergence in the Dantzig-
Wolf algorithm, one can hope that the proposed algorithm will prove
to be effective under certain conditions. It may prove more effective if the number of participants and the number of global resources are increased (possibly tenfold or more). It is particularly
interesting to test this algorithm under stochastic and integrality
conditions, when it is especially important to damp local solutions
of the cells.

From our view of the essence of money as an economic invariant,
it follows that in principle it can be used as a means of control in
any economic system. The difference in the systems, of course,
will primarily consist in the way monetary assets are formed.
Moreover, we can assume that the proposed approach to the definition of money has general systems significance. Thus it is
feasible to consider energy an analogue of money in physical systems. With the mechanical approach to physical systems there
are only first-rank shadow prices — force and pressure. Their
set reflects the set of initial parameters belonging to objects in
the system such as their coordinates, volume, etc. With the
thermodynamic approach there arises a new type of shadow price
that is of the second rank — temperature. It appraises the general

universal constraint of the object — the amount of energy (it can be expressed through work and thereby through a first-rank shadow price — work expresses forces and the path traversed).

As we know fruitful analogies have been established between physical and economic systems that make it possible to obtain a number of quite effective means for analyzing and solving economic problems (for example, analogue models for solving economic problems through the methods of mathematical programming). Interesting attempts are now being made to use physical analogies to find the state of equilibrium in Geil's economic models of equilibrium.[18] The use of this analogy also raises hopes for the formation of new types of algorithms to solve economic problems in the optimal allocation of resources. Such algorithms can simulate the inclusion of money in the model in the sense discussed above.

Value Invariants in Production Systems with Human Participation

The inclusion of man in the system of production leads to the emergence of a number of new phenomena. Let us examine those that are associated with the price mechanism and are invariant relative to vertical or horizontal mechanisms. We shall initially mention such invariants of economic systems as excise taxes and contour money. In the following two chapters we will examine in greater detail such invariants as stimuli for increasing the effectiveness of performance, inflation, and color markets.

Excise Taxes, Subsidies, and Limited Commodities

The individual system of preferences for products may be such that it clashes with the interests of society no matter how the latter is understood. Among such products are, for example, drugs, alcohol, tobacco goods, and so on. Society may disseminate propaganda explaining the harm that these products cause the individual, i.e., attempts may be made to alter the system of people's values. However, the path of changing the system of individual preferences is very difficult and in many respects even dangerous for both the social and physical health of the nation. For this reason, in order to limit the consumption of such products, society introduces restrictions on their production. Society may entirely prohibit the production of such products, i.e., they may be banned (see Chapter 7

118

for more detail). It does so for the products most destructive to social life, e.g., drugs. (Naturally, this does not refer to the production and consumption of drugs for medical purposes.)

For products that are relatively less disruptive of social life, restrictions are introduced on their production, i.e., they are limited commodities. Within the framework of the price mechanism, these constraints are realized by raising consumer prices. Here we refer to a price higher than one that would reflect the individual preferences of people and the existing production potential without any additional constraints on them.

Such raising of prices on commodities whose consumption is to be limited can be expressed formally, for example, in the following model of scalar optimization. Explicit in it are the factors that distort price when there are constraints on the consumption of commodities and their relationship to expenditures.

In this model we will differentiate between two types of constraints: direct constraints on variables and functional constraints. Among the former are constraints directly imposed on variables, such as their nonnegativity, and the domain of their permissible volume. Among the latter are mediate constraints connected to variables through corresponding functional dependences, for example, methods of production.

The optimality criterion in this model $f(x)$ is given in the set of individual functions of all participants consuming market basket x.

Constraints on the production potential are adopted as functional

$$A x \leq b.$$

If there were no other constraints, then by virtue of the high utility, say, of alcohol to many participants and the relatively low expenditure of resources on its production, its consumption would be so high that it might have a negative impact on society. As we noted above, the principal way to diminish the consumption of products of this type is to institute constraints on their production

$$x^* \leq \alpha ,$$

where x^* is the set of limited products (x^* is the subvector of vector x);

α is the maximally permissible volume of production of limited products.

In accordance with this model the price of this type of limited product $p^* = \dfrac{\partial f(x)}{\partial x^*}$ rises. This rise will be expressed in the growth of expenditures. (Here we construe expenditures in the broad sense of any type of action associated with overcoming the constraints.) Expenditures grow as a result of the inclusion of the shadow price of direct constraint λ^* in addition to expenditures of production resources proper $A\lambda$

$$p^* = A\lambda + \lambda^*.$$

In all developed economic systems the state restricts the consumption of such products. It establishes higher prices, e.g., on alcoholic beverages, tobacco, etc., in the form of excise taxes. The economic essence of the excise tax is expressed in the shadow price of the constraint on the sale of commodities of this type.

Constraints on the sale of a commodity may also be established from below, i.e., no less than a given quantity of the commodity should be sold. If this quantity exceeds the population's demand based on normal prices under the given conditions, the price should be correspondingly lowered relative to the expenditure of resources. A negative shadow price of such a constraint on the volume of consumption of a number of products determines the economic essence of the corresponding type of subsidy.

The state resorts to this type of subsidy, for example, in order to disseminate certain types of books when the population has not purchased them for "normal" prices. The state's primary motivation in doing so — the education of the population or propaganda — is another matter.

Contour Money

We know that in society there are many producers (either organizations or individual persons) the results of whose activity cannot in principle be sold — the activity of the army, the state, persons studying basic science, etc. — or which it may also be for some reason inexpedient to sell — free schools, hospitals, and so on. All these producers cannot be assessed in terms of profit, and thus they are called nonprofit institutions (we note again that in a specific case they may be individual persons).

At the same time, these producers require resources to carry out their activity. The resources may be given to them by higher-echelon organizations or by all sorts of independent social organizations: charitable societies, foundations, and so on. In other words, nonprofit institutions may receive resources within the framework of vertical and horizontal mechanisms of functioning.

They may obtain these resources in physical or in monetary form. In the latter case the additional problem arises that the personnel of the institution receiving the money may spend it for their selfish interests. They may spend more of this money to increase their wages, to organize pleasure trips, etc., than on the purchase of equipment, supplies, and so on. Since an organization (or an individual) financing nonprofit institutions cannot monitor the value of the result through its purchase, it must monitor the expenditure of money. Such control is exercised through an estimate of expenditures, i.e., in constraints on the expenditure of money according to corresponding lines in the estimate. Within the limits of the sum of money on a line in the estimate, the participant may be granted independence in making decisions about the purchase of the necessary resources. We call money whose degree of universality is limited "contour" or "estimated" money.

Thus contour money is invariant relative to the system's mechanism of functioning. Differences in the mechanisms of functioning affect the structure of contour money and the flexibility of change.

If one takes an arbitrary level of the hierarchy in the vertical mechanism, generally speaking, it experiences the pressure of higher-echelon agencies and itself regulates the activity of lower links. Here strictly formal bureaucratic principles are more important in regulating activity. Within the framework of these mechanisms there is a more detailed breakdown of expenditures into various items.

Thus rigidity in the distribution of money among various items in the estimate is also more characteristic of vertical mechanisms. In these mechanisms it is considerably more difficult to be flexible in the redistribution of money among various items of expenditure. In market-type horizontal mechanisms contour money can be used more flexibly. For example, the owner of a small fund can finance scientists less formally, accepting to a greater degree their peculiarities, the possibility of trusting them, and so on.[19]

* * *

Summing up the first two sections of this chapter, we can state that the theory of duality, which has been so successfully developed in mathematics, especially in the last three decades, has made possible considerable progress in economic science. This progress is primarily connected with the construction of algorithms for finding optimal solutions and, on their basis, appropriate methods of control.

At the same time, the theory of duality has been developed mainly for convex functions. It has not yet been sufficiently developed for more complex cases in which its generalization could provide new ideas for building constructive procedures. Of interest in this connection is the generalization of the theory of duality problems with integer variables. As was shown above, with integer variables and prices on resources there are also such economic parameters as subsidies and superprofits. Speculation develops as to whether these parameters are valuations of integer constraints.

Further, in the algorithm we discussed above that uses the penalty function there emerged a parameter like the penalty. However, the methods for finding its magnitude are in practice based on the intuition of the person doing the calculations; unlike the existing methods of finding prices, there are no regular procedures whatsoever for establishing the magnitude of a penalty. We know that in both economic and legal literature the problem of setting a penalty is also controversial. We can assume that the joint effort of economists, jurists, and mathematicians could help create regular procedures to set penalties for comparatively simple situations for which appropriate algorithms could be devised.

Thus further generalizations of the theory of duality both for instances of more rigid demands on the type of functions used in the formulation of economic problems and for situations in which new economic institutions (such as penalties) are introduced may promote the further progress of economic science.

Soviet Experience in the Use of the Price Mechanism

The economic invariants we have examined help us to better understand the theoretical and practical problems entailed in forming a price mechanism in planned economies of the Soviet type and the reasons for the major errors committed in building this mechanism in the USSR.

Theoretical Substantiation of the Price Mechanism by Soviet Economists

The classical scholars of Marxism believed that the price

mechanism was the offspring of the spontaneous market system. Since developed commodity exchange in the market system cannot take place in physical form, it unequivocally requires prices, money, and other value categories. Capitalism, in which commodity relations have attained the greatest development, has become a synonym for such mechanism.

Reactionaries called for liberation from the price mechanism through a return to a subsistence economy devoid of developed exchange relations. And communists considered the price mechanism the spawn of the devil, since it was linked to a spontaneous mechanism, the possibility of enrichment, people's worship of the power of money, and so on.

The communists were romantics on this issue. They called for a society based on developed exchange relations. But since future society, in the opinion of Marx and Engels, would be based on the planning principle, the need for spontaneous market exchange in it would be obviated. And since there would be no spontaneous exchange, there would be no attendant value parameters.

The classical scholars of Marxism conceived of future society as a system in which everything would be obvious. People's goals would be obvious, as would the available resources and methods for transforming them into the products needed by the population.

Marx and Engels used at least three images to picture the economic mechanism of future society. In the first volume of Capital Marx used the example of Robinson Crusoe to show that when man deals purposefully with production problems, he does not have to resort to the services of the price mechanism. Second, it seemed that the price mechanism was not used in primitive tribes, since all work in these tribes was directly planned.

Finally, Marx and Engels evidently pictured future society as an analogue of the nineteenth-century factory, which represented for them the model of organization, unlike the anarchy of the market mechanism. Indeed, if one takes the routine work of a textile mill, for example, it has few degrees of freedom. The product mix is given. Production technology and resources are fixed. Under these conditions it simply remains to distribute tasks between spinning, weaving, and dyeing production facilities. In principle this can be done quite simply, in physical terms, without resorting to the services of all sorts of complex mechanisms, including the price mechanism.

Thus the implicit use of the price mechanism in the life of Robinson Crusoe and a primitive tribe or its negligible role in the

established life of a rigidly organized enterprise served the classical scholars of Marxism as bases for proving the historical
limitation of the price mechanism.

Soviet economists faced the problem of justifying a price mechanism under the conditions of a planned economy where, it seems,
there was no place for it.

The ideal embodiment of the Marxist interpretation of the role
of the price mechanism was found in the USSR during the period of
war communism, so called largely because the bulk of the resources were allocated directly without any value parameters.
Such a concept of communism serves as the basis for the leaders
of such underdeveloped countries as China and Cuba to proclaim
the superiority of the system created by them, since they hardly
use the price mechanism.

As we attempted to show in the first part of this work, the price
mechanism is required to organize the effective, autonomous
decision-making of economic cells that have degrees of freedom.
Let us see to what degree in the period of war communism in the
USSR and in the situation that has developed in China and Cuba it
is possible and necessary for the price mechanism to be used by
the leading participants in the economic system: consumers, producers, engineers, and the state.

Consumers have no opportunity to select the requisite market
basket, since the level of production is low and the assortment is
limited. In such a situation it is essentially clear what people need
to survive, and it is very convenient to use a ration system to distribute consumer goods.

As regards managers of enterprises, their basic task amounts
to fulfilling the established output target in physical terms. It is
specifically on this task that the authorities focus the attention of
relatively unskilled managers and workers. Getting the managers
to attain the requisite output with less effort is too difficult a job.

Nor do engineers have a particular need for prices, since their
basic task is to copy existing foreign models of armaments and
production technology.[20]

Finally, let us take the heads of state. Their application of effective methods of planning the use of the price mechanism would
make it possible to accelerate the economy's rate of development.
However, they do not have such tools at their disposal, since a
sufficiently effective methodology of national economic planning
does not yet exist.

Marxism oriented these leaders and the theoreticians serving them toward revolution, and it relegated to tenth place or, more precisely, even basically denied the need to work out beforehand methods for managing a future planned society. As we have already noted, it seemed to Marx and Engels that everything in future society would be obvious and that it would be child's play to organize the planning process in such a society. The most important thing was to make the revolution and to destroy the old world, with its hated price mechanism.

Thus the absence of methods for effectively managing an economic system and, on the other hand, the possibility of functioning within the framework of outright directives on engineering, production, and distribution meant that a low level of development of the science of mechanisms of functioning of the economic system and a low level of development of production and its cadres were generally presented as good, as the ideal of future society.

As the Soviet economy develops, as the living standard of the working people rises, as its own research and development base is created, and as the cultural level of management rises, the question of the need to have an effective price mechanism becomes more and more urgent. Yet the nature of this mechanism in a planned economy has remained vague to Soviet economists.

In keeping with Marxist doctrine, the majority of Soviet economists are sincerely convinced that the price mechanism is engendered by transitory factors, that it is a temporary phenomenon, and that it is necessary only for the period of transition from socialism to communism. Under communism the price mechanism will disappear.

Thus when out of practical necessity it began to apply the price mechanism following the introduction of NEP, Soviet economic science could not explain its essence. As a result great difficulties ensued in using this mechanism. Economists sought an answer to these difficulties through theoretical comprehension of the nature of the price mechanism assuming the peculiarities of the planned Soviet economy. They perceived these peculiarities in the existence of two forms of ownership — state ownership and collective-cooperative ownership — in the existence of labor with different skill levels, in the isolation of factories (specifically factories and not another level in the hierarchical formation) that had to compensate their expenditures by the sale of their product, and so on.

Only in recent years has the view also developed among traditional Soviet economists that the price mechanism will remain even under communism in connection with the need for decentralization. Unfortunately, the explanation for this is vague and obscured by all sorts of statements about money performing the role of accounting money, etc.[21] But even such a view is subject to fatal criticism from the position of the withering away of commodity production under communism.[22]

The lack of clarity in Soviet economists' understanding of the principles of the price mechanism leads to various difficulties of both an ideological and economic quality. During the Soviet economic reform, when the USSR began implementing measures aimed at decentralization and at strengthening the role of the price mechanism, some economists in the West proclaimed the convergence of the systems, that the USSR was sliding toward capitalism. However, a price mechanism is not the prerogative of capitalism. This mechanism will be inherent in any economic system. The only difference is that in less developed systems it does not appear in explicit form but can be used by people intuitively. Therefore it is by no means necessary to slide toward capitalism or to unify economic mechanisms in order to employ a developed system of value parameters.

Thanks to the aforementioned factors in their interpretation of the nature of the price mechanism, however, Soviet economists are unable to resist their Western colleagues who understand the price mechanism as an invariant. Hence some Soviet economists, who hold very conservative positions, in a number of cases agree with some of their Western colleagues but also declare, for example, that the use of a value category like profit is borrowing from bourgeois categories. For these economists there is a contradiction in the fact that, despite the global criterion of optimality for society through maximum satisfaction of the needs of its members, maximum profit can still be a local criterion for an economic unit. They essentially demand the curtailment of the role of the price mechanism.

Other Soviet economists make all sorts of excuses for using value parameters under socialism. First, they believe that value parameters are only a temporary phenomenon that will wither away under communism. Second, they try to proclaim the genuinely socialist nature of these parameters and their harnessing.

If we set the demagogy aside, in reality planned systems create in principle conditions for the more orderly use of value parameters. But this requires the construction of these systems on the basis of modern advances in science and, of course, above all the preservation of the diversity of economic mechanisms within the framework of political democracy. Otherwise the use of price mechanisms may be ineffective.

The Practice of Using the Price Mechanism

We shall now examine in more detail some aspects of actual Soviet practice in using a number of value invariants such as price, subsidies, and superprofits.*

Prices

Prices in the USSR, as we know, are built on the basis of calculation of labor inputs.[23] The calculation of the shadow price of land, its mineral deposits, and so on, has been totally rejected.[24] As a result of such cost figuring, the overall value of output is lowered, to say nothing of disruptions in proportions between prices on various products.

During the last decade a number of economists tried to incorporate rent and interest on capital in the calculation of costs. Proponents of the theory of optimal planning have most consistently developed this point of view. An appreciable number of traditional economists, i.e., economists who in fact do not know Western economic theories of price formation, have also drawn attention to the basic need to take these economic phenomena into account. However, their arguments for including the categories of rent, rate of interest, etc., are inconsistent, which has led to simplifications in practical implementation.

Also simplistic, moreover, has been the calculation of labor that lies at the root of Soviet price formation. The theory of labor value still enthralls the majority of Soviet economists by the clarity with which it measures inputs in terms of working time (calculated working time).

We shall present a hypothetical model on whose basis the key concept in the Soviet system of price formation through labor inputs is evidently demonstrated.

Let the planning system pursue the goal of maximizing the function of social well-being F, the value of which depends on the volume of consumption of consumer goods $x = \{x_1, \ldots, x_e, \ldots, x_m\}$

*Chapter 6 details Soviet practice in using shadow prices of labor resources and penalties. On the use of money in the USSR, see the work of G. Grossman.[25]

$$F(x_1, \ldots, x_e, \ldots, x_m) \to \max.$$

We shall take the existence of only one type of labor in volume L and technological conditions as constraints. Technological conditions are characterized by the fact that every product is produced by only one method, and this method is expressed by a linear function. To put it more simply, a_e — labor inputs in the production of a unit of every product — are fixed.

Taking the foregoing into account, the optimal planning problem will assume the following form:

$$F(x_1, \ldots, x_e, \ldots, x_m) \to \max.$$

$$\sum_{e-1}^{m} a_e x_e \leq L.$$

From the necessary conditions of the extremum it follows that at the optimum point for all x_e differing from zero, the following equality is fulfilled

$$\frac{\partial F(x_1, \ldots, x_e, \ldots, x_m)}{\partial x_e} = a_e \lambda.$$

From this it follows that at the optimum point, the marginal labor inputs are proportional to marginal utility with an accuracy of the multiplier. If we designate the marginal utility of product e

$\dfrac{\partial F(x_1, \ldots, x_e, \ldots, x_n)}{\partial x_e}$ as u_e, then for arbitrary products e and e'

$$\frac{u_e}{u_{e'}} = \frac{a_e}{a_{e'}}.$$

Thus, since for the formation of prices their relationships are mainly important, in the given instance both labor theory and the theory of marginal utility will produce the same results. (The Russian economist M. I. Tugan-Baranovskii called attention to this fact in his day.)

In this case prices can also be based on labor inputs. Let us designate the vector of prices obtained in this way as $p' = \{p'_1, \ldots, p'_e, \ldots, p'_m\}$. [16]

This method of criticizing the labor theory of value can conditionally be called immanent criticism. The method is analogous, for example, to the method of criticism of classical mechanics from the standpoint of the theory of relativity. Characteristic of immanent criticism is the fact that there can be found a theory with a system of axioms that yields all the inferences deducible from the previous system of axioms. Naturally, the new theory is richer since its axiomatics make it possible to draw a larger number of conclusions. At the same time, it allows us not to refute the conclusions of the old theories, since it permits us to see under precisely which <u>conditions</u> the inferences from the old theory are correct.

Thus as a special case the axiomatics of the theory of marginal utility make it possible to draw conclusions that agree with the theory of labor value.

Since wages exist in the USSR, there further arises the problem of distributing goods by the price mechanism. In what way within the framework of the investigated model are wages coordinated with the quantity of goods to be received?

If we are concerned only with the consumer goods sold by the trade system (public goods will be involved in the latter) and denoted by the index i $(i = 1, \ldots, n)$ then the total amount of labor expended on the production of these goods is

$$L_i = \sum_{i=1}^{n} a_i x_i .$$

We know that under socialism wages depend on the quantity and quality of labor. If one hour of labor is taken as the monetary unit, the total mass of wages, denoted W_i, will be

$$W_i = \sum_{i=1}^{n} w_i x_i$$

where w_i is the wage paid for production of one unit of an i-th good.

The price of a certain commodity p_i is equal to the wage paid for the production of this commodity $p_i = w_i$. The total value of the produced consumer goods denoted Π_i is

$$\Pi_i = \sum_{i=1}^{n} p_i x_i .$$

On the basis of our assumptions the total sum of wages is equal to the value of the produced goods, and therefore this amount of wages will be completely covered by goods

$$W_i = \Pi_i .$$

Let us now assume in the system that there are public goods (for example, the services of the army, the state, etc.), means for accumulation, etc. Their distinguishing feature is that expenditures on all these goods are not included in direct costs of the production of consumer goods paid for, i.e., distributed by means of prices. In such a case how can one coordinate the wage fund with the available quantity of paid consumer goods, with expenditures on their production, and with prices?

Subsequently, for the sake of simplicity we will speak of two types of goods in the system: consumer and public goods. Let us designate the volume of production of a public good as $x_s = \{x_{n+1}, \ldots, x_s, \ldots, x_S\}$ and labor inputs in the production of a unit of public goods as a_s. Then total labor inputs in the production of these goods will amount to

$$L_s = \sum_{s=n+1}^{s} a_s x_s.$$

Labor inputs in the production of all goods throughout the system will be

$$L = L_i + L_s.$$

Total wages paid in accordance with the socialist principle of distribution according to labor will equal total labor inputs

$$W = L.$$

Thus a discrepancy develops between the amount of wages paid throughout the system W and the value of consumer goods produced — Π_i. This discrepancy is equal to labor inputs in the production of public goods, an adequate sum of wages W_s, and values Π_s.

In such a case how can the wages paid be equalized with the value of consumer goods? There are several methods. One of these methods is based on introducing income taxes; the sum of taxes has to equal the value of public goods. But because in reality there are a lot of intermediate goods, this method has some technical disadvantages. If it is used, one must deduct a significant amount of income tax at every step of the process of producing goods. The disadvantages of this method are more clear if one keeps in mind another method to equalize the amount of wages and the value of consumer goods. This method entails adding to the prices of consumer goods on the basis of direct expenditures a sum equal to the value of public goods. This operation can be made once, at the stage of passing the commodities from the producer to the consumer.

130

In the Soviet economic literature all public goods and accumu-
lations are usually called the surplus product. In fact this is not
a rigorous definition of the surplus product, since in all cases
free services rendered the population are not surplus product
but are only a form of distribution of consumer goods.

For the sake of simplicity we shall subsequently use the surplus product concept adopted in the USSR and designate its mass
as Π.

It is necessary to keep the proportions of the prices of commodities equal to the proportions of their marginal utilities. This
is a necessary condition for selling consumer goods. Since in the
case we are analyzing marginal utilities are equal to the labor
expenses, it is possible to separate the labor expenses for the
production of public goods and relate them to consumer goods in
the same proportion as labor expenses for their production.

The new price of a certain consumer good denoted $\hat{p}_i$ is

$$\hat{p}_i = p_i(1 + \tau),$$

where τ is the coefficient that expresses the relationship of the
mass of the surplus product to the mass of labor inputs in the production of consumer goods $\tau = \dfrac{\Pi}{L_i}$.

Measured by the new prices, the value of consumer goods

$\Pi_i \left(\Pi_i = \sum\limits_{i=1}^{n} p_i x_i \right)$ will now be equal to the wages paid throughout

the system

$$W = \hat{\Pi}_i.$$

It is this model that essentially underlies the Soviet system of
price formation. Let us now attempt to examine this system of
price formation in somewhat greater detail, while remaining within
the framework of rather simple models.

We shall now examine the implications of the fact that there are a
number of commodities going into accumulation, i.e., that the process of producing consumer goods is not instantaneous. With
multistage production of consumer goods it would be possible to
distribute the surplus products at all stages of production in proportion to labor inputs. In a stationary process (the rate of
growth is equal to 1) the sum of such inputs at the various stages
would be equal to the value of consumer goods at a given time.
Under nonstationary conditions the balance of wages and the value of consumer goods would not be secured given such a distribu-

tion of the surplus product. What is more, such a method of distributing the surplus product, as noted above, is technically unwieldy compared with the method of including these costs in the last stage of production before the product is released to the consumer. It is the latter method that has been used in the USSR for a long time. It engendered a category like turnover tax, [26] which as early as 1940 comprised 58.7 percent of all budget revenues, and today accounts for about 30 percent.

Thus, assuming the inclusion of the aforementioned inputs in the costs of producing consumer goods, one could be theoretically and practically satisfied with turnover tax alone. However, another category — profit — has also been taken into account in the Soviet practice of establishing prices.

Let us increase the complexity of the model slightly and assume that there are several producers of a given intermediate product. The labor inputs of each of the producers differ for one reason or another. Here the problem of calculating production costs is solved quite simply: they are established at the level of average costs. In this case planned profits and losses would arise only as a result of the deviation of individual costs from average costs (technical, organizational, and other features of individual economic cells would make themselves known). Of course, these deviations are not so harmless if we consider that a very definite system of rewards and punishments lies behind the words "profits" and "losses." But at any rate, such a system of calculating costs has been adopted in the USSR.

Our subsequent exposition, however, will be devoted to another source of planned profits. At the dawn of the introduction of the planned system of price formation, a 3 to 5 percent planned profit was added to planned average production costs at the intermediate stages in establishing prices. It is difficult to find in the literature today an explanation of the reasons for introducing such planned profit. As far as I know, the argument for including profit in price involved the convenience of regulating the economy. Since in the course of implementing the plan a branch may have unforeseen difficulties and may increase costs compared with the plan, the existence of such planned profit may offset this increase. An increase in the share of profit in price, especially after the 1965 reform, was dictated by the government's effort to create for enterprises the opportunity to decentralize somewhat, given the organization of incentives for personnel and the improvement of production processes. The formation of the corresponding enterprise funds is based specifically on withholdings from profits.

Thus in Soviet economics profit has been isolated from the surplus product. Naturally, if prices are stable, then with changes in costs the branch will either have a superprofit or require a subsidy.

Since prices rarely change in the USSR and in the majority of branches costs are reduced, such profit does occur. Deductions from profit today make up a large part of budget revenues. (In this connection we call the reader's attention to the following situation in the USSR: frequent changes in production plans and infrequent changes in prices.) Thus profit in the USSR has no economic justification whatsoever from the standpoint of expressing the shadow price of production factors. It has been introduced to regulate production, including minor decentralized decisions.

Let us further complicate the model and see how the problems of price formation are resolved in the USSR in the case of producing several consumer goods by several resources or, more precisely, several different types of labor.

In conformity with the principle of optimality, we must coordinate the investigated aspects of the system of production and distribution as follows

$$F(x_1, \ldots, x_i, \ldots, x_n) \to \max.$$

$$\Sigma a_{ij} x_i \le l_j,$$

where l_j is the quantity of the j-th labor, $j = 1, \ldots, j$; a_{ij} are inputs of j-th labor in the production of a unit of i-th product i. From the necessary extremal conditions it follows that

$$\frac{\partial F(x_1, \ldots, x_i, \ldots, x_n)}{\partial x_i} = \sum_{j=1}^{J} a_{ij} \lambda_j .$$

The price of the product p_i, which is equal to its marginal utility where

$u_i = \dfrac{\partial F(x_1, \ldots, x_i, \ldots, x_n)}{\partial x_i}$, must equal expenditures of various types of labor weighted on the basis of their shadow prices $\sum_{j=1}^{J} a_{ij} \lambda_i$.

(Through the criterion these prices also reflect distribution principles adopted in the system from the standpoint of the social demands on them.)

Personnel will be paid on the basis of the assumption that wages are equal to the price of labor

$$W_i = \sum_{i=1}^{n} \sum_{j=1}^{J} a_{ij} \lambda_i x_i .$$

The value of consumer goods produced Π_i will equal $\sum_{i=1}^{n} p_i x_i$. At the same time, within the framework of the given model it is obvious that $W_i = \Pi_i$.

The comparison of various types of labor, as we know, is the Achilles's heel of Marxist political economy (see Chapter 4).

The system of prices in the USSR does not involve prices on labor. Labor expenses are measured by wages, which <u>partly</u> reflect the scarcity of labor.

Let us denote by ρ_j the existing coefficient of reduction of the wage paid for j-th kind of labor to base unskilled labor. Then the expenditures of production of a certain consumer good, denoted c_i, are

$$c_i = \sum_{j=1}^{J} a_{ij} \rho_j .$$

The price of a consumer good based on these expenditures is denoted p_i^ρ; $p_i^\rho = c_i$.

Because wages and shadow prices on labor in the Soviet Union do not coincide, the equilibrium price p_i, generally speaking, is not the same; therefore the proportions in these prices are also not coincident. In order to effect distribution on the basis of equilibrium prices, it is necessary to alter the proportions between prices obtained on the basis of the theory adopted in the USSR for measuring expenditures. It is necessary to introduce some sort of artificial tax mechanism to raise some prices and lower others vis-à-vis the aforementioned expenditures. At the same time, the value of the consumer goods sold will, naturally, equal the sum of production costs.

Above we have revealed the reason for turnover tax in the USSR. Now we can see why it is differentiated for various products: because it is necessary to coordinate market-type distribution by means of the price mechanism with the calculation of costs on the basis of labor expenditures reduced through distribution factors.

If the collective product is now introduced into the model, one faces only the problem of adding labor inputs in the production of collective goods to expenditures on the production of consumer goods in order to balance prices on consumer goods and the wages paid. Redistribution factors retain the same function of assuring correspondence between prices on consumer goods and equilibrium prices.

Such is the simplified model for coordinating prices and expenditures on the production of consumer goods in the Soviet economy. From this model it follows that in the USSR the system of prices not only ignores the value of such production factors as natural resources, limited means of production existing at the beginning of the planned period, and production time, but it even calculates the labor inputs themselves without properly taking them into account as scarcity resources.

The aforementioned operation of redistributing the surplus product essentially applies only to consumer products, since only consumer products are distributed through a mechanism that requires equilibrium prices. As for the means of production, they are distributed primarily on the basis of rationing. Prices on these products reflect only the average expenditures of labor on their production plus profit; these prices are very far from equilibrium prices. The fact that there are great differences in the percentage of turnover taxes on various consumer goods is evidence of this.

By virtue of all the foregoing, in the USSR in the production sphere it has proved impossible to coordinate the various functions of price. Coordination of the function of price as a means of balancing supply and demand for consumer products with a price function like providing sources for growth and for the production of public goods works to the detriment of the price function that is meant to promote autonomous decision-making by the economic unit about the effectiveness of measures it implements.

Subsidies and Superprofits

The reasons for the subsidies and superprofits that exist in the USSR are essentially rooted not in a rational mechanism of planning but rather in its imperfection. The imperfections of this mechanism are determined by the very essence of the Soviet system of planning.

First, the system of price formation on the means of production is based in the USSR on average expenditures for a branch plus a certain percentage of profit. Such consistent adherence to the theoretical principle that price must reflect average socially necessary expenditures of labor in actual practice proves to be a contradiction between planning in physical and value terms.

Indeed, from the standpoint of the goal of producing certain types of products (we shall consider this goal to be rational), given the existence of enterprises with different types of technical structures and scales of production, it may prove advisable to include in the plan production at different enterprises. At the same time, from the standpoint of the adopted theoretical principle of price formation based on average expenditures, enterprises with worse equipment and an insufficient amount of profit to be added to costs will operate at a planned loss. If the laws of the price mechanism were followed, these enterprises would have to be closed down. Enterprises with better equipment would realize an artificial gain.

Thus a gap would develop between the physical and value aspects of the plan. In order to bridge this gap, when an enterprise has planned expenditures higher than the established price, it receives a planned subsidy. To be sure, in such a case the subsidy does not come from the budget but is brought about through intraministerial channels for the redistribution of profits. But this does not alter the core of the matter.

Moreover, the existence of such redistributive relations has a negative impact on the mechanism of the functioning of the economy. Enterprises whose planned expenditures are lower than average receive excessive profits. They pay part of them into the enterprise fund, but they still get part of their income from having better resources. We do not want to deny that an enterprise that has more effective resources should receive additional incentives to optimally preserve these resources. But clearly this should be part of the rent and interest on capital received by them rather than withholdings from average costs. Under the indicated procedure for paying profit withholdings into the enterprise fund, enterprises whose expenditures are above average will not receive withholdings for the enterprise fund even if they work more intensively.

A number of industrial branches tried to resolve these difficulties by introducing so-called accounting prices. Accounting prices were constructed within the branch in such a way that each enterprise received a planned target for expenditures in accordance with its potential. In this case the actual profit for an enterprise, which was the difference between its planned and actual expenditures, accurately expressed the effectiveness of its work.

With accounting prices relations between sales and supply agencies were, as before, built on prices based on average branch expenditures plus a certain percentage of profits. Therefore, while they were freed from one of the shortcomings in the theoretical principle of price formation based on average expenditures, the customers nonetheless received distorted information about expenditures in the branch, since marginal expenditures were not reflected.

Lack of flexibility to alter prices is the other reason for subsidies in the Soviet economy. Wholesale prices rarely change: once every five or six years. Prices have a certain stability. However, when there is a significant change in input-output volumes, prices must be changed.

Since in many branches, especially in the extractive industry, there has been a rise in costs largely due to the growth of wages, given artificial price stabilization, losses were inevitable. These

losses were offset by subsidies. Naturally, it would be possible
to avoid subsidies through timely price revisions. We can assume
that the failure of the authorities to understand the role of prices
and their relationship to the plan is <u>ultimately</u> the factor that
causes delays in changing prices. Comprehension of this role
would make it possible to calculate prices along with the plan and
would not lead to the artificial mechanism of subsidies.

In other branches of industry that have lowered costs, superprofits have originated from fixed prices. In addition, artificially
inflated prices on new types of products have been a source of
superprofits. Superprofits were highest at enterprises belonging
to the Ministry of Instrument Making, Automation Equipment, and
Control Systems and the Ministry of Construction, Road, and Mu-
nicipal Machine Building, where the share of new types of products is highest.

6

Economic Incentives
and the Soviet Experience in Using Them

A considerable amount of literature has been devoted to the problem of work incentives in the Soviet economy. Here I would like to touch on some relatively less illuminated aspects of this problem. They include the following:

1) incentives for personnel and the creation of conditions for their activity;

2) incentives and inflation;

3) incentives, envy, and social manipulation;

4) incentives and anticipatory mechanisms.

First, several general comments.

In the USSR wages are based on the principle that they cover expenditures on consumer goods. Direct taxes on wages represent a relatively small part of budget revenues. The basic sources of budget revenues are indirect taxes: turnover tax and, largely artificial, profits (see Chapter 5). Thus in 1973 direct taxes from the population made up 8.4 percent of the state budget, while turnover tax alone accounted for 31.5 percent.[1]

Hence differences in nominal incomes in the USSR are not as great as they might be if wages were based on shadow prices of labor. As a result of the existing practice of calculating wages in the USSR, the stimulating role of income is appreciably reduced, to say nothing of the incorrect calculation of labor costs.

The overwhelming majority of Soviet economists and executives do not understand the role of wages as shadow prices of labor. In their opinion taxation only increases the volume of bookkeeping work, and hence taxes on wages should be eliminated in general. This attitude was reflected in the Program of the Communist Party of the Soviet Union adopted in 1961.[2] Thus the number of population groups not subject to taxation in the USSR is increasing, even though not as rapidly as had been anticipated by the party leadership.

138

Incentives and the Nature of Workers' Activity

On the Relationship between Expenditures to Maintain a Worker and Incentives to His Greater Efficiency

As the first premise for this problem, we shall assume the elementary fact that the volume of activity a person can perform during his lifetime depends on the market basket of goods he receives (this dependence can be expressed by a convex function).

As the second premise we shall assume that people differ in their natural abilities. Moreover, it is impossible to train every person for every occupation or to endow him with creative abilities.

The third premise is associated with expenditures on training personnel. Today it takes as long as twenty years to train a highly qualified engineer or scholar. As regards skilled personnel, the cost of their training does not include just expenditures on their education. Enormous outlays of resources and time entailed in training highly skilled cadres go directly into their obtaining knowledge and skills on the job. The errors these people learn from require large expenditures that are difficult to assess in concrete terms.

Proceeding from these premises, the following qualitative conclusion can be drawn: other things being equal, the lower the level of development of production, the greater the disparity between the abilities of people and the expenditures on their training, the greater must be the disparity between the quantities of consumer goods received by persons in the various occupations. As production grows, these disparities will lessen.

In other words, within the framework of the given premises, despite their simplification, the basic reason for nonegalitarian distribution is the need for a differentiated approach to maintaining personnel that depends on their influence on the development of the system as a whole.

In formulating our premises we have ignored the fact that everyone is aware of the differences in wage levels.

Assuming that a person has a free choice of occupation, differentiation of incomes from the standpoint of creating conditions to maintain workers turns into a means of stimulating people to choose more effective jobs and perform them better. I call particular attention to this dual role of income because the opinion is quite widespread that nonegalitarianism is based on the need to stimulate workers.[3] Without denying the stimulating role of income, I would like to note that it is insufficient to explain the reasons for non-egalitarianism.

In fact a person is stimulated to perform a specific job by a number of factors: in addition to material benefits, a person is interested in working conditions, in enjoying the creative nature of his labor, and so on. Thus, for example, a person capable of creativity may subjectively be interested in performing an important job even if the level of its remuneration is lower than a job that is creatively less interesting!

This situation may occur, in particular, under the following conditions. Growth in a person's general educational and cultural level is primarily dictated by the need for comprehensive development of his personality. This development, in turn, is required for his participation in the democratic mechanism of management, which presupposes the availability of competent people to cope with the complex modern organization of life. An uneducated person will fear initiative, will be afraid to make decisions on his own, and will try to shift decision-making to "powerful personalities" simply because he cannot grasp what is going on around him. The modern level of military technology similarly dictates the necessity of having people in society with a high general educational level.

At the same time, the technical level of production organization may be such that many jobs are still nonautomated and still entail performing a large number of unskilled tasks that do not interest an educated person. The creation of efficient, highly automated production requires a great deal of time as well as considerably more than raising the general educational level of members of society. Under these conditions, in order to encourage people to do unskilled jobs, it may prove expedient to pay them higher wages than skilled personnel. The latter are compensated for their lower pay by more interesting work.

However, while noting the possibility of such a situation, it is important to realize at the same time that the absolute level of wages of skilled personnel should be adequate for them to realize their potential. Otherwise, even though people are hired for skilled jobs, "their coefficients of efficiency" may be low and may entail enormous losses of the competent people whose numbers are limited by nature, as well as huge expenditures on training a skilled work force.

For all its obviousness, this proposition has definite significance

for better understanding the differentiation of incomes in various
countries.

As we know, in recent decades in the United States there has been
a narrowing of the income gap between skilled and unskilled personnel. Even now the income of individual groups of workers, e.g.,
plumbers, is comparable with the pay of university professors.
Without discussing the legitimacy of the rates of reducing differences in the pay of various personnel groups, we should note that
in the United States the gap is being bridged under conditions of a
high absolute level of income for skilled personnel, and this provides them opportunities to display their abilities.

The situation is different in the USSR. There, given the overall
low level of incomes, the gap between the incomes of workers and
of engineering-technical personnel is also systematically diminishing.[4]   This is confirmed by the table on page 141, adopted from
a table compiled by Professor Peter Wiles.[5]

Even now in the USSR there are numerous enterprises at which
the average pay of workers is higher than the average pay of
engineering-technical personnel and clerical employees. In Moscow one sees advertisements offering 120 rubles a month for subway cleaning women. Yet a student who has graduated from a
higher educational institute receives approximately 95-105 rubles
a month when he starts work as an engineer.

Understandably, the Soviet government is now compelled to increase the income of unskilled personnel, since the sharply increased general educational level of the population makes it hard
to find people to do unskilled jobs. Local interests entirely justify
these changes in the wages of personnel with different skill levels.
But integral interests suffer in the process. The absolute level of
incomes of skilled personnel in the USSR is extremely low. Even
if we assume that the pay of engineering-technical personnel is
approximately 170-180 rubles a month, according to the official
exchange rate for the dollar (which is obviously understated with
respect to consumer goods), this amounts to approximately $220
a month. This speaks for itself!

The low absolute income level of engineering-technical personnel
has an extremely negative impact on their productivity. Moreover,
the change in recent years in the relationship between the incomes
of workers and engineering-technical personnel also affects the
makeup of student enrollment. At higher educational institutes
there has been a significant decline in the number of young people
with average abilities — the basic group. These youngsters (as

Table 1

Earnings of Soviet Occupational Groups

	Manual workers*	Engineers and technicians† (various sources)		Clerical employees‡	Peasants§	Workers and employees in education and health
1928	100	—	172	—	—	—
1932	100	263	193	150	—	—
1934	100	—	192	—	—	—
1935	100	236	182	126	—	—
1940	100	210	—	109	—	93
1941 plan	100	204	170	98	—	—
1950	100	175	—	93	—	87
1955	100	165	—	88	—	—
1960	100	151	—	82	47	73
1970	100	—	—	—	68	—
1972	100	130	—	83	—	76

*Rabochie.

†Inzhenersko-tekhnicheskii personal.

‡Sluzhashchie (note that this word often includes engineers and technicians in other contexts).

§Kolkhozniki.

well as their parents if they are not themselves intellectuals) prefer to become blue-collar workers — drivers of passenger vehicles, etc., whose earnings are quite high.

Thus the Soviet Union faces a rather complex situation. As a world power that has modern military technology in hypertrophied amounts, it requires large contingents of literate people (it is no accident that district military commissariats keep track of the education of young people in general education schools). As a country in which people have considerable latitude in the choice of jobs, it needs an economic mechanism to draw people into various jobs. At the same time, the USSR has a relatively low level of production of material goods. As a result a conflict arises between production's need for large numbers of relatively unskilled workers and the existence of a considerable able-bodied population with a relatively elevated general educational level. As we have shown, the resolution of this conflict causes the sacrifice of the system's long-term efficiency for the sake of current interests.

Incentives and "Flation"[6]

Incentives can be offered by increasing workers' nominal or real wages. Generally speaking, a rise in the nominal wage is a more effective means of increasing labor productivity, since it makes it possible to directly link the results of a person's activity to his income (naturally, assuming that prices are more or less stable). With a rise in real wages caused primarily by a decline in prices there is no direct incentive to increase productivity, since a single person cannot count on the influence of his activity on a future decline in prices.

At the same time, a rise in the nominal wage may engender difficulties in balancing it against the increased production of consumer goods. Among these difficulties we should note principally those that stem from the nature of a person's activity.

To attract workers to new regions or other branches and to keep them there, depending on the circumstances they must be offered a sum that is no less than a certain amount; a person may not react to a lesser amount. The situation is similar when one offers workers incentives to increase the volume of their activity. At the same time, simply because of physiological limitations a person can increase the volume of his activity only to a certain degree. Under the given conditions growth in income does not always match growth in output: the increase in output may even be smaller. In principle the gap between the rates of growth of income and output can be compensated by introducing higher taxes, by stimulating savings, and by raising prices. Thus the limitations of human psychology dictate that the development of the system requires simultaneous use both of accelerators — the growth of income — and of decelerators — increased taxes and savings, higher prices.[7]

With an increased nominal wage the central place in the process of striking a balance between supply and demand belongs to prices. This can be explained by the fact that tax policy is quite conservative, and the effort to increase savings collides with the limited potential for growth in interest rates. Here inflationary processes emerge that, when there is creeping inflation, become a factor in economic growth.

From what I have said it follows that inflationary processes are invariant with respect to any economic system.

Inflation has played various roles at various stages in the development of the Soviet economy. These topics have been examined in considerable detail in the works of Western economists, particularly those of Franklin Holzman.[8] Here I would like to dwell briefly on only a few points that characterize relations between the growth of the nominal wage and prices on consumer products in the USSR during the period following World War II.

Prior to 1953, even in those sectors of the national economy in which economic methods of management had been adopted, emphasis nonetheless fell on administrative means organically augmented by demagogy. Specifically, this was done by fixing basic wage rates and salaries within the enterprise.[9] If a piece-rate worker increased his productivity, his wages increased for awhile, whereupon the norms were revised and his wages gradually returned to their previous level. For piece-rate workers, who were a majority in industry and construction,[10] such revisions of norms were made in the first quarter of every year. Since so-called experimental-statistical norms were usually in force, it was easy to revise the norms.

We know that during the pre-1953 period the discrepancy between basic wage rates and wages was very high in various branches of the national economy and was artificially maintained thanks to the significant percentage of overfulfillment of norms.[11]

Even though "time-rate workers" received a fixed salary (basic wage rate), their wages were usually not fixed. This was because these categories of workers received bonuses depending on their performance. It was quite a simple matter to regulate the wages of these groups of workers. Among the numerous conditions that had to be fulfilled in order to receive a bonus it was always possible to find an excuse for saying that one condition or another was not fulfilled (or incompletely fulfilled) and for reducing the bonus. In 1950-51 there were months when bonuses in general were cut by 25 percent on the basis of a corresponding decree of the USSR Council of Ministers. (I know because I worked at the Moscow "Frezer" plant during these years.) Thus the bonus fund was regulated to prevent the growth of wages of "salaried persons" ["okladniki"]. The intensiveness of their activity was increased by means of an annual increase in plans through the well-known method of so-called planning based on the already attained level.

Holding down the level of money wages could not be an adequate means to preserve the balance between incomes and the available quantity of consumer goods. This was due to the fact that through-out the nation the wage fund was increasing as a result of consid-erable growth in the number of workers and employees. This meant that the growth rates of the number of personnel exceeded the growth rates of the production of consumer goods and services.

Under such conditions the government resorted to administrative measures in the form of taxes to preserve the balance between the level of incomes and the available consumer goods. However, for demagogic purposes this action was cast in the form of loans to which the working people subscribed "voluntarily" each year. At the same time and also for demagogic purposes, the prices of con-sumer goods were lowered each year despite the general shortage of such goods throughout the nation.

The policy pursued during this period had its reasons. In order to expand military might it was necessary to increase labor produc-tivity. Consumer goods production had to be kept at a low level.

It was dangerous under these conditions to stimulate the growth of productivity by increasing money wages. Unless prices and taxes were increased, this would have led to the accumulation of spare cash, with all the ensuing negative consequences. In addi-tion a systematic, significant growth of prices and taxes bore a markedly negative ideological character, especially for a victorious socialist country. Hence it was easier to correlate consistent im-plementation of a rigid policy of militarization with administrative methods of increasing labor productivity. Such a policy for the USSR national economy was supported during the postwar period until 1953.[12]

After 1953 material incentive methods were intensified in the USSR, as is evident from the appreciably higher growth rates of money wages.

Table 2

Dynamics of the Average Monthly Wage (in rubles)
in the USSR between 1950 and 1975[13]

| Year | Average wage | Increase during five-year period | |
		absolute	in %
1950	64.2		
1955	71.8	7.6	11.8
1960	80.6	8.8	12.3
1965	96.5	15.9	19.7
1970	122.0	25.5	26.4
1975	145.8	23.8	19.5

Simultaneously there was a substantial rise in the income of Soviet collective farmers after 1953. Pensions and scholarships sharply increased. (These questions have been widely discussed in the literature, and we will not deal with them.)

Yet after 1953 there was also a price rise that was largely "bashful." Prices of individual types of foodstuffs, clothing, furniture, automobiles, etc., rose under the guise of improved quality. Insignificant changes in a commodity brand caused appreciable increases in price.[14] We should note that the rise in prices, which is usually painful to consumers, was damped to a considerable degree by the devaluation that occurred in 1960. With the shift from prices expressed in large sums to prices reduced tenfold it was possible to make the price increase quite unnoticeable to the consumer. From inertia consumers continued to think for quite a long time in terms of the old price scale.[15]

Another way to increase prices entails the so-called "erosion" of inexpensive commodities. In official statistics there are no data on these commodities. But on the basis of my personal observations and the observations of my colleagues, I can say with sufficient assurance that the "erosion" of inexpensive commodities has gone on all these years. It is especially evident from the example of television sets, the prices of individual types of which fell.[16] At the same time, inexpensive small-screen sets, which had previously proliferated, gradually disappeared. They were more and more replaced by relatively costlier sets with larger screens (even though, I repeat, the prices of these sets were lowered!). "Erosion" of inexpensive commodities has affected meat, macaroni products, and so on.

But the rise in prices (despite insufficient production of consumer goods) could not offset the increase in the population's money income. All this led to an artificial increase in spare cash. While between 1950 and 1960 the average sum of money on deposit in savings banks increased by 905 million rubles a year, and by 3.569 billion rubles between 1960 and 1970, between 1970 and 1973 the annual increase was 7.3 billion rubles.[17] In 1973 deposits in savings banks amounted to 68.6 billion rubles.[18] We can assume that the population has yet another one fourth of this sum in hand ("under the mattress," in safes).

The surplus of spare cash results to some degree from the population's reluctance to buy poor-quality consumer goods — especially clothing and footwear.[19] However, the basic reason for the existence of "spare cash" lies in the shortage of consumer goods.

Yet we note that all this time the ratio of commodity stocks to total deposits in savings banks (not counting the population's cash on hand) has been declining. From Table 3 it is evident that while in 1950 the ratio of commodity stocks to total deposits was 530 percent, in 1973 it was only 76.0 percent. Thus the overall spare cash in savings banks alone already appreciably exceeded total commodity stocks in the USSR.

Table 3

The Ratio of Commodity Stocks (in Retail and Wholesale Trade and in Industry) to the Population's Deposits in Savings Banks[20] (in millions of rubles)

Years (at year's end)	Commodity stocks	Total deposits	Ratio of total commodity stocks to deposits (in %)
1950	9,821	1,853	530.0
1960	24,483	10,909	224.4
1970	45,693	46,600	98.1
1971	48,298	53,215	90.8
1972	49,707	60,372	81.8
1973	52,239	68,660	76.0
1974	56,050	78,905	71.0
1975	58,203	90,985	64.0

Naturally, this fact, generally speaking, should not be considered negative, since to do so one must ascertain the rational relationship between commodity stocks and savings under corresponding conditions. We are not able to calculate this norm. However, in all cases we can say that since this relationship has a pronounced tendency to decline and is a magnitude less than 100 percent, it provokes alarm. It creates a threat to the existence of a price-monetary mechanism for the distribution of consumer goods and may require the introduction of a rationing system. Indeed, in the event of panic the population may use its "spare cash" and begin hoarding. This can lead to a shortage of commodities in stores, to the emergence of a black market, to runaway price rises, and so on. The chance for such a panic does exist in the USSR, since consumers, lacking accurate information on impending measures to change prices, the monetary system, and so on, tend to believe all sorts of rumors. (At the end of the 1960s Soviet newspapers had to squelch rumors about a supposedly impending change in bank notes because panic loomed.)

Of course, since the Soviet state concentrates in its hands incomparably greater power over various realms of society than do the Western countries, it has more chances to prevent this inflation or to damp it more rapidly.

But it is important to note at the same time that the threat of runaway inflation can also exacerbate the political struggle in the incumbent USSR leadership and may promote a victory of the conservative forces. Indeed, since it is difficult to overcome the threat of galloping inflation without undermining the population's savings, without decelerating the growth of military power, and without creating a more flexible socioeconomic mechanism that can guarantee increased production of consumer goods, administrative methods of solving the problem can prove to be very tempting. And this gives an advantage in the struggle to those groups in the party that vividly recall Stalinist times and continue to remind us that under Stalin prices fell, the country's power grew, the people were satisfied, and the world trembled before the USSR. And if it was necessary to draw off spare cash (as it was during 1947 monetary reform or during the loan subscription campaigns), the people greeted this move with enthusiasm...

Incentives, Envy, Manipulation of Personnel

Since the number of highly skilled jobs and the number of persons needed to fill them are limited, such jobs and the corresponding income from them are by no means open to all. Thus the positive aspects of income differentiation turn into its negative side: envy.

Envy plays a negative role, disorganizes the individual, and impels him to egalitarianism. Under these conditions, in order to extinguish envy it is very important to appropriately educate people, including taking legal steps against those who want to forcibly alter the principles of distribution, thereby robbing in one form or another people with higher income under the guise of struggle for just distribution of incomes.[21]

Envy has been explained as the attitude of people with relatively low income toward people with high income. If we now look at relations between people from the standpoint of the attitutde of a person with higher income toward a person with lower income, we can see that some people with high income suffer to some degree because

148

their income is higher than that of others. (Of course, the majority of people do not suffer from high income but, on the contrary, enjoy it.)

Economic science now has mathematical models that seek equilibrium taking into account the fact that the level of satisfaction of each participant depends on his perception of the level of satisfaction of other participants.[22]

In the USSR for various reasons, among them tradition, envy of people with higher incomes plays a decisive role in the social life of society. That the government must cope with it has been shown, in particular, by unofficial discussions on the pay of scientific workers. Each of the disputing sides noted some aspect in the system for paying scientists: the need to create better working conditions for scientists, the role of incentives to draw personnel into scientific work, or the negative influence of scientists' high pay on the other strata of the population. Note that these factors above, taken together, show how difficult it is to solve the problem. Yet it is obvious that if differences in pay are reduced simply to the role of incentives, the existing disparities in the remuneration of workers and scientists must be reduced, since the working conditions of scientists are more attractive thanks to the chance for creative work. But if one considers only the contribution of scientists, their limited number, and expenditures on their training, then from the point of view of maintaining scientists, these disparities should be increased. If only the influence of the population's envy is considered, then scientists' pay should be reduced.

We know that these discussions have borne both theoretical and very serious practical importance. Thus during the reign of Khrushchev the question was raised very seriously of reducing the wages of science personnel. Supposedly, a decree of the USSR Council of Ministers was even prepared on this matter. Soviet scientists were "rescued" from an income slash by their American colleagues. Not long before the projected signing of the decree by Khrushchev, he was visited by the head of the American Academy of Sciences. In a talk with Khrushchev he emphasized that the USSR owed its success in outer space largely to the comparatively high wages of its scientists. As proof the head of the American Academy of Sciences described the status of scientists' pay in the United States, which at that time lagged considerably behind the USSR in the conquest of space. Subsequently the gap between the wages of scientists and workers in the USSR lost its acuity thanks to the substantial growth of workers' wages.

Yet the problem of envy on the part of the populace remains very serious with respect to leading officials in the party, Soviet, and economic apparatus who receive sizable incomes. Moreover, the problem of distributing income with respect to this cohort is augmented by the stimulation of their allegiance.

Following Marx's behests, which were based on the experience of the Paris Commune, and Lenin's principles postulated in his State and Revolution, it was felt in the USSR that the average wage of leading officials should not significantly deviate from the wage of skilled workers. Even shortly after the revolution it was found that such a demand did not satisfy the new class of leading officials. In particular, in order to preserve outward conformity to Marx's and Lenin's principles, these officials were given additional income in kind and perquisites. This situation has persisted to this very day in the USSR and is widely known in the West.[23]

In this respect we would simply like to focus attention on some facets of this principle of forming the income of leading officials. We shall formulate the following law, which can be regarded as one possible manifestation of the socialist principle of distribution according to quantity and quality of labor: the higher the place a person occupies in the social hierarchy in Soviet society, the higher is the share of payments in kind and perquisites in his income. Thus while the entire income received at an enterprise by a machine-tool operator consists almost entirely of money income, the money part of the income of a CPSU Central Committee secretary (who is not a candidate member or member of the Politburo) is on the order of one third; two thirds of his income consists of payments in kind and perquisites that he receives in accordance with the position he occupies.

Naturally, the high income level of leaders makes it easier to maintain them and at the same time is a powerful incentive to obtain such positions, especially thanks to the opportunity to obtain commodities that cannot be bought in stores.

Moreover, the existence of considerable payments in kind in the income of these persons, and especially the perquisites they receive, also promotes the authorities' more skillful manipulation of cadres. The existence of payments in kind and perquisites does not let executives officially accumulate significant money resources and become more independent, on the one hand, and on the other hand it means a sharp drop in their living standard if they lose their high position.

The Soviet elite is not satisfied with such income instability.

Against the background of the rebirth of a primordial Russian tradition, particularly pride in belonging to the Russian aristocracy (we recall that back in the 1920s and 1930s the door to higher education was barred to the children of Russian aristocrats), this dissatisfaction assumes what appears at first glance to be whimsical forms. Thus some of the elite share the view (which was even expressed at a quasi-official meeting by Belashova, a secretary of the Union of Soviet Artists) that the USSR should restore something like service nobility strata, whose privileges would be preserved for life whatever positions they held. It seems that to some extent only corresponding members of the academies of various sciences and academicians who receive a considerable lifetime sum for their titles enjoy such privileges in the USSR.[24]

On the whole the Soviet leadership is glad to receive higher income, payments in kind, and perquisites that are unavailable to other strata of society. The overwhelming majority of people, if they have the opportunity, strive to obtain higher executive positions. The top leadership uses these inclinations as incentives to draw loyal persons into executive work. Envy of leading officials' incomes is quite severely repressed. I know of a case that took place in the late 1950s at a party meeting held at the Ministry of Communications, when a rank-and-file communist criticized the system through which the leadership of one of the chief departments received goods in kind, in his opinion, to the detriment of the department of rank-and-file personnel who were in dire need. For his statement this communist was persecuted and repeatedly censured at various levels of the party hierarchy; he escaped expulsion from the party because he "admitted" his errors and was a participant in World War II. Isolated instances are also known of executives being oppressed by their income privileges and experiencing a feeling of altruism.[25]

Incentive and Anticipation

Contract, Plan, and Incentives

In the process of its functioning, any developed economic system is faced with essentially the same problem: how to coordinate the interest of the personnel of the economic unit in increasing the effectiveness of their work with the increased effectiveness of work in the system as a whole.

The basic principle in paying workers should evidently be constructed so that the increased effectiveness of the work of their unit is accompanied by growth in their income, especially thanks to growth in nominal income. Given such an approach the interests of the personnel in any unit are coordinated quite explicitly with its contribution to the increased effectiveness of the system as a whole.

In simplest form the stimulation of the unit to increase the effectiveness of activity is embodied in a bazaar (or auction) economic system. I understand bazaar to mean a variety of market in which the results of workers' activity are revealed only as an aftereffect. Put more succinctly, the participant produces a commodity, compares its price with his expenditures, and realizes income from his activity.

Other things being equal, under such a system the more a participant produces, the lower his expenditures, the more he increases his income. There are no constraints whatsoever on the growth of income. However, the system of work based on aftereffect is fraught with major difficulties. There is a real threat that the participant's efforts will prove to be in vain because the customer may not need the commodities he produces.

The introduction of contracts between participants acts as an anticipatory system that lowers the probability of a unit performing useless activity. Contracts do not abolish the aftereffect mechanism, since the effect is ultimately felt through sales, but they substantially limit it.

The anticipatory system is at the same time a constraint. Responsibility must be borne for its observance: a penalty must be paid for nonfulfillment of a contract. Hence a new game situation emerges in the course of the functioning of the economy, as well as the new problems it entails for incentive methods. Other things being equal, when concluding a contract, on the one hand a participant tries to sell a larger quantity of commodities. But on the other hand he displays caution, since he bears responsibility for fulfilling the contract. This caution will increase in proportion to the participant's fear of risk and the size of the penalty for the nonfulfillment of a contract. Thus in the development of a market in which there are anticipatory mechanisms there emerge forces that in a certain sense limit the striving of workers for increased effectiveness: the fear of nonfulfillment of contracts.

For many reasons the system of contractual relations — for all their significance — does not make it possible to properly coordinate the actions of participants that are directed toward increasing the effectiveness of the entire system. There is a vast body of literature devoted to these problems — criticism of a market economy not restricted by the government — and I will not discuss them here.

In order to overcome the difficulties that arise in a market economy, under certain conditions it is necessary to introduce basically new institutions that permit the government to monitor the development of the economy. Among these institutions an enormous role is played by the stabilizers built into the economic system. These stabilizers are controlled by the government and are intended to regularize the market. The distinguishing feature of stabilizers is that to a greater or lesser degree they operate on the basis of aftereffect.

Therefore, under certain conditions it is also important for the government to have institutions that make it possible to anticipate the development of the economic system. The plan is such an institution. The plan offers an anticipatory coordinated action program for maximum production under existing conditions (also including the political structure of the system, and so on). Unlike the contract the plan is not a voluntary act of a limited group of participants. The plan, which is elaborated by central government institutions, is law for all participants. Like every law it limits the actions of participants and at the same time can help them attain their own goals. Naturally, as in the case of every law, the degree of its usefulness is dictated by the mechanism of its elaboration. If it is a democratic mechanism, it somehow reflects the opinion of the majority.

The plan can be elaborated in physical terms or in a dual form for the prices of resources and products. For us it is not now so important how the central agency presents the plan. But it is important in this regard to call attention to the emergence of a new institution by means of which normative anticipatory development of the system takes place.

It must be remembered that for all its attractiveness, the plan cannot be all-embracing. For this reason the planning mechanism should not, generally speaking, exclude the market mechanism (and also the bazaar mechanism) but should merely limit them. The degree of such limitation may vary, and this largely shapes the diversity of types of economic systems.

The advent of the plan immediately raises the question of how workers will be stimulated to fulfill it. The answer to this question depends primarily on the degree of obligatoriness in following the plan. If we bear in mind that the plan helps steer the economy in the required direction and yet may be imperfect, the obligatory observance of the plan by the participants should be moderated as much as possible. Hence the system of incentives should provide a reward for a participant who follows the plan. The existence of a system of rewards, unlike the system of penalties, moderates the negative aspects of the plan as a normative institution and represents the essence of the indicative system of planning.

It is the possibility of getting a reward for following the plan and the possibility of realizing a gain for deviating from the plan that form the basis of the game that the participant now plays with other participants in the economic system.

Depending on various conditions, responsibility for fulfilling the plan may increase or diminish. Rewards for following the plan may be supplemented by penalties and all sorts of other administrative measures. The degree of strictness of the administrative measures will depend, on the one hand, on the degree to which — given the threat of loss to society from deviations from the plan — the compilers of the plan are in a position to obligate executors with a given income level to follow the plan. On the other hand it will depend on how serious to the plan executors is the threat of losing a certain amount of income or the reward for deviating from the plan indicators.[26]

Thus in a developed economic system it is necessary to link an improvement in workers' performance with a system for stimulating them that takes into account both the limiting effect of contractual institutions and planning principles.

The Plan and Incentives in the USSR

What then is the distinguishing feature of the Soviet system for stimulating personnel to increase the effectiveness of their activity?

In the Soviet economic system the plan plays a decisive role in the economic mechanism. The plan has suppressed the effect of other institutions that could serve as a basis for developing the economy. Contractual relations have been turned into ways to itemize the plan in terms of assortment and time.

In the Soviet economy the incentive system ignores payments for increasing the effectiveness of production. Here we have in mind the fact that in the USSR wages do not depend on the degree to which a given unit has increased the effectiveness of its production compared with the preceding period. Incentives are based primarily on the degree to which the plan is fulfilled. The entire system of incentives revolves around fulfillment of the plan.

This system of incentives for fulfilling plans was introduced under Soviet conditions in the 1930s, when the rigid political system with a dictator at its head created under Lenin was developed. The introduction of strict principles of stimulation was principally a consequence of the low level of consumer goods production. If income had increased under these conditions, the result could have been rampant inflation.

Hence it was necessary to hold incomes at a certain level. In such a case, given the existence of a planned system, it is very convenient to make wages dependent on fulfillment of the plan. Planned income also includes a certain percentage of bonus from projected overfulfillment of the plan.

However, given a low level of production of consumer goods, material incentives for fulfilling the plan may not be strong enough. This means that a working person cannot be severely punished in a material sense in the event of the nonfulfillment of the plan, since under these social conditions it is essential to maintain his minimum income level. This is expressed in the maintenance of an executive's salary as long as he occupies his position. In the 1930s there were proposals and even experiments at individual enterprises to make the executive's salary dependent on the percentage of plan fulfillment (similar to a piece rate for workers). But this system of paying executives was perceived as punitive, and it did not become widespread.[27]

The impossibility of using monetary penalties as a sufficient means for stimulating personnel to fulfill plans led to the intensification of nonmonetary administrative measures. However, such administrative measures as reprimands from higher-echelon leaders, etc., have comparatively little influence on a person, since they do not significantly influence his status. On the other hand, the use of judicial measures as a direct punishment for nonfulfillment of the plan may prove to be excessively strong, since it is impossible to imprison every manager who fails to meet the plan. To be sure, in the 1930s the USSR indirectly invoked strict judicial measures against individuals who failed to fulfill the plan by accusing them of sabotage, with all the ensuing consequences.

In view of the ineffectiveness of administrative reprimands and the excessive severity of judicial measures, there emerged in the Soviet economic system, in addition to other incentive methods, what was evidently a unique method of stimulation: through workers' membership in the Communist Party. Membership in the Communist Party entails some positive stimuli, since the chance to move up the hierarchical ladder necessarily requires membership in the party. At the same time, membership in the party also entails powerful negative stimuli. A system of various types of reprimands, including even expulsion from the party, is widely used as punishment for executives who transgress in their economic performance. If a person receives a certain number of reprimands, he is stripped of the opportunity to transfer to other work; expulsion from the party actually deprives a person of the chance to hold certain jobs, and so on.

The mechanism underlying the functioning of the economic system and its incentive system created in the 1930s remain basically the same today. Ongoing discussions in the USSR during the post-Stalin period about ways to improve the incentive system have been of a hierarchical nature, reflecting the depth of possible changes in the mechanism of production management and, accordingly, in the system of incentives.

The most radical proposals have been connected with the possibility of sharply expanding the role of a market mechanism based on well-known economic incentives. Unfortunately, the works of Soviet economists who stressed the need to strengthen the role of market mechanisms did not set out modern forms of a market mechanism and appropriate incentive systems. We can assume that Soviet economists working on the idea of decentralization will arrive at the need to introduce a system of indicative planning and the appropriate incentive principles.

The overwhelming majority of Soviet economists have discussed improving the economic mechanism through preservation of the dominant planning system. Economists in the "opposition" first proposed strengthening the role of economic incentives to improve production under the planned economic system and eliminating the party's influence on production, and thereby its administrative measures. Even though it was impossible to proclaim the separation of the Communist Party from the economy in official Soviet literature, the economic reform of 1965 in fact revolved around this very issue.

We shall further examine proposals by Soviet economists to improve economic incentive methods proper in a planned system. They can be divided into two groups. The first includes proposals to offer incentives to workers for increasing the effectiveness of production.[28] Mathematical models have been used to show how the increased effectiveness of an economic unit should be reflected in a local criterion. Constant shadow prices are used to measure this effectiveness. Naturally, the research data must be developed in order to rigorously ascertain the conditions under which such a criterion is suitable.

Unfortunately, proposals by the authors of this point of view are confined solely to incentives for growth in effectiveness and do not take into account responsibility for fulfilling contracts and the plan.

The second group of proposals made by Soviet economists to improve the incentive mechanism revolves around remuneration depending on the plan. The basic idea of all these proposals is to stimulate personnel to adopt a more intensive plan and to fulfill it in the best way.

The overwhelming majority of proposals by economists to improve incentive methods revolve around such issues.[29] A number of their proposals were implemented in the course of the economic reform. They have been analyzed in great depth in the work of Joseph Berliner, and they have been presented in very precise mathematical form in the work of Martin Weitzman.[30]

We note that only the economic aspects of the problem have been examined. Since administrative, particularly party, responsibility of executives for fulfilling the plan remains in the USSR, economic measures introduced to stimulate personnel to adopt more intensive plans could not produce the desired results even if they were perfect.

Nonetheless, perfecting the economic incentive mechanism in planned systems is of unquestionable interest in itself. It may somewhat improve existing practice and, most importantly, may create a reserve for future development if it is combined with the introduction of a more developed economic mechanism freed from unnecessary administrative fetters. Thus the USSR's existing system for stimulating personnel to adopt intensive plans is based on the following indicators: the plan proposed by a given economic unit, the plan proposed by a higher-echelon organization, and finally, the actual fulfillment of the plan.

Setting the amount of reward is based on the principle of working deviations from the two aforementioned plan parameters: the plan proposed by a given unit and the plan proposed by the higher-echelon organization. The more the plan proposed by workers exceeds the plan of the higher-echelon organization, and the less the actual results of the work are understated compared with the adopted plan, the higher will be the workers' reward.

Thus this inventive principle sees workers' pay fluctuating around a <u>fixed salary</u>. The fluctuations depend on the deviations from parameters of the plan. The relationships of coefficients used in calculating the bonus fund for the adoption of a higher plan and in the event of the nonfulfillment of the plan for which the workers will adopt a highly intensive plan are shown in Weitzman's work.[31]

If one plan period is examined, this method of incentives will promote increased effectiveness in an economic unit's operation. However, if we look at the planning process in dynamic form, with planning cycles repeating, this incentive method engenders certain difficulties associated with the establishment of plans by the higher-echelon organization. The influence of plan fulfillment in a given cycle on the plan projected by a higher-echelon organization for the following cycle also shapes the behavior of enterprises in that cycle. If it assumes that the existing practice of establishing plans on the basis of the level attained plus a certain percentage of growth will be maintained, an enterprise will naturally be cautious in fulfilling the plan, fearing that it will get a more intensive plan for the next period.[32]

But let us assume that the Soviet planning system is improved and that plans are compiled on rigorous scientific grounds. In all cases the attained level of fulfillment of the plan is taken into account in compiling the new plan. If for the sake of simplicity we now assume that the new plan which the personnel may propose equals the plan proposed by the higher-echelon organization and that its fulfillment strictly corresponds to 100 percent, the remuneration of the personnel remains at the previous level. The fact that the personnel attained greater effectiveness in the preceding cycle will be reflected only once in their remuneration, while their fixed salary will not change.

Of course, increasing the stability of the plans and issuing long-term plans to economic units as the basis of their incentives can eliminate to some degree workers' fears about increasing the effectiveness of production by adopting and overfulfilling more intensive plans. The question of increasing the stability of plans, known in Soviet economic literature as the question of introducing long-term norms, has been the subject of broad discussions among economists. These discussions originated in the 1960s in the works of E. G. Liberman.[33]

Finally, a further vulnerable point in the system of incentives is the method by which higher-echelon organizations formulate plans.

Generally speaking, there arises in the hierarchical structures the theoretical problem of coordinating the processes of planning and stimulation between different levels. The central question revolves around the responsibility of higher-echelon organizations for the plans they formulate. To what extent will higher-echelon organizations abuse the establishment of plans if the well-being of the plan executors depends on their fulfillment?

In the USSR the party and government agencies that approve the national economic plan try to make it as intensive as possible, yet they bear no responsibility for its fulfillment. At the intermediate levels a desire does exist to get a smaller plan, since responsibility must be borne for its fulfillment.[34] At the same time, in some sense there is still no responsibility at these levels for the establishment of a correct plan. The game situation played out between the higher-echelon and lower-echelon organizations in the planning process lies in the fact that the plan is compiled by the higher-echelon organization in a power struggle with the lower-echelon organization. The higher-echelon organization attempts to impose a more intensive plan on the lower-echelon organization, which tries in turn to obtain a less intensive plan. This situation and the ensuing consequences have been described in detail in Soviet and Western literature. I shall only briefly review what is already known.

Given the aforementioned power struggle, the output plan is frequently unrealistic, since in fact it lacks the necessary material backing (for example, a plan will include the receipt of supplies from capacities slated in the plan to go into operation but which, as is known beforehand, actually will not start up, and so on). In the process of assigning more intensive plans, the higher-echelon organization is guided by the key idea that if a participant gets an intensive plan, it will nonetheless try to fulfill it, and thus there will be a greater increase in the effectiveness of production. If it should turn out that the participant cannot fulfill the plan, at the end of the plan period there will be a chance to correct the plan and make it fulfillable.

However, since personnel are uncertain about a chance to correct the plan, this leads to corresponding negative phenomena. On the one hand, workers use every means to fulfill the plan, violating processing technology, lowering the quality of output, and so on. On the other hand, the higher-echelon officials on whom plan correction depends are corrupted, because under the existing system of planning they can often use deliberately jacked-up plans to discredit objectionable personnel.

Approaches to locating responsibility for formulating valid plans have been discussed in the Soviet economic literature. Thus, for example, V. S. Nemchinov proposed replacing the planning system with a contractual system.[35] He intended to base the relations between organizations at all levels of the hierarchy (also including the highest level of the economic hierarchy) on the elaboration of mutually advantageous plan orders that are essentially contracts. These orders were to resemble the system of relations in Western countries between the state and firms making military products. Such relations are formed on a contractual basis.

I do not rule out vertical contractual relations between various participants in the Soviet economy. Moreover, as the production of consumer goods grows and as society becomes liberalized, the role of these relations should grow. However, as follows from what I have already said, contractual relations are, generally speaking, inadequate and do not rule out the need for a normative planning principle.

The problem of responsibility for formulating the plan, especially at the higher level that sets the tone of development for the entire system, is a very complex sociopolitical issue. Its solution returns us to our discussion of general problems entailed in the functioning of modern economic systems. (Unfortunately, in the Soviet economic literature the discussion of such issues with respect to the USSR is practically impossible.)

Thus research on stimulating personnel to adopt intensive plans and to overfulfill them has made possible substantial progress in the theoretical elaboration of this question. At the same time, there is a vulnerable point here, since the stimulation of personnel to directly increase production efficiency is ignored. The threat remains that plans confirmed by not sufficiently responsible higher-echelon organizations will prove to be very intensive and that sooner or later (more likely sooner than later) the attained fulfillment of the plan will be taken into account in the organization of the planning and incentive system. This is why the organization of a system of incentives that excludes direct payment for the increase in effectiveness attained by a given economic unit and that revolves only around the plan may prove insufficiently effective.

The Contract and Incentives in the USSR

As we noted above, in the USSR the contractual system plays a secondary role. Contractual relations do provide penalties for nonfulfillment. However, the penalties are in fact rarely invoked, even though contracts are frequently not fulfilled.

The reasons for such a situation should be sought in the system of planning. The plan, as we know, is usually drawn up in a way that provides for totally satisfying the demand for resources, particularly by commissioning new capacities during the year or by suppliers overfulfilling the production plan. Contracts between suppliers and customers are based on the plan. However, from experience it is known that the commissioning of new capacities on schedule is highly improbable, and the percentage of plan over-fulfillment may prove small. Yet all customers have received warrants for products; accordingly, under these conditions there will not be enough production for some customers. Specifically which ones is not known! Thus a situation occurs in which demand exceeds supply, with all ensuing negative consequences.

In order to describe this situation, let us examine a model of a game that we will arbitrarily call "120 chairs." (It is similar to "musical chairs.") The idea of the game is for 120 chairs to be arranged on a stage and for 121 people to come out. The one who fails to get a chair loses. And even though only one person may be left without a chair, there is a "scuffle" on the stage, the possessors of chairs are "bribed," and so on, since every participant will try to get a chair. Here one clearly sees the phenomenon of control, i.e., when a small quantity of energy can bring enormous masses into play (pushing a button raises a massive sluice gate).

Let us return to the implementation of the plan referred to above. The situation in the "120 chairs" game is enhanced by the appearance on the scene of a figure like the "pusher." Every enterprise, fearing that it will be the one that lacks the essential product and that it will fail to fulfill its plan and suffer all the ensuing consequences, determines to send its agent (pusher) to intercept the requisite product. [36] The pusher illegally presents a large number of gifts to the "necessary" people in order to secure the necessary products. An unofficial system of stimulation of personnel to transfer commodities to a given enterprise emerges that carries with it the negative consequences characteristic of corruption. Here we would also like to call attention to another aspect of this "game." Under the given conditions, when demand sharply exceeds supply it is very difficult to improve product quality, to attain the requisite assortment of output, etc.,[37] even if there is a system of penalties for delivering poor-quality, incomplete products. This is a result of "reciprocal amnesty" between supplier and customer.

If the customer fines the supplier for breach of contract, the latter may deprive him of the product he needs, and then no pusher will be able to help.

Thus under this system of planning, when demand exceeds supply not only does the system of penalties for the nonfulfillment of contracts not function, but there also appears a system of unofficial gifts for the right to get scarce commodities, and this entails the inherent negative characteristics of corruption.

The problem of increasing the efficacy of the system of penalties for the observance of contracts actually becomes the more general problem of introducing competitive mechanisms in planned systems.

Theoretically, even with equality of supply and demand throughout the system as a whole, enterprise personnel who are dissatisfied with the fulfillment of the contract by the supplier may demand that he pay a penalty. However, in order for supply and demand to coincide in the event of a breach of contract, there must be reserve resources in the form of corresponding products (or means for their production). The formation of these reserves must be provided for in the plan itself. Such reserves can be seen as second-order incentives, as distinct from resources that directly satisfy consumer demand. The point is that for the producers the formation of such reserves can be conceived as competition. Producers try to produce more than customers need altogether. But since it is not known beforehand which producers will prove to be "overboard," this stimulates them to more effective activity.

The foregoing can be represented in simplified form by the same model of "120 chairs." Keep the 120 chairs with their owners standing behind each chair. Now bring another 119 people on stage. The owner of the chair who fails to find a person for his chair will be the loser. At this point the control phenomenon will operate in reverse direction. A commotion will develop among the owners of the chairs: each of them will persist in offering his own chair. Thus by means of a small quantity of surplus resources it is possible to arouse a large number of producers to positive activity. Under this competitive mechanism the planning agency plays the part of a buyer of surplus commodities or commodities of lower quality for lower prices.[38]

An objection may be raised against this argument: "Is it possible to resort to the production of second-order incentives in the face of a shortage of products?" In my view the answer to this question can be affirmative. After all, when the plan is compiled the wishes of all customers are not completely satisfied. The plan balances supply and demand in the face of given limiting resources and scientific-technical knowledge. By reducing the satisfaction of the need for a product by a small amount at a given time (attention was also called to this circumstance in the model of "120 chairs"), on the whole we increase the effectiveness of production, since it also depends on delivery schedules for complete sets of products, their quality, etc.

Thus the competitive mechanism can in principle be introduced under the conditions of planned socialist systems (see p. 69). This point of view has been maintained by a number of Soviet managers and economists.[39] In particular, it was even developed in a series of measures introduced by the Soviet government in the late 1960s that were meant to accelerate technical progress.

Competition in the design of war materiel was introduced in the USSR as far back as the Stalin era. Tupolev and Miasishchev competed in the production of heavy aircraft, Iakovlev and Mikoian competed in the production of fighters, and so on. This competition was subsequently incorporated in the production of missiles. A decree of the Central Committee of the CPSU and the USSR Council of Ministers "On Measures for Increasing the Effectiveness of the Work of Scientific Organizations and Accelerating the Utilization of Scientific and Technological Advances in the National Economy" was adopted in 1968. The decree recommends the introduction of competitive mechanisms in the field of research and development.[40]

However, the expansion of the competitive mechanism has naturally affected many other aspects of the functioning of Soviet society. As is evident from the facts enumerated above, in principle competition is possible in the USSR, even with the existing political regime. But since this competition is organized in an autocratic regime with a centralized system for issuing resources and assignments that entails the intervention of the party apparatus, it assumes a distorted form. Therefore the further development of the competitive mechanism inevitably requires its liberation from party guardianship and subsequently the possible curtailment of the role of state ownership and the attendant system for the allocation of resources and assignments.[41]

The Soviet leadership thus faced a very urgent alternative. One possibility was to relinquish a certain amount of the political power of the party and of the central authority by permitting the introduction of developed competitive mechanisms, thereby increasing the effectiveness of production, the power of the state, and hence their own political power. The other path was to preserve the existing political mechanism, which gave immense powers to the leaders, and try to find the answer to the question of increasing production effectiveness within its framework.

The second point of view prevailed at the beginning of the 1970s. It was formulated rather clearly in a report by P. N. Demichev, then secretary of the Central Committee of the CPSU for ideology and candidate member of the Politburo, at an ideological conference in 1971.[42] Demichev objected in general to introducing competition into the Soviet economy. His arguments against doing so actually relate more to more developed forms of competition that, indeed, require substantial renunciation of strict centralized planning (but not centralized planning in general, as Demichev wrote) and the decentralization of ownership. However, Demichev's assertion that unemployment, inflation and higher prices, and the irrational expenditure of resources result from competition is erroneous. All these negative phenomena are not the necessary companions of competition. They can also be seen in such centrally planned economies as the Soviet Union, which Demichev defends. (See, for example, the first section of this chapter.)

It must be noted that, as is evident in his article, Demichev's objections to competition were part of the general criticism of the possibility of introducing developed market mechanisms in the Soviet economy, softened, to be sure, by the inertia of preceding discussions on the liberalization of the Soviet economy. (This was expressed in Demichev's criticism of the rigid economic system in China.)

But the analysis of this issue goes beyond the purview of this work.

7

Market Colors and the Soviet Economy

The control of developed economic systems requires the use of a very complex price mechanism, as we have shown in Chapter 5. Under the conditions of a planned socialist system, in which the role of formalized control processes is sharply increased, great difficulties arise in utilizing these mechanisms.

But the main difficulties in a planned socialist system stem from the fact that people take part in it. These people are endowed with human features and do not want to be robots. Their features are expressed in the fact that people have different desires and values, they make mistakes, and so on. In varying degree people have natural vices, i.e., they try to get life's pleasures by illegitimate means.

The Marxist ideology adopted for planned socialist systems is based on arousing people's interest in improving their well-being and obtaining life's pleasures. It thereby fosters in people the appropriate stereotypes of well-being, which differ from those in introverted cultures. At the same time, Marxism denies people's natural vices and assumes that they are merely the result of a social order based on private ownership.

However, as shown by the experience of the Soviet Union, where private ownership was abolished in the early 1930s and socialism was proclaimed in 1936, human psychology has not changed there. For a long time the attempt was made to explain human vices in the USSR as remnants of capitalism in people's minds. "Creatively" developing Marxist theory, which considered economic changes the basic, decisive factor in all social change, Soviet ideologues declared that people's minds have inertia and memory of the past. Such an explanation could have been accepted for the generation that was born and reared under the capitalist conditions of tsarist Russia, or at worst during the NEP period. But how can one explain human vice in generations that were born and reared after the building of socialism? It may be that there are "remnants of socialism in the people's minds" that are in no way different from the "remnants of capitalism." Still, there remains the hope that people's psychology will change only under communism. But communism has already been promised twice to the present generation of Soviet people — by Lenin and Khrushchev — and it still has not come to pass.

Finally, let us note that the structure and culture of the main population in Russia, where the construction of socialism began, also have their own peculiar features which have not caused the many problems that have arisen in the planned system but which have to a considerable degree exacerbated them. The Russian population consists primarily of peasants. For various reasons it was not reared in the spirit of respect for the law. While in the past people's morality was not very stable, religion nonetheless significantly restricted their behavior.

The relativistic morality introduced by Marxism and the denial of absolute moral principles, accompanied by the persecution of religion, largely deprived the people of fundamental moral principles. For the sake of the triumph of communism, any amoral act is permissible; such acts are consecrated by official propaganda. But people who have become accustomed to using illegitimate means for the sake of bright ideals also begin using them for the sake of their own interests. And if the law punishes them for these illegitimate means, people believe that the law is bad and not that they are guilty before the court of their conscience or social absolutes.[1]

All that I have said helps us approach a more detailed examination of the reasons for the formation in the planned system of markets that both implement and supplement the centralized mechanism of planned management. These markets may be for all sorts of goods, services, and labor resources, but we shall examine only a number of markets for selling goods and services.

The planned system generates a spectrum of markets (see Table 4). We will designate the various markets by different colors which, perhaps, will help us understand how these markets are perceived by the authorities.

We will differentiate types (colors) of markets according to how the authorities assess the markets from the standpoint of advancing their target functions under the given constraints. (The authorities' target functions are primarily the growth of the scope of their power, the growth of military potential, etc.; human psychology is

Table 4

Basic Characteristics of Market Colors in the USSR

Market number and color	Degree of legality			Holder of goods	Receiver of goods	Typical reward or punishment for increasing sale of goods	Possible market development in future	
	of goods sold	of source of goods	of method of sale				immediate	distant
I. Legal markets								
1. Red	legal	legal	legal	managers of state store	public	bonus	expansion	expansion
2. Pink	legal	legal	legal	public	public	bonus	expansion	expansion
3. White								
a. soft goods	legal	legal	legal	public	public	market tax	contraction	contraction
b. foodstuffs	legal	legal	legal	collective farmers	public	market tax	contraction	contraction
II. Semilegal markets								
4. Gray								
a. consumer goods	legal	legal	semilegal	public	public	fine	expansion	contraction
b. means of production	legal	semilegal	legal	state managers	state managers	party reprimand	expansion	contraction
III. Illegal markets								
5. Brown								
a. consumer goods								
i. scarce on red market	legal	semilegal	semilegal	state store workers	public	dismissal, severe party reprimand	expansion	contraction
ii. privately imported	legal	semilegal	semilegal	visitors from abroad	public	ban on foreign travel	expansion	contraction

Market number and color	Degree of legality			Holder of goods	Receiver of goods	Typical reward or punishment for increasing sale of goods	Possible market development in future	
	of goods sold	of source of goods	of method of sale				immediate	distant
b. means of production	legal	illegal	illegal	state enterprise workers	collective farms	severe party reprimand	expansion	contraction
6. Black								
a. goods with limited production or import								
i. legally produced	legal	semilegal	illegal	profiteers	public	prosecution	expansion	contraction
ii. stolen	legal	illegal	illegal	plunderers of state property	public	prosecution	expansion	expansion
b. goods with restricted sale	legal	legal	illegal	profiteers	public	prosecution	expansion	contraction
c. goods not imported or produced for public	semilegal and illegal	illegal	illegal	currency and clothes speculators, prostitutes	public	prosecution	expansion	expansion

one of the constraints.) This assessment can be expressed by the degree of the markets' legality from the standpoint of the commodities sold on them, the sources from which goods are obtained, and the ways they are sold. The degree of legality is measured by the scale of reward or punishment for an increase in the sale of commodities.

Hence we shall examine legal, semilegal, and illegal markets.[2] Each has its own subdivisions that also reflect the degree of desirability any market has for the authorities. Thus within the legal market we distinguish the red market for state sale of consumer goods and services, which is most in keeping with the state's interests in the existing situation. Its participants receive bonuses for increasing commodity sales.

We next note the pink market, which is also actively supported by the state even though it is controlled to a lesser degree. Finally, we examine the white market, which although legal and supported by the state, holds less significance for it. This market causes difficulties in economic management because it forces the state to coordinate its stricter centralized planning with a market mechanism that in principle functions spontaneously. Participants in the white market are taxed.

In the semilegal gray markets the public rents means belonging to private individuals, services are rendered, or resources are redistributed between economic units. These markets actually give the authorities a chance to boost their target functions because, with given resources, the mechanism of functioning created by the rulers themselves is not adequate, and the negative consequences engendered by these markets are not so great for them. Participants in the semilegal markets are subject to mild administrative punishment, are fined, or receive party reprimands.

We differentiate two types of illegal markets. The first is the brown market. It is the result of the existing mechanism of functioning under which a scarcity of commodities is created artificially, and managers use illegal methods to find resources for fulfilling the plan. As a result of the considerable negative consequences of this market for the authorities, its participants are more severely persecuted. However, the persecution is confined solely to administrative punishments, including dismissal from work, a ban on foreign travel, and the imposition of severe party reprimands. But as regards the black market, whatever its origins, its existence impinges deeply on the target functions of the powers that be. The authorities resolutely combat the participants in this market — profiteers, plunderers of socialist property, prostitutes, and currency speculators — and prosecute them.

Thus the planned socialist economic system in the USSR has generated a multitude of markets. Following the principle of invariants, we can provisionally outline three groups of factors that shape the three corresponding groups of markets in the planned socialist system.

The first group consists of markets that are immanent in developed society as such; we will provisionally call them immanent markets. They are the offspring of large economic systems in which people function who are endowed with various human passions. These markets include the red and pink markets and the part of the black market involved in the sale of commodities banned in any civilized society.

The second group consists of markets generated by the planned system and state ownership. They are the gray market in the means of production and partly the black market involved in the theft of socialist property. We will provisionally call these markets socialist markets proper.

The third group consists of markets that have emerged in the USSR chiefly as a result of specific historical conditions in the development of a peasant country with a population having a low standard of living and low cultural level. We will call them rudimentary markets. They include the white market, the gray market in consumer goods, the brown market, and so on.

In keeping with our classification of markets, it is possible to forecast, as we have tried to do in part in this work, the future for these markets in the USSR. In order to avoid repetition, the following exposition is based on the classification of markets according to the degree of their legality.

Legal Markets

The Red Market

People living in a society with a planned economy also have different systems of values, and even with the same income, they prefer to consume different market baskets. The more differentiated the incomes, the greater the diversity of consumer goods produced, the more flexible must be the system for the distribution of consumer goods.

Take a period with the extremely low level of consumption that is especially characteristic of wartime. In such a period there is little variety in consumer goods, and people need essentially all of them. Under these conditions goods can be distributed directly through a system of rationing. Of course, the actual variety of human values will make itself known even here. As a result a parallel system will emerge to redistribute products obtained by ration cards. This happened during World War II in the USSR when a rationing system for consumer goods was introduced. The very fact that tobacco products were rationed although some people do not smoke while for others tobacco has the greatest value led to the emergence of "redistributive relations." Girls sometimes exchanged bread for stockings, and so on.

In principle the formation of such a parallel market had positive features for the state because it became possible to raise the level of satisfaction of the state's wards. Yet this market also had its negative features. In centralized systems the authorities generally have a negative attitude toward any mechanism they do not directly control. Such a negative attitude toward uncontrolled mechanisms is actually justified to the extent that such mechanisms potentially can have a direct negative impact on the authorities' target functions.

Indeed, the market for the redistribution of rationed commodities soon produces middlemen. In themselves middlemen are, generally speaking, a positive phenomenon, since they promote more effective exchange. But since this exchange is not controlled by the state, the middlemen are not restricted in the amount of income they receive. Hence the incomes of the middlemen may exceed the incomes of producers dozens of times. This may induce active people, whom the state needs for its immediate goals, to become middlemen. For this reason middlemen are proclaimed profiteers, and a rather relentless struggle is waged against them.[3]

Since even when there is an acute shortage of consumer goods it is hard to distribute them by rationing, it becomes particularly difficult to do so when there is a greater saturation of commodities. Hence the acute need to introduce a flexible mechanism that in principle permits each participant to obtain the market basket he needs within the limits of the money he has (a universal constraint).[4]

Practical workers in the USSR realized, based on their intuition and experience, that under certain conditions it is possible to use the price and money mechanism for the flexible distribution of consumer goods. Thus a market was created to sell consumer goods, and the direct rationed distribution of the means of production was preserved. Strictly speaking, this mechanism for the distribution of consumer goods should be considered a quasimarket, since the state establishes both prices on the commodities as well as incomes. At the same time, it has essential market features: the existence of an option in people's actions, the chance to select both various types of activity and different market baskets of consumer goods, and the inverse influence of this selection on the actions of state agencies.

It is commonly assumed in theory that with progress toward communist society, the role of the red market should diminish and the role of the free distribution of services must increase. In our view however, as the well-being of the Soviet working people improves, the role of the red market should grow. It will also become useful to gradually draw into this market commodities now distributed gratis. We can assume that the free distribution of such goods is largely due to the low standard of living (we have in mind mainly medical care and education).

Generally speaking, it is hard to imagine a society in which products can be distributed according to needs. However high productivity, there will always be constraints. They are dictated simply by the fact that the survival of mankind will always be menaced by external natural forces. Even if a high degree of stability is attained within the confines of the earth's atmosphere, there will still be a threat from outer space. The assessment of this threat to people will grow as the probability of survival on earth increases. At the same time, the acceleration of the rate of technical renewal of consumer goods requires considerable resources for their production.

From what I have said we can assume that the balance of resources that must be allocated to satisfy the population will, evidently, always be strained. Hence every person will in principle be able to obtain only a limited amount of resources. It is likely that the distribution of resources by means of money and prices is most flexible from the standpoint of the peculiarities of each individual's consumption. This is one side of the problem.

The other side of the problem is that the existence of a money economy permits effective monitoring of the economic units' activity and of the volume and quality of the work they do and their production costs. Evidently, money is in principle an effective means for the functioning of any complex system, especially under stochastic and uncertainty conditions. The existence of money serves as the general expression of the values received by the system and the general constraint on its possible activity given the existence of degrees of freedom. The comparison of values obtained and expended is the general criterion of the effectiveness of a system's activity. Yet the sum of values received may also play the role of a feedback mechanism by coordinating the activity of one system with other systems that assess ingredients obtained through the first system.[5]

The Pink Market

People living in the USSR, like Homo sapiens in general, are prone to err. In particular they may make mistakes in the purchase of various items. It often happens that an unfortunate purchase becomes apparent only after an item has been used several times. Since it is frequently impossible to return purchased items to the store, the customer can correct his error only by selling the mistakenly purchased commodity to people who need it.

Soviet man, like man in general, with time changes his mind. In some cases it becomes important for him to acquire a new commodity. But he may not have the necessary money at his disposal. In such a case, in order to obtain money he will be ready to sell some of the commodities he has previously acquired and that have less value for him compared with the new commodity in the new situation.

Fearing the development of a spontaneous market for people's resale of commodities and the possibility of its becoming a black market replete with profiteers, the state has created a special network of government commission stores to sell clothing, furniture, and books. Their only purpose is to adjust consumers' actions, since the consumers themselves use the overwhelming majority of the goods they purchase.

Since the number of commission stores is comparatively small (there are several dozen of them in Moscow, for example), they have not required significant capital resources. The operating costs of the stores are borne entirely by the people who bring their goods to these stores. They pay roughly seven percent of a commodity's sale price for the store's services.

Commission stores are fully guaranteed against losses that might result from the unsalability of a commodity, since money is paid for an item only several days after its sale. The state quite carefully monitors the activity of commission stores. In order to prevent them from being used to sell stolen goods or privately produced commodities, a person bringing an item to a commission store is registered by his identity card. Through these stores the state monitors prices and does not permit the sale of commodities at prices higher than the state price.

At the same time, unlike in the conventional network of state stores, at the commission store prices are fixed by the staff of the store itself. These prices are very flexible. They may be lowered as fast as needed if an item taken on commission does not find a market. Naturally, the store lowers the price only with the consent of the person selling an item.

Finally, we should note the buy-up variant of the commission store, whose raison d'être is as follows. Some people need to get money immediately for the items they sell, but at the conventional commission stores one has to wait until an item is sold. The state network of buy-up stores has been created specifically for cases in which a person has to sell an item immediately. Since the store assumes the risk for the sale, the person selling the item receives a substantially smaller sum than the sale price. The difference between the price for which an item is sold by a buy-up store and the sum received by the person selling an item fluctuates according to the demand for the item.

Thus the USSR has created a network of state stores that perform the middleman functions needed to adjust consumers' actions. Since these stores are the property of the state and the people employed in them are state employees, we have here a situation analogous to the red market. A number of other government constraints on the activity of store personnel in accepting commodities on commission and setting limit prices at the level of state prices also makes them resemble the trade enterprises in the red market.

Yet there are also significant differences between these stores and state stores. As we have already noted, the basic difference is the setting of prices by store personnel, especially in buy-up stores. This creates considerably greater opportunities for the staff to illegally increase their income. It is the basic reason that commission stores are not red but pink.

What are the prospects for the development of the pink market in the USSR? The pink market will also be retained in the distant future, since it is born of factors that are part of human nature. As the well-being of society and the quantity of commodities consumed increase, the role of this market will grow. Naturally, structural changes will also occur in the nature of the commodities sold on the pink market: given the relatively low prices of clothing, used clothing may be sharply devalued. But at the same time there may be an increase in the role of passenger automobiles sold through commission stores.

One can also suggest that in terms of the <u>method of its function-</u><u>ing</u>, the pink market may prove competitive with the red market. It is conceivable that Soviet trade methods may be improved by organizing the work of the state retail trade network on a true commission basis with enterprises producing consumer goods. Of course, such a trade reorganization requires appropriate socio-economic measures to define the responsibility of the participating parties. The so-called cooperative trade in the USSR, headed by Tsentrosoiuz, is essentially a state system. It operates on the basis of the same principles as state retail trade but differs from the latter chiefly in that it serves primarily inhabitants of rural areas.

The White Market

The white market also belongs among legal markets. A peculiarity of the white market compared with the pink market is that here the owners of the commodities are the direct sellers. The white market, even though it is controlled by the government, is managed by the state to a lesser degree than the pink market.

Two types of white market can be discerned. One of them is primarily a market in soft goods, while the other is primarily a market in foodstuffs. The reasons for their emergence are quite different.

Soft Goods

Since the pink market is not very powerful, in many cities state agencies officially authorize the sale of old items at special markets the people call "flea markets" [barakholka]. The state imposes taxes on these markets and checks to see that new items are not sold there (new items can be returned to the state store where they were bought or to a commission store). The state places no restrictions here on prices. The owners themselves sell their goods at these markets.

So poorly controlled a market can quite easily become a nesting place for profiteers. For this reason the state does not encourage these markets and closes them down if they become major centers of illegal trade. This happened in the 1950s when the large Moscow

Perovskaia "flea market" was shut. A similar market in Kiev bearing the name "storm cloud" [tucha] was closed in 1975.

We shall characterize in somewhat greater detail another type of white market that plays a large role in the USSR.

Foodstuffs

The specific conditions underlying the development of the planned socialist system in Russia, a country with a small-scale peasantry, supplemented by Stalin's foreign and domestic policies, led to the emergence of a collective farm market in the country.

Stalin's policy of industrialization at the expense of the peasantry was accompanied by the introduction of the corvée system in the form of collective farms. The state shed its responsibility for the welfare of the peasants and left them to fend for themselves. This was the basic reason for the emergence in the USSR of two forms of ownership — public and collective farm-cooperative. The corvée system of agricultural organization was the easiest way to confiscate the largest percentage of agricultural products from the peasantry: it is easier to force the peasants to work in the fields of the landlord, which was the state, than to take from them the lion's share or even the entire product produced by them on their own land.

For their labor on the collective farms the peasants received some pay, usually in the form of a small percentage of the grain or vegetable harvest. The peasants' basic source of income was their private plots. (Prior to 1952 the plots were also taxed by the state.) Thus peasants received incomes in kind from private plots and from the collective farms.

Since the structure of products available to the peasants could not satisfy their needs, while on the other hand city dwellers' demand for a number of foodstuffs was also not entirely satisfied by state trade, a means had to be found to organize the exchange between town and country. It would have been possible in principle to organize this exchange through the appropriate state trade system. But this would have required diverting considerable labor resources to the delivery of commodities and their sale. Moreover, the peasants have a considerable amount of free time that is of little value to them. They are willing to spend this time delivering and selling goods in the city and purchasing the goods they need. They even have an interest in doing so, since with their low income level they are reluctant to pay for middleman services.

All this led to the organization of the collective farm market in the USSR,[6] which we will provisionally call white. The white market is less desirable to the state than the red market because it is less controllable. However, as an official market it is restricted by the state not only from the standpoint of certain hours of operation but because the state also defines the <u>upper limits</u> of prices. These prices may not exceed prices of similar products in state stores, evidently, more than threefold.

The state does not usually intervene directly in prices on the collective farm market. But when crop failures occurred in the late 1960s and in 1975, limit prices were set. This quickly led to the white market being augmented by another, an illegal market. At the same collective farm market, the same sellers were now selling required commodities "under the counter" for higher prices. Products of poorer quality stayed on the shelf. The inevitable risk to the sellers increased the prices still further: they were one and a half to two times higher than the official limit prices.

The usual theoretical assumption in the Soviet Union is that with progress toward communism, the role in the economy of state property must constantly continue to grow. This means that state farms should play a larger part in agriculture, private plots should be eliminated, and hence the collective farm market should disappear. But it is possible that as a result of the increase in peasants' incomes on collective farms, accompanied by the introduction of money wages and the reduction of the marketability of private plots owing to the reluctance of peasants to work extremely hard in the absence of commodities on which to spend their money, the mass of commodities sold on the collective farm market will decline even independently of the growth of state property. Existing Soviet statistics seem to confirm this trend. Thus the relative role of the collective farm market in overall trade turnover is clearly diminishing. Even in the overall sales of foodstuffs in actual prices between 1950 and 1972, the share of the collective farm market declined from 28.7 to 7.7 percent.[7]

As regards the absolute volume of sales, it is basically growing in money terms but has evidently been declining, especially in recent years, in physical terms. Thus the volume of sales of agricultural products on the collective farm market in the city increased from 3.7 billion rubles in 1960 to 4.3 billion rubles in 1972, i.e., it grew by only 17 percent;[8] the rise in prices on the collective farm market during this period was substantially higher.[9]

All that I have said does not negate the enormous role that the collective farm market plays even today in supplying cities with certain high-quality products, especially potatoes, meat, and so on. But here we intended only to note trends toward change in the role of this market.

Semilegal Markets

The Gray Market

Consumer Goods

The commodities on the gray market are items of personal consumption (and services) allowed by the state that are "brought" to the market and sold by their legal owners. The illegality of these operations lies only in the fact that the transactions are not officially recorded and the resulting incomes are not taxed. Among the commodities on this market are rented urban apartments and summer dachas, lessons by "private" instructors, home repairs, and so on.

Let us examine in somewhat greater detail the reasons for the formation of the gray market for individual commodities.

In the USSR houses in cities are built chiefly by the state, which formally distributes them among city dwellers through district soviets of workers' deputies. Most urban dwellers receive their housing from the institutes and enterprises where they work. The importance of a given institute or enterprise and its need for personnel determine the amount of housing allotted to it by the state.

The system for housing distribution in the USSR is shaped by the use of housing as an additional incentive to attract people to a given job. Additional wages could not play the part performed by housing in this situation. Such allocation of housing also makes it possible for a person to lose his housing if he quits his job at some enterprise. And this does happen when it is necessary. [10]

Only a person who does not live in a certain city may get accommodations in hotels. He confirms his nonresidence to the hotel management by his identity card on which his place of permanent domicile is listed by the militia. By himself he cannot rent temporary housing.

Yet for various reasons city dwellers need housing the state cannot supply. Thus students who move to the city to study cannot always find space in a hostel. A young married (or unmarried) couple that wants to live apart from their parents also sometimes seeks housing — they would rather rent than live with their parents.

The demand for additional space creates a supply. Some families find themselves in dire need due to the death of the family head, or they need money for good medical treatment (see below), and so on. Such families or single people rent one of their rooms or part of a room.

People looking for a place to live quite often find it through their friends or acquaintances or through advertisements. But for some time the major cities have had certain places (usually the exchange office) where people renting and people looking have unofficially congregated.

Unlike state prices for apartment rent, which are independent of location, the availability of an elevator, or other conveniences, prices on housing rented on the gray market, like all other market prices, also take into account the qualitative parameters of the place rented.

Thus in Moscow a separate one-room apartment with all amenities (gas, electricity, running water, bathroom) located near a subway station will cost approximately 600 rubles a year (remember that the average annual wage in the USSR is approximately 1,800 rubles). A room in an apartment with all the amenities occupied by the family renting the room, near a subway station, will cost approximately 350 rubles a year, and so on.

Summer recreational housing is another commodity on the gray market. In the summer the cities are quite hot, the air is saturated with gasoline fumes, and houses are not air conditioned. [11] Intellectuals, who generally speaking pay more attention to health and rest, try to spend the entire summer outside the city or visit an area suitable for recreation.

It is impossibile to make such arrangements "on an organized basis," since the state does not have houses for rent in resort areas. During Khrushchev's times, as reported in the press, the state was planning the construction of many thousands of suburban houses for the recreation of Muscovites. But like many other of Khrushchev's "projects" aimed at improving the well-being of the working people, this effort did not get off the drawing board. As for state sanatoria, rest homes, young pioneer camps, and similar institutions, accommodations in them can be acquired only for a limited time — usually for a month. Only a small segment of the intelligentsia has private or state-owned summer cottages. It is possible to build a private cottage legally if an enterprise allocates the land, or it is even possible to buy a finished cottage. But this

entails major expenditures and efforts on maintenance (it is difficult to acquire materials for repairing cottages, etc.).

Here the private owner [chastnik] comes into play who offers
part of his suburban home to a city dweller for the summer. Let
us note at this point that living conditions in the country are very
difficult. There are few food stores and other service institutions;
there are few privately owned motor vehicles; after work one has
to get part way to the cottage on a crowded suburban train and then
walk the rest of the way. Moreover, one has to bring a large part
of the groceries from town (especially meat and vegetables). Thus
the payment for the cottage becomes payment for such limited resources as fresh air, a place to swim, and so on.

The leasing of part of a suburban home may be an important
source of income for the lessor. A summer cottage near Moscow
(depending on the area, number of rooms, etc.) costs between 150
and 300 rubles for the season, i.e., its rent equals one or two
months' salary for an average engineer or two or three months'
income for suburbanites, many of whom work on collective farms
or at small suburban enterprises.

About ten years ago the government tried to put a stop to the
renting of summer cottages, particularly because the additional
sources of income for suburbanites made them less interested in
their basic work. The attempt was made right on the eve of the
summer season. But the state quickly found that a large number
of families could not arrange their vacation under these conditions.
The central authorities were showered with complaints and appeals
to lift the ban on renting dachas. I do not know why the authorities
reacted to letters from working people, but the ban on dacha rentals
was shortly lifted. This was officially reported in the local press
(particularly, in the newspaper Evening Moscow [Vecherniaia
Moskva]), which stated that, generally speaking, it was forbidden
to rent houses for the summer, but that one could invite relatives.
And since the degree of kinship was not indicated, the practice of
renting dachas was reinstituted.

Other commodities on the gray market are educational and health
services that adjust the free system of education and medical care.

Given the Soviet system of secondary school education, it is usually difficult to obtain sound knowledge of a foreign language. In
the overwhelming majority of schools the study of a foreign language
begins only in the fifth grade. There are thirty-five to forty pupils
in a class, and the classes are usually held twice a week.

First-generation intellectuals generally do not know foreign lan-

guages and have not heard foreign speech at home. Yet they try to
provide their children some knowledge of foreign languages and
hire private instructors to help. First-generation intellectuals
themselves also begin studying foreign languages as adults. This
is because in the post-Stalin era contacts with scholars from Western countries have increased, it has become possible to read
Western literature in some fields, and so on. This knowledge is also
usually acquired through private instructors. Even though it is not
expensive to attend evening foreign language courses, it is difficult
because classes are large and the program is quite intensive. Free
foreign language classes for individuals (or for small groups) are
primarily a privilege of the elite.

Private instructors receive three rubles a lesson (one academic
hour). This is approximately two and a half times more than a foreign language instructor gets in a school.

Another reason for hiring private instructors relates to admissions to higher educational institutes for which the corresponding
entrance exams must be passed. Intellectuals strive to give their
children a higher education. Practically all children of intellectuals
try to get into higher educational institutes, naturally, the best
ones. But roughly since 1968 it has become more difficult for the
children of intellectuals to get into higher educational institutes.
Significant advantages have been accorded the children of workers
and peasants, many of whom are admitted to higher educational institutes, without going through the general system of examinations.
Such admissions of worker and peasant youth to higher educational
institutes evidently result from the authorities' desire to paralyze
the activism of the student body.[12] (See Chapter 2.) Children from
Jewish families, which traditionally try to provide their children
an education, experience special difficulties owing to the policy of
anti-Semitism.

The limited number of places generates intense competition
among the children of intellectuals for admission to the best higher
educational institutes. Of course, "competition among parents,"
corruption, etc., inevitably crop up here. But in any case, the extent of a pupil's preparation also plays some part. Hence parents
try to improve their children's knowledge of the subjects in which
they must pass examinations. This applies in particular to mathematics, which many higher educational institutes require for the
entrance examination and which traditionally is quite difficult for
many school pupils.

In order to improve the children's training, private instructors are called in, especially during the summer months just before entrance examinations to higher educational institutes. Depending on his qualifications, such an instructor receives up to ten rubles per hour per pupil. Instructors from higher educational institutes and secondary schools, as well as students, perform such private teaching activities, which are a very appreciable source of income for all of them.

The gray market in the health field emerges as follows. Medical care in the USSR is free. Yet good physicians are frequently concentrated in hospitals attached to higher educational institutes or research institutes not connected with the compulsory system of health care for the inhabitants of any area. Even if a hospital is obligated to serve the inhabitants of some area, the patient does not have the right to choose his physician. The number of good physicians is limited, and they may more or less choose their patients. Naturally, the patients want to get the best physicians. The demand for good physicians exceeds their supply. A balance is struck because patients pay considerable sums to the best physicians: up to 150 rubles for an operation in some clinics or 25 rubles for a house call. Here such payment is not gratitude for good treatment but goes to secure the doctor's agreement to select a specific patient.

It is also a common practice in hospitals to pay nurses' assistants ten rubles a night to sit at the patient's bedside. The nurse's assistant on duty usually does not take good care of patients — there is no incentive to do so.

We know that the sphere of paid services to the population is underdeveloped in the USSR: it was assumed that the so-called productive sphere, which is primarily connected with creating military power, had to be developed first. At one time Soviet propaganda even considered it an advantage of socialism that a considerably larger percentage of the gainfully employed population in the USSR worked in the so-called productive sphere than did so in the West, especially in the United States.

Let us examine in greater detail specific factors that prompted the advent of a number of services on the gray market.

Apartment repair is a very common form of service on the gray market because almost all housing in the cities belongs to the state. Apartment rent in the USSR is indeed very low. An apartment (including heat, water, plumbing) with thirty to thirty-five square meters of living space (excluding kitchen) costs on the order of ten rubles a month (i.e., approximately four percent of a family's monthly wage). Such apartment rent is obviously too low, but the state refuses to change it primarily for ideological reasons. Low apartment rent is used to propagandize the Soviet way of life in the West, where the cost of housing constitutes a considerably greater percentage of the family budget.

Low apartment rent, however, engenders a multitude of negative consequences, including poor maintenance: there are insufficient funds to repair the buildings. Tenants must pay out of their own pocket for routine repairs to their buildings. Since there are few state apartment repair shops, lines are long and prices are high; tenants prefer to hire a private repairman. These repairmen are usually construction workers who earn extra money in their spare time. It should be noted that the quality of service by the private repairmen is generally quite low. Common corruption on the primary job — low quality of work, lack of responsibility for meeting targets, especially owing to hard drinking — also crops up directly in work done on a private basis. Rarely does a privately hired worker do his work neatly and on time. He usually tries under various pretexts to get an advance (and many fall victim to such requests) and then disappears for a long time to drink up the money he has received.

Cobblers, tailors, and the like quite often work on a private basis. There are private tailors, for example, thanks to the low quality of clothing in state stores and the low quality and slow schedule of individual tailoring in the state shops. A good private tailor charges approximately two or three times more than a state shop. The recent drop in the number of private tailors is basically due to the appearance of attractive imported clothing (in state stores and on the black market).

Finally, flowers are a commodity on the gray market. The point here is that the sale of flowers on the official collective farm market is limited in time — the markets close at six in the evening — and in space — there are very few markets and they are far from the busiest areas. The number of state flower stands is also small and their assortment is limited. But since the need for flowers is very great in the evening — they are a pleasant and relatively inexpensive present — and the commodity itself is entirely legal, the powers that be have officially authorized the private sale of flowers. The place of sale is basically a secondary question. Even though there may be misunderstandings here in the sense that the militia may oust flower vendors, the authorities are usually indifferent to this type of trade in busy places and are reconciled to the illegal methods of sale: the vendors do not pay taxes on the goods they sell.

Flowers reach the gray market from two different sources: they are brought in by inhabitants of southern regions, or they are grown by suburbanites who have plots of land near their homes.

The sale of flowers from the southern regions has become quite big business. There are even people who devote all their time to this business, as well as wholesale flower dealers. In large cities wholesalers sell to local inhabitants who organize retail trade. This business is partly run by inhabitants of southern regions who move to the major cities for a considerable period of time. The retail trade in flowers is primarily in the hands of married women who cannot be accused of parasitism.

The growing of flowers near large cities has become an important source of income for suburbanites, some of whom even build hothouses. In the early 1970s there was an article in the Soviet press (Literary gazette) [Literaturnaia gazeta] attacking such flower growers because they were restoring private production. Here we approach the general problem of the admissibility of private production in a victorious socialist country, a discussion of which is the subject of special research.

Thus since in the Soviet economy there are consumer goods (and services) for which the state cannot entirely satisfy the demand, there appear people who can provide these commodities from their own resources or produce them with their own labor. Since the satisfaction of the demand for these commodities generally does not contradict the interests of the leadership and their source is entirely legal, the state primarily prefers not to impede this spontaneous process. Thus the gray market is a market for the sale of legal commodities from legal sources in illegal form.

With the growth of the intelligentsia in a society that prizes health, recreation, education, etc., the demand for this type of benefit will increase. We can assume that the USSR is going through a phase in its development when the number of intellectuals will increase at a more rapid rate than any change in the conditions that promote the gray market. As the wealth of the country increases, it will be possible to build more boarding hostels in the countryside; the state will be able to introduce higher housing rent, to make it easier to purchase and rent housing, and to increase the differentiation of schools according to quality of instruction. This should lead to a reduction in the role of the gray market.

Market Colors

Means of Production

All sorts of means of production — primarily various types of
materials, spare parts, etc., that are directly used for the production of commodities belonging to the state — appear on the gray
market. Exchange on this market is physical. Owing to the semilegal nature of the formation of resources, many participants do
not know that others control resources.

As we know, the planning system in the USSR is based largely
on the "power play" principle. Starting with Gosplan and ending
with the work place there is a struggle between the rulers and the
ruled to set the plan. The ruled try to obtain the smallest possible
plan for output and to include in the plan as many expenditures as
possible. If large planned expenditures are "coaxed" from the
higher-echelon organization, surpluses will turn up at the lower
echelon. Since claims for various resources are unevenly
"chopped" by higher-echelon agencies, the size of these surpluses
is usually not uniform.

At the same time, an economic unit may lack resources for a
number of items. This shortage either stems from shortfalls in
deliveries, since there was an imbalance built into the plan itself
(deliveries of products from enterprises slated to start up that,
as a rule, are not put into operation on schedule), or is due to de-
fective production. Such imbalances between supply and demand
for various types of resources are evident at all levels of the hierarchy in the Soviet economy, all the way down to the work place.
The art of participants in the Soviet economic system, then, lies
in exchanging their surpluses for the items they lack. Only the
very skilled know who has what and can organize an exchange
through their unofficial communication channels.

Government officials understand the need for such redistribution
of resources. They also realize that here people are essentially
operating within the framework of the planning mechanism they
have themselves created, from which favorable plans should
emerge. Hence higher-echelon organizations "close their eyes"
to the sources of surplus resources. They authorize an exchange
between participants that is carried out quite legally at all levels
of the hierarchy. For example, at the enterprise level it happens
when participants exchange the appropriate official letters and appropriate entries are made in their accounts at the bank. Moreover, if the commodities are not part of the fixed capital and are
not funded, such an exchange of letters is adequate for the exchange.

But if the commodities are funded and belong to fixed capital, then in all cases authorization from a higher-echelon organization is required for the exchange. It is usually no trouble to obtain this authorization, which is a purely formal act. But under the conditions of state ownership of the means of production, such monitoring is inevitably required.

Thus the gray market in the means of production operates legally but derives from semilegal acts committed in the process of the functioning of the economic mechanism.

We should also note that the existence of the market in the means of production has a corrupting influence on the people who take part in it. It legalizes illegitimate means — lying and corruption — insofar as it permits the realization of what was attained by these means in the course of compiling the plan. And where a first step has been made toward corruption born of the very system of planning, there will also be other steps that lead, as we shall see below, to a black market.

We can assume in principle that improving the mechanism of functioning of the Soviet planned economy (in this connection see the second section of Chapter 6) will make it possible to reduce the role of this market.

Illegal Markets

The Brown Market

The basic impetus to this market is the so-called scarcity of goods. Scarce commodities exist among the means of production and consumer goods. The reasons for the scarcity of these commodities greatly vary: nonfulfillment of the plan, errors in planning, the absence of flexible direct ties between suppliers and customers, and so on. Below we will examine only the scarce goods market characterized by the fact that the very existence of scarce commodities is consciously "built into" the plan itself.

We will examine separately the formation of the markets for scarce consumer goods and for means of production.

Consumer Goods

Scarce goods on the red market. In the USSR prices of a number of consumer goods are lower than equilibrium prices. For this reason the demand for these commodities surpasses their supply and they are scarce. Note that for a number of other commodities, the need for which is also not entirely satisfied (i.e., if their prices were lowered or if incomes increased, the consumption of these commodities would grow), equilibrium prices have been established, and the supply and demand for these commodities have been equalized (this applies at least to the consumption of bread, potatoes, cheese, and other foodstuffs in many cities).

Scarce commodities include many types of women's clothing, rugs, imported furniture, refrigerators, passenger cars, [13] building materials, etc. Note that scarcity does not apply to such vital necessities as bread, sugar, potatoes, ordinary clothing, etc. It would seem that in such a case the state could raise the prices of scarce commodities without fear of popular protest, since this rise would not affect particularly vital items.

Nonetheless it is likely that scarce commodities exist because the state fears raising prices in the face of possible public discontent. In a private talk I heard the following explanation of scarce commodities from quite a prominent official involved in price formation. He believed that the unduly low prices existed because politically they made it possible to delude the public that such items are available, that in principle even a person with a small income could buy them if he is willing to stand in line. Hence it is now impossible to buy some things without standing in line supposedly only because of temporary difficulties, a temporary shortage of commodities. As the production of scarce commodities increases, the lines will grow shorter.

In my view some other indirect conclusions also follow from this position. Since in the USSR there is no mechanism for fighting to increase wages and since there are, generally speaking, unlimited opportunities to raise prices, such artificial restraining of prices is a sort of evidence that constraints do exist for the authorities, that they are afraid to stir up the public. The fact that the government agrees to create lines and the dissatisfaction they cause influences the state and prompts it to increase the production of consumer goods.

Let us now examine the negative aspects of scarce commodities and determine the price society pays for the illusions created here by the state.

The existence of scarce commodities generates an illegal system for selling goods in the state network. The mechanics of this vary. For example, a store clerk tells her friends when a scarce commodity will be delivered. The customer comes, stands in line, and buys an item, or else the clerks "put it aside" (they write "sold" on hard-to-get furniture, stash hard-to-get clothing, etc.). While additional payments in such cases are lower than for profiteers, it is more difficult to find clerks who are willing to run this risk with strangers. Clerks often deal with a "reliable contingent" of customers and profiteers.

It can safely be said that the overwhelming majority of the clerks in stores selling soft and durable goods make this kind of sale of scarce goods — after all, there are scarce commodities in practically all stores. Even if a young clerk is honest, she is forced to do these things by the department head to whom she must give part of her income. The latter, in turn, must give part of his income to the store manager, who must pay part of his income to the trading depot that supplied him with the scarce commodities (after all, they could have given these commodities to someone else), and so on to the very top of the trade hierarchy. The exposure of abuses in trade in the late 1950s showed that a USSR deputy minister of trade was involved in them.

All that I have said about the sale of scarce commodities by trade network personnel refers both to the red and the pink markets. It is the impossibility of officially fixing higher prices on the pink market as well that begets the same artifically created scarce commodities as on the red market.

What then compels trade personnel to resort to illegal selling methods? On the one hand, their low standards of living and low wages. A store clerk earns approximately 1,000 rubles a year. On the other hand, there is the direct chance to make money illegally (an engineer could also trade under the counter with scarce resources, but he does not have them). At the same time, these methods of selling scarce commodities are relatively safe, since it is hard to prove that a clerk telephoned someone or put a commodity aside. Moreover, militiamen whose job is to combat such trade methods themselves get low pay and are easily corrupted.

The creation of opportunities to amass considerable sums of money in the trade system leads to the widespread corruption of people who work in that system. Given the low cultural level of trade personnel, they spend the bulk of their easily acquired money on alcohol. This is especially noticeable in furniture stores, where the clerks have very high incomes owing to the scarcity of commodities (as much as several hundred rubles on certain days). Usually these clerks "are not dry" but are always "slightly tight." Drunkenness among women working in trade is also sharply on the rise.

Let us note yet another type of scarce commodity that is found on the brown market — illegal service by passenger vehicles not privately owned. The major cities of the USSR have for the most part organized urban transit, especially and chiefly subways. [14] However, the taxi fleet in many large cities is inadequate to meet demand because rates are unduly low, there is insufficient incentive for drivers to make long runs, and so on. Again, the individual comes to our aid here. The price of his services is approximately the same as for taxis.

Passenger cars illegally offered for hire usually belong to offices and enterprises. In the USSR the heads of enterprises and offices have passenger cars at their disposal. Whatever their age and status, the executives themselves do not drive the cars: there are staff drivers to do so. [15] The wages of these drivers are usually low — lower than the average wage in the USSR. In order to keep good drivers (and executives are very interested in keeping them) executives try somehow to increase drivers' incomes. The following is one of the means of doing so. The driver of a passenger automobile gets permission to use the car to transport private persons at a time that is convenient for the executive to whom the driver is assigned. The driver's additional income in such a case amounts to approximately half his salary.

Privately owned imported commodities. By no means does the Soviet Union produce all types of commodities needed by its people. Many high-quality commodities, especially footwear, clothing, and furniture, are officially imported and sold in state stores. Nonetheless the quantity of imported goods is inadequate and the assortment is limited. At the same time, the importation of goods into the USSR, especially goods made of synthetic materials, is very profitable. The relationship between the prices of these goods in the West and in the USSR is such that for many of them the purchasing power of the dollar is as much as ten times higher than that of the ruble. For example, an overcoat costing $25-35 in the United States will bring up to 350 rubles on the Soviet pink market.

In the USSR there are entirely legal private sources for obtaining imported commodities from the West. Such goods are usually brought in by sailors, Soviet actors performing in the West, athletes competing in Western countries, etc. These people spend quite a long time abroad and can legally accumulate a sufficient amount of money to purchase goods in the West that are very fashionable in the USSR. (Tourists or delegates to scientific conferences spend a comparatively brief time in the West and use the limited amount of currency they have to buy clothing only for their families.) To be sure, Soviet customs restricts the importation of goods beyond a certain amount. But customs personnel usually do not examine the luggage of actors and athletes who perform in the West. The state views the additional income obtained by Soviet citizens from the sale of items purchased in the West essentially as an additional reward to them. It also, perhaps, compensates for the fact that the currency these citizens get for performing in the West or for working in international institutions is almost totally confiscated by the state. [16]

Goods imported privately into the USSR can be sold officially through the state network of commission stores. However, using this network entails certain inconveniences, although their prices are quite high. In order to sell an item on commission, one must display one's identity card. The very fact that this transaction is recorded is in itself very unpleasant for the seller and, assuming fairly frequent sales, is also quite dangerous for him, especially if new Western goods are involved. Moreover, the commission stores must be paid for their services.

All this fosters the brown market in imported goods which, as we shall see below, becomes a black market when both owners and profiteers participate in the sale of these goods.

Thus for the state the existence of a brown market in consumer goods is in principle undesirable, since it creates an artificial redistribution of incomes among the population and is a source of easy money. Nonetheless the state does not severely persecute participants in the brown market and confines itself to firing them and similar methods. Perhaps the state sees this market as a way to draw personnel into activities important to the state for which it is thus possible to pay a comparatively low wage.

We shall examine below some consequences of a scarcity of commodities and prospects for developing the market it stimulates as we characterize the black market and its profiteers.

Means of Production

Scarcity of the means of production is also built into the plan. We shall examine only one group of scarce commodities directly associated with our topic.

The USSR is short of spare parts, especially for machines that are in wide use — tractors, automobiles, farm implements. This parts shortage has a multitude of sources, one of which has received little attention in the press. In the USSR the processing technology for the machines I mentioned, as well as for others, is designed principally to produce great military potential and opportunities for very rapid conversion to war materiel. In wartime the service life of tanks, motor vehicles, mortars, and other types of weapons and equipment is quite short. Hence there is no need for machines with a long service life; spare parts for these machines are also needed in comparatively limited quantities. This suggests that the capacities of Soviet machine-building plants and the proportions between assembly and machine shops are set up to maximize military production if it is needed.

However, since the production of peacetime products requires different proportions between the production of machines and spare parts, a conflict arises. It is resolved in favor of military objectives. Therefore the shortage of spare parts relative to the demand for them is built into the plan.

Agriculture suffers most from the shortage of spare parts and the system for their rationed distribution. It is a major consumer of these parts and yet is considered a less important branch than heavy industry, transport, construction, etc. For this reason agriculture is usually the first to be refused funded spare parts. Yet the managers of agricultural enterprises bear very great responsibility for the harvest. They try to obtain parts by all sorts of legal methods, and they are joined in this effort by the regional and district party committees held particularly responsible for deliveries of agricultural products. The committees compel enterprises under their party custody to produce spare parts for agricultural machines.

Still, all these legal methods are not always sufficient. Since collective farms have greater opportunity than state enterprises to use the money they have on deposit in the bank, their managers stimulate the organization of the brown market in spare parts. Its dark color stems from the fact that the collective farms purchase stolen spare parts. These parts are manufactured for the collective farms on the basis of personal agreements with plant workers who then illicitly ship the parts to the collective farms. Collective farm managers sometimes enter into such illegal relations with managers of state enterprises. The enterprise manager gets quite a significant sum of money for spare parts received from the plant.

In terms of the methods used on this market it should be classified as black. However, there are attenuating circumstances here. Collective farm managers who urge plant personnel to steal are not pursuing their own personal gain or enrichment so much as the stability assured by fulfilling the plan for delivery of the requisite agricultural products to the state.

These attenuating circumstances permit us to believe that here we are dealing with the brown market and the corresponding administrative, rather than criminal, system of punishment for its participants. In the future the brown market for the means of production may be seriously curtailed. This depends, in particular, on the leadership's assessment of the threat of war. If the possibility of war can be removed, the ways military potential is built can be changed. Military potential can be enhanced through a more effective structure of production in peacetime: by increasing the service life of machines and the production of spare parts. The economy realized here may subsequently make it possible to expand military potential to an even greater degree.

The Black Market

We will call the market whose participants are persecuted by the state and convicted as criminals the black market. We will examine the structure of the black market from the standpoint of the degree of legality of the goods circulating on it. These properties of the commodities have also given rise to special terms for their owners, who participate in the activity of this market.

Goods with Limited Production or Import

Legally produced. The existence of myriad domestically produced and imported scarce consumer goods also results in the transformation of the brown market stimulated by them into a black one. This market is characterized by the emergence of a special group of people who buy up commodities for resale — profiteers. The crux of the matter here is that the state store personnel who operate on the brown market are frequently afraid to deal with the many random customers for scarce commodities. Despite a certain degree of danger, they prefer a regular specialized wholesale buyer — a profiteer.

It is also often disadvantageous for the owners of imported commodities to sell them in commission stores, since they have to register, the prices are sometimes not high enough, and so on. Soviet sailors, actors, and athletes returning from the West do not always have enough acquaintances to whom they can conveniently sell the things they have brought with them. As a result the commodities brought in from abroad are sold by their owners through profiteers, i.e., on the black market.

This black market "feeds" on the body of other markets, especially the white market. In a number cities, especially port cities (Odessa, Tallin, and others), imported goods are usually sold "under the counter" at "flea markets," since it is forbidden to sell new commodities there. In cities where there are no "flea markets," such as Moscow, for example, imported commodities form a special market — the commodities are purchased in profiteers' homes.

Foreign tourists are another important source of imported goods. This is especially true of Finnish tourists for whom it is very easy to spend a weekend in Leningrad. Since in Finland there are certain restrictions on alcohol consumption that do not exist in the USSR, a trip to the USSR helps Finns avoid these obstacles. These tourists often bring all sorts of cheap nylon clothing from Finland to sell in the USSR, where nylon clothing is very expensive. They also use the services of profiteers.

As we have already noted above, the state does not tolerate profiteers, even though they essentially perform for it the function of balancing supply and demand. Since profiteers run the risk of being caught and convicted, they set higher prices.

It is rather hard to say how much higher profiteers' prices are than those in state stores. Price markups vary depending not only on the degree of a commodity's scarcity but also on the number of hands through which it has passed, i.e., whether a profiteer has purchased a commodity in a store or bought it from someone else, whether the profiteer is trading in "fast-moving" items in large quantities (profits from turnover) or dealing in small quantities of luxury items. Roughly speaking, we can assume that a profiteer's markup within the range of 40 to 100 percent of the state price of a commodity is normal. Sometimes profiteers sell their place in line, i.e., they stand in line for a scarce commodity and then sell their place in line to a person who needs the item. It is somewhat cheaper to buy a place in line than to buy the commodity from the profiteer.

It is difficult for me to assess the number of profiteers in the USSR, since even a person who wants to buy goods from a profiteer has trouble finding one. But I would venture to say that the number of profiteers approaches several hundred thousand. For the most part they are married women entitled not to work. There are also profiteers who combine profiteering with their basic job, particularly janitors in large cities who work primarily at night and in the early morning. During that time they take their place in lines for stores expected to receive scarce commodities.

The presence of profiteers has a corrupting influence on society and generates a substantial stratum of people prepared to risk criminal punishment to make large sums of money. Even though the threat of punishment offsets the large income, the fact that the state generates the source of these incomes, for which one must pay with prison, is a diabolical temptation for people.

Petty and major profiteers are not the only ones who flourish in the realm of scarce commodities. There are also swindlers who cunningly exploit the shortage of goods. Some of them are true masters of their work and are worthy of Ostap Bender in terms of their inventiveness.[17]

It may be assumed that the role of the black market (as well as the brown) in consumer goods will grow in the next few years if the production and importation of commodities needed by the public do not increase significantly. The reason is the sharply increased sum of the population's cash on hand (approximately 100 billion rubles), which is in large measure awaiting commodities to buy. If in the more distant future the level of the population's well-being grows, it may be assumed that the state will abandon exploiting the illusion of opportunities to buy commodities together with all its attendant negative consequences.

Stolen goods. The black market examined above sprang from commodities legally obtained in the trade network.

To some degree the Soviet black market also originates from illegally produced commodities, which are ultimately consumer goods, since only for them can cash be obtained; given the current border controls, smuggling is virtually impossible in the USSR. Plunderers of socialist property are participants in the black market who obtain legal commodities by illegal means. On this black market there may be scarce and nonscarce commodities; the important thing is that all of them are produced from stolen materials at state (cooperative) enterprises or are stolen in the trade network. When we were examining the sources of the gray market in the means of production, we noted that the system of "power planning" that exists in the USSR generates reserve resources for enterprises. Enterprise managers normally use these reserves to fulfill and overfulfill their plans. Since the managers are not personally enriched in such cases but only preserve their position and receive comparatively low bonuses for the fulfillment and overfulfillment of the plan, we were inclined to believe that a gray market emerged here.

But in a number of cases such reserves are used to produce products that ultimately go to consumers, while the money (very substantial sums of money) is pocketed by the wheeler-dealers. The reserves thus generated, generally speaking, also create opportunities to use them for personal enrichment. Illegal methods of generating reserves also facilitate their use for self-seeking ends, for personal gain. If reserves can be used for illegal production, personnel in the higher-echelon agencies get large bribes to establish higher norms for the expenditure of supplies, equipment, etc. Major trials that are conducted from time to time in the USSR show that in the planning system itself there is potential for illegally producing commodities by artificially jacking up the norms governing the expenditure of resources.

The chains of illegal production of consumer goods can be quite long. Thus enterprises in light industry (or more precisely, artels that did not have high-quality materials to produce high-quality elastic braid) purchased stolen supplies from aviation enterprises to which high-quality materials for manufacturing parachutes had been allocated. The production of consumer goods from stolen materials is set up by the manufacturing enterprise itself.

We note that artels for producing consumer goods that existed in the USSR before the end of the 1950s actually produced goods illegally quite often — the artels' status stimulated them to steal. On the one hand, the artels were supposed to operate on the basis of scrap materials, and they did not receive funded raw materials from the state. On the other hand, high-quality production was demanded of them. Their small scale of production created a private situation in which it was easy to produce commodities illegally.

In the central regions of the USSR, Khrushchev's amalgamation of the artels and their conversion into state factories, coupled with the introduction of severe punishment for illegal production (up to execution by firing squad), sharply reduced the illegal production of commodities. However, in a number of republics, and especially in Georgia, where the authorities were very corrupt, mass illegal production has existed until the last few years. This is confirmed by trials that have recently been conducted in Georgia.

Illegally produced products, since they resemble legal ones, are usually sold through the state trade network, particularly through small state stores or stalls at collective farm markets. The unmonitored sale of commodities is significantly easier in these stores and stalls, which frequently do not have stock records and cash registers.

Commodities stolen from wholesale trading depots or from stores themselves are another source of commodities for the black market generated by plunderers of state property. Here the methods of theft are myriad, specifically taking the form of writing off supposedly spoiled goods, short-weighing the customers, etc. The commodities obtained are usually sold through the state retail system, whose constraints on the sale of illegally obtained commodities are circumvented. For example, a state trade enterprise that has cash registers, stock records, etc., sets up open sales of illegally obtained commodities in its district (this is quite typical in the summer). The clerk behind the counter takes in money directly; stolen goods can also be delivered to him directly, bypassing the warehouse, and so on. The store manager justifies setting up open sales counters by saying that the stores do not have enough space to fulfill their plan.

Finally, we should note that some commodities are stolen from state enterprises and are sold directly to the public — principally building materials, many of which are in short supply. Materials that are not scarce are sold at a low price on the black market — lower than in the state stores, since the buyer of stolen goods also risks punishment.

Goods with Restricted Sale

All the scarce commodities we examined above are commodities that the state would try to sell more of if it had the appropriate resources to do so. But some scarce commodities in the Soviet economy originate from the state's attempts to reduce their consumption. Wines and spirits stand out among these items.

It is well known that excessive consumption of alcohol is a Russian tradition. In the USSR these "glorious traditions" have multiplied. One of the reasons is that, given the prices existing in the USSR for food, clothing, automobiles, and similar products, the greatest quantity of positive emotions per ruble of expenditure can be derived from alcohol. The difference between the USSR and the West in this regard is that in the West the prices for strong alcoholic beverages are comparable with prices for clothing and footwear: the price of a good shirt or pair of shoes is comparable with the price of a half-liter bottle of strong wine. In the USSR, on the other hand, a bottle of vodka costs between one fifth and one tenth the price of a good shirt, a pair of shoes, etc.

The state's attitude toward alcohol is ambivalent: on the one hand, it is negative — alcohol is the scourge of production, one cause of crime, and so on. On the other hand, it is positive — alcohol is a tremendous source of budget revenues (on the order of ten percent), and most importantly, it is a means of psychological relaxation for the masses. When the negative aspects become especially alarming to the powers that be, they issue yet another decree aimed at curbing alcoholism. Among the measures incorporated in one such decree in the last decade was the following: the sale of vodka was forbidden before eleven in the morning and after seven in the evening. Thus it was anticipated that the workers at least would not drink before work or at the beginning of work and in the evening. However, a decree cannot abolish the demand for vodka both in the morning and in the evening. And it is unrealistic to buy a reserve of vodka because if there is vodka, it will be drunk up.

Thus vodka became a scarce commodity in the morning and evening. And as it always happens in such cases, a black market springs up. It begins right in the state trade network. Clerks of stores trading in wines and spirits assume the role of profiteers, sell vodka under the counter in the morning and evening, taking approximately an extra ruble (twenty-five percent of the price) for their services.

The black market in alcohol then spreads to people who combine their basic jobs with the illegal profiteering sale of alcohol. Cab drivers, who can easily be found at cab stands, usually carry on this trade. Finally, there are also professional bootleggers. For the most part they are middle-aged women; there have also been cases in which teenagers have become involved in scouting for customers.

The restriction on the sale of such legally circulating commodities as wines and spirits is one reason for the higher prices of these commodities relative to the expenditure of resources on their production: the price also includes the shadow price of the constraint on the maximum production of these commodities. [18]

The possibility of producing spirits inexpensively in the home has led to a market in a semilegal commodity like homemade liquor ["samogon"]. Vladimir Treml, who made a very interesting study of the "wine and spirits balance" of the USSR, estimates that homemade liquor equals approximately one third of the total consumption of alcoholic beverages produced by the state. [19] The production and consumption of homemade liquor is especially typical of rural areas.

Most homemade liquor is, evidently, consumed by its producers. But some of it is sold on the black market. Unfortunately, it is not yet possible to provide a more precise quantitative picture of the role of homemade liquor on the black market.

We can assume that a major reason for the comparatively low level of sale of homemade liquor is the quite severe penalty for selling it. (The penalty for producing homemade liquor for own consumption is much less severe.) Thus the sale of homemade liquor carries a prison term of one to three years with possible confiscation of property.

It would be interesting to ascertain the relationship between the penalty for the sale of homemade liquor and the income from such operations. However, it is difficult to determine such income, since there are only fragmentary data on the prices of homemade liquor on the black market. Moreover, the data do not take into account the quality of the homemade liquor, the opportunities to buy vodka in a given region, and so on.

Goods Not Imported or Produced for the Public

Semilegal commodities basically include some consumer goods not officially imported by state institutions. Ideological considerations are the main reason for this. Thus certain types of clothing are not normal for Soviet citizens and are associated with the Western way of life, e.g., blue jeans. Brightly colored Western dresses and neckties suggest foppery, are considered immodest, and so on. Modern music, including pop music, is incomprehensible and apolitical, that is, it does not fit the measure of socialist realism. We can say that in autocratic systems like the USSR, the leaders prefer the conventional for the sake of stability. Any deviation from the conventional usually promotes disruption of mental stereotypes. And if something new comes from "overseas," it also inspires people's respect for other countries in which new types of clothing exist, etc. Hence the authorities attempt to suppress an increase in diversity in the system by limiting the assortment of imported goods.

However, in the USSR, a country with an extroverted culture, there are quite a few industrious people who want to stand out from their fellows, which they can do with unconventional clothing. Therefore in the USSR there is a demand for such undesirable, "semilegal" goods. Meeting this demand can be very profitable for private citizens traveling from the USSR to Western countries for some time or for foreigners coming to the USSR. For example, blue jeans that cost $15 to $20 in the United States sell for 70 to 100 rubles on the black market in the USSR.

Semilegal goods in the USSR are available in comparatively small quantities. Petty profiteers who sell these goods (and also such illegal goods as, for example, foreign currency) are called "fartsov-shchiki." The state relentlessly combats these profiteers also because they deal with foreigners.

Some commodities in the USSR may not be bought and sold by private citizens and are illegal. This refers primarily to foreign currency, gold (in bars), narcotics, etc. But even these goods are bought and sold in the USSR. It is mainly people who are involved in the black market and who have sizable incomes that need foreign currency and gold. For general reasons they feel it is wise to keep their wealth in various forms, particularly that of foreign currency and gold. Soviet citizens traveling abroad also sometimes buy foreign currency because their currency is limited for buying commodities they can sell at home.

Foreign tourists, as well as people who have saved since the 1920s dollars (pounds sterling) that they received from relatives living abroad, are sources of foreign currency. At one time Soviet citizens returning from abroad could also bring in currency and use it to purchase goods in special stores. However, it has been several years now since a rule was introduced requiring that foreign currency brought into the country be exchanged for certificates (nominal) with which one can buy commodities in the same special stores.

On the black market gold circulates primarily in the form of the gold coins from tsarist Russia, but it is also possible to acquire bar gold and gold dust. The sources of this gold may be quite fantastic, including gold stolen from the gold fields.[20]

The price of currency on the black market is quite stable. A dollar costs on the order of five rubles. People who operate on this black market are usually professional currency speculators.

The system of penalties for the sale of currency in the USSR is very severe — up to execution by firing squad. Until the early 1960s the punishment for participating in currency operations was relatively mild — two or three years in prison. Some people felt such mild punishment made it wise to do currency deals that promised a large income. It was possible to earn tens of thousands of rubles in this way. Even if one were jailed, the money could be used to make prison life easier. Later one could live quite well even without trading in currency. However, when Khrushchev decided to halt currency operations, a new law was introduced; in violation of the principles of Roman law, "currency speculators" were tried and convicted under the new law for earlier offenses.

A number of "currency speculators" were sentenced to shooting.
A wave of protests from the world community against Khrushchev's
lawlessness, including a statement on this score from Bertrand
Russell, could not stay Khrushchev's punitive hand. Some "currency
speculators" were shot.[21]

Narcotics are also sold on the black market. The demand for
narcotics is generated by the same factors as in the West: primarily
by young people's desire for violent sensations.

Morphine is the basic narcotic. It comes from hospitals where
it is used as an anesthetic in chronic cases. Morphine is stolen
from hospitals and sold on the black market at a price per am-
pule — one injection — on the order of one ruble. Hashish and
opium are also sold on the black market. They are supplied illegally from regions of Central Asia and Azerbaijan where the plants
are grown, and they are also stolen from pharmaceutical industry
enterprises that use them in preparing drugs. It is practically impossible to buy the narcotics used in the West on the Soviet black
market: it is difficult to bring them into the USSR, and the risk of
punishment for seller and buyer is too great.

Finally, we should mention the illegal commodity prostitution.
Unlike in the capitalist West, where prostitution is also illegal but
where it is a part of the gray market (the police close their eyes
to prostitution), in the USSR, as in other socialist countries, prostitution is a commodity on the black market.[22]

It is formally assumed that there are no prostitutes in the USSR
and that the phenomenon of prostitution has been eradicated. I know
of no open trials of prostitutes. In the USSR as in the West, however, there is a demand for prostitutes, especially in the large
cities where there are many travelers, military personnel, etc.
Demand generates supply. Most prostitutes in the USSR are women
who have a job somewhere. Professional prostitution is difficult
since, according to Soviet law, a young unmarried woman must
work: otherwise, she will be declared a parasite.

The reasons prompting women to engage in prostitution are the
same in the USSR as in the West. According to members of a commission to combat prostitution in Moscow, prostitutes feel that one
reason for their actions is the low earnings from their main job
plus the desire to be well dressed. If one recalls that a pair of
fashionable women's boots costs as much as seventy rubles (slightly
less than the monthly wage of these women, which is approximately
eighty or ninety rubles a month), the arguments made by the prostitutes become understandable. Since a prostitute charges between

five and fifteen rubles per client, she can earn enough money to buy good clothing. Responding to a commission member's comment that prostitution may make it difficult for girls to marry, one of them replied that, on the contrary, prostitution helps them be well dressed and better looking, and this could help them find a husband.

In the USSR the state actively combats prostitution. In addition to the reasons that all countries have in common for combating prostitution, the active fight against prostitution in the USSR also stems from possible links between prostitutes and foreigners, each of whom is viewed in the USSR as a potential spy. This does not prevent the KGB from using alliances between prostitutes and foreigners for its own purposes.

The future of the black market in the USSR is dark, as it is, strictly speaking, in many other countries as well. In principle the following structural changes in it are conceivable. The number of profiteers may decline for the same reasons that the role of the brown market will diminish. The introduction of convertible currency in the USSR may prompt a reduction in the number of currency speculators. However, given state ownership and considering human nature — the existence of people predisposed to get their income by illicit methods — we can assume that the volume of economic crime will grow throughout the nation. As for prostitution, with the growth of large cities and the easing of the housing shortage, etc., it may also grow.

*   *   *

We can draw the following conclusions from all that we have said. Multiform immanent markets will remain in both the immediate and distant future in the USSR, and they will expand.

Socialist markets proper will also remain in the distant future, even though major improvements in the socioeconomic mechanism of the functioning of the economy may substantially diminish their role.

As for rudimentary markets, we can suppose that they might even expand in the immediate future; but under appropriate conditions in the distant future, they may be eliminated in practice.

Notes

Chapter 1

1. In the early 1920s an attempt was made in the USSR to construct a proletarian physics. Proletarian physics was distinguished by the fact that it studied energy processes as a whole and viewed them as a homogeneous formation. In the opinion of its authors, this could have direct significance in helping the proletariat — as a whole formation — to recognize its energy capacities and how to implement them. Bourgeois physics, on the other hand, was concerned with studying the structure of processes and probed into all kinds of subtle effects. This reflected the heterogeneous bourgeois world as well as bourgeois refinement and remoteness from practical problems.

In later years as well some new areas of science, such as genetics and cybernetics, were proclaimed bourgeois.

2. We suggest that the reader who is less familiar with the role of invariants in the exact sciences solve the following problem (see Figure 1). It shows how the idea of invariants makes it possible to order the process of searching for a solution and minimize the effort required.

Figure 1

Figure 1a is given. It is to be transformed into Figure 1b with a minimum of rearrangements of the dots.

Usually many people solve this problem, but it takes them a long time, many errors, and a number of variations. But using the idea of invariants makes it possible to solve the problem quickly and elegantly.

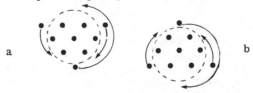

Figure 2

First, one finds the part of the structure common to both figures — that is, the part which remains the same when one figure is transformed into the other. We enclose this common part in a broken line (see Figure 2). After the invariant is found, it is readily apparent that Figure 1a can be converted into Figure 1b by rearranging three dots (indicated by solid arrows in Figure 2). The smallest number of dots permitting this transformation is three.

3. S. Kuznets, Modern Economic Growth: Rate, Structure, and Spread (New Haven: Yale University Press, 1966).

4. Edward Ames, Soviet Economic Processes (Homewood, Ill.: R. D. Irwin, 1965); D. Gale, "On the Theory of Interest," American Mathematical Monthly, vol. 80, no. 8, October 1973, pp. 853-68; J. Montias, "Soviet Optimizing Models for Multiperiod Planning," Mathematics and Computers in Soviet Economic Planning (New Haven: Yale University Press, 1967), pp. 201-45.

5. E. Z. Maiminas, Protsessy planirovaniia v ekonomike: informatsionnyi aspekt (Moscow: "Ekonomika" Publishers, 1971). A critical analysis of this work from the standpoint of a narrow interpretation of the realm of invariants within the framework of conventional concepts of philosophy and political economy (in the Soviet sense of the interpretation of philosophy and political economy) was given in part by me in a review of the book. See Izvestiia Akademii nauk SSSR, seriia ekonomicheskaia, 1972, no. 6, pp. 167-71.

6. In the USSR I tried to develop a general systems approach to economics, particularly to analyze prices, profit, and other categories as economic invariants. Along this line, I published "Metodologicheskie problemy upravleniia slozhnymi sistemami" in the collection Problemy metodologii sistemnogo issledovaniia (Moscow: "Mysl'" Publishers, 1970), pp. 87-126. However, the views on economic invariants expressed in this work (as well as in related publications by me) went unnoticed, even though they offered an entirely new approach to explanning the reasons for price-monetary relations under socialism, compared with the views accepted in the USSR.

7. What should a management agency do to avoid such a contradiction, that is, to see to it that, in the price, the expenditure of resources equals the effect of consuming the produced commodity?

We focus attention on the answer to this question, since it helps us understand why in the USSR even those who advocate establishing prices at the level of marginal expenditures do not consistently implement this principle. They fail to take into account the fact that price should not only be marginal but should also equalize the effectiveness of all production methods incorporated in the plan through the appropriate revision of prices on scarce resources.

Let us assume that presses are the only limiting factor in the expansion of production. Let us then divide expenditures on the production of these items into two parts: depreciation of the presses and miscellaneous expenditures (wages, electrical power, capital charges, etc.). Let depreciation be 30 rubles and all other expenditures be 70 rubles per unit of output under the old method. According to the second, new method, depreciation is reduced from 30 to 20 rubles (since 50 percent more output is produced per press). Other expenditures increase from 70 to 82 rubles. Thus total expenditures per unit of output prove to be 2 rubles higher under the second method than under the first. Naturally, assuming that prices for plastics remain the same, enterprises cannot be economically motivated to convert to the second method.

The first conclusion that can be drawn from this example is that the high effectiveness of plastics (under existing conditions) requires that prices on them be raised; on the one hand, this should stimulate expansion of the production of plastics, and on the other, it should promote their economical use and the substitution of other types of products for plastics in certain cases. But raising prices on plastics without also correcting prices on resources used in making them would mean an unjustifiable increase in the profits realized from production by the first method and would make the use of the second disadvantageous. Obviously, in order for both methods to be equally effective and to be used in parallel to produce the required quantity of items, it is necessary to revise prices on presses, that is, to strictly indicate the source of income growth.

In our example this requirement is met by the price of the press, which exceeds the initial price by not less than 20 percent. It must also be reflected in the price of the item, which must rise. But raising prices is obviously justified by the effect the national economy gains from using these items. In the case being studied expenditures under the first and second methods of production will become equal: for the first method, 36 rubles + 70 rubles = 106 rubles; for the second, 24 rubles + 82 rubles = 106 rubles.

The example shows that prices must not be established directly at the level of the new "worst" method of production, and that changes in prices on the limiting resources — in our example on the presses — must be taken into account. This consideration leads to the conclusion that the new price on plastics should be 106 rubles rather than 102 rubles.

I have not touched here on the economic aspect of the production of presses and the entire chain of associated production processes. But the situation in that regard is similar to the case under investigation, since additional limited resources are required to expand the production of any product for the given coefficients of expenditures per unit of output.

8. H. Levine, "Pressure and Planning in the Soviet Economy," in Industrialization in Two Systems: Essays in Honor of Alexander Gerschenkron, ed. by H. Rosovsky (New York: John Wiley, 1966), pp. 266-85.

9. The use of dual valuations of constraints in the problem, which appears to be necessary only for its mathematical solution, allows a deeper understanding of a number of phenomena in structural mechanics. See A. A. Chiras, "Primenenie metodov lineinogo programmirovaniia pri raschete uprugo-plasticheskikh balok i ram i ikh realizatsiia na ETsVM," in ETsVM v stroitel'noi mekhanike (Moscow: Stroiizdat, 1966). Mention can also be made of the work of University of Chicago Professor R. Malliken on creating a theory of molecular structure based on studying the motion of electrons within molecules. In the most complex mathematical calculation of the levels at which electrons may be found in the molecule, each stage in the calculation is characteristically reinforced with an interpretation.

10. H. Scarf, The Computation of Economic Equilibria (New Haven: Yale University Press, 1973).

Chapter 2

1. V. I. Lenin initially believed that the revolution in Russia did not preclude

the possibility of revolution immediately beginning in developed countries: it was simply easier to begin world revolution through an underdeveloped country. After the successful culmination of the civil war in the USSR, Lenin evidently began to give up the idea of immediate world revolution. Other possible considerations here were Lenin's personal motives and his passion for power plus the threat of losing his prestige should revolution triumph in the motherland of Marxism — in Germany — and in other developed countries. This is shown, for example, by Lenin's work Detskaia bolezn' "levizny" v kommunizme, written in 1920 after the successes scored in the civil war. Here Lenin openly declares that the October Revolution in Russia was not limited to a backward country. Its experience has international significance. In the same vein is Lenin's claim as victor that he could show labor parties in other countries, especially in Germany and Great Britain, ways to prepare for revolution. Here the emphasis was not on immediate revolution in these countries but on gradual preparations for the revolution even through participation in reactionary parliaments, all sorts of compromises with other parties, and so on.

Yet on the very first page of this work one glimpses Lenin's fear a proletarian revolution will succeed in other countries: "... it would be an error to lose sight of the fact that after the victory of the proletarian revolution, even in only one progressive country, there will in all probability be a sharp turnabout; specifically: soon thereafter Russia will become not an exemplary but once more a backward (in the "Soviet" and socialist sense) country" (V. I. Lenin, Sochineniia, vol. 21, 3rd edition, p. 171).

2. A. A. Fel'dbaum, Osnovy teorii optimal'nykh avtomaticheskikh sistem (Moscow, 1965).

3. Virtually no country today accepts patent designs for perpetual motion machines. Great Britain seems to be the exception. The likelihood that an idea contained in a perpetual motion machine project might prove useful justifies somewhat the consideration of such projects.

4. While there is a great similarity between Marxism and Christianity, there are also profound differences. Christ promised happiness and brotherhood on earth if people renounce their riches and begin living modestly. The Qumran communes — the forerunners of Christianity — were organized precisely on the principle that the people joining them renounced their individual wealth and led a modest and obedient life. Marxism, on the other hand, promised a rich, active life combined with brotherhood. Moreover, in brotherhood Marx saw a powerful force for attaining unprecedented social wealth and creating a heaven on earth. Such a combination of Christian ideals with the values of people who prize earthly goods proved to have enormous magnetism.

5. The migrating story of the golden fish, which is known to me in particular from Russian and Chinese tales, is an expression of this fact.

6. A professor from the University of California at Berkeley related the following curious case to me. Before World War II his father was a well-known communist in Canada. Every week he came to his brother, who was an engineer, with a new idea about how to build a perpetual motion machine.

7. I have made certain comments in this regard in "Metodologicheskie problemy upravleniia slozhnymi sistemami," in Problemy metodologii sistemnogo issledovaniia (Moscow: "Mysl'" Publishers, 1970), pp. 87-126.

8. Experience in the organization of so-called joint teams in the USSR is also

interesting in this respect. The essence of these teams is as follows. Automatic and semiautomatic lathes are widely used at ball-bearing plants. The set-up personnel usually service them in three shifts. Serious difficulties in organizing labor to operate these lathes arise during the transfer of set-up equipment between shifts. The point is that the wages of the set-up man usually depend on the number of pieces produced during his shift. Toward the end of the shift the lathe sometimes begins to go out of alignment. However, the operator does not stop the lathe to adjust it since this might reduce his output for the shift. He tries to "make do" until the end of the shift. The next operator then has to spend a lot of time setting up the lathe, much more time than it takes the first operator to set up the lathe, since the lathe was not so far out of alignment at the beginning. Thus organizing the labor of set-up personnel individually has significant flaws, since it has a negative influence on the general productivity of the equipment and the earnings of the operators.

The foremen of such automatic sectors use various types of administrative methods to induce the set-up personnel to transfer the lathes between one another in alignment. However, the foremen do not always succeed, since it is hard to determine when a lathe began to go out of alignment.

Taking the minuses of individual organization of labor on automatic machines into account, at the First State Bearing Plant Burov decided to create "joint teams," i.e., to unite the set-up personnel of all three shifts servicing a given group of automatic machines. Thanks to the changeover to the collective organization of labor and to a system of wages based on the results of the work of the entire team, the productivity of the automatic machines and workers increased and so did their incomes.

Burov's initiative was approved by the Ministry of the Automobile and Tractor Industry and was recommended for introduction at branch enterprises. As usually happens in the USSR, a campaign to introduce such teams everywhere was launched at plants belonging to the ministry. However, "joint teams" are by no means always effective. An indispensable condition for their organization is that every team member have values that promote an awareness of the collective interest. But not everyone has this interest. Thus, for example, some workers are lazy and try to "snip off" part of others' income. Some young workers spend a considerable part of their evening having a good time. The next day their capacity for work is diminished. Moreover, these workers prize earnings less. On a joint team, side by side with such young workers there may also be middle-aged workers with families who are more interested in a high income. Young workers of the type described are very satisfied with working on a joint team, since they can work with a smaller return while not losing much from their earnings: they get part of the income of others from the "common pot." As a result of the organization of "joint teams," productivity has dropped on many teams owing to the incompatibility of the members' values. As a result, the idea of these teams was discredited. In the majority of cases individual organization of labor was resumed.

In the USSR a similar situation characterized the introduction of collective forms of labor organization and wages in a number of branches of the ore extracting, coal, and timber industries and in construction, where there were collectives of workers in different occupations united by the production of the same commodities. Still other difficulties cropped up in the organization of links on the basis of collective income in agriculture, since the authorities' interests were affected (see Chapter 3 for greater detail).

9. K. Marx and F. Engels, Sochineniia, vol. 34, p. 236.

10. Ibid, vol. 23, p. 6.

11. It seems this idea was suggested to Khrushchev by I. I. Kuz'min, who was then the head of the industrial section of the Central Committee of the CPSU. Kuz'min had a brilliant career after Khrushchev's victory: he unexpectedly became chairman of USSR Gosplan. But, alas, this career was short-lived. Whether Kuz'min displeased Khrushchev in some way or Khrushchev did not want to be dependent on his "benefactor," at any rate a short time later Kuz'min was sent into honorary exile as ambassador to Switzerland. But even there he supposedly exceeded his ambassadorial powers by interfering in domestic affairs. The story has it that he wrote a letter to the Swiss government protesting that cows with bells went by his suburban home and disturbed his sleep. At any rate, Kuz'min was recalled from Switzerland shortly after his appointment. He returned to Moscow and tried to find work teaching at economic institutes. His subsequent fate is unknown to me.

12. If one compares fascism in Germany, Italy, and Spain, it is evident that fascism and nazism are not identical. Spanish fascism did not generate nazism, did not generate the idea of the greatness of the Spanish nation. Franco did not even claim to be the leader of the Spanish, even though he was sympathetic to them throughout the entire world, and it seems he even helped communist Cuba in some ways.

13. It may be that the difference between fascism and Marxism largely lies in the stand taken on the continuity of old economic institutions. It is therefore possible that in countries under fascist regimes an incomparably smaller number of people were destroyed and a smaller number of people left the country than under Marxist regimes. Moreover, this might mean that fascist regimes are more amenable than Marxist regimes to evolution (in this connection, see the pamphlet by F. M. Burlatskii, Ispaniia: korrida i kaudil'o [Moscow: "Pravda" Publishers, 1967]).

14. Even so fervent an annihilator as Stalin expressed indignation at this. See his Otnositel'no marksizme v iazykoznanii (Moscow: Gospolitizdat, 1950).

15. "The new invention does not destroy the old one but only narrows the area of its application. After all, while prose developed later than poetry in art, poetry has remained." V. Shklovskii, Zhili-byli (Moscow: Goslitizdat, 1964), p. 394.

16. Tevosian, the head of the metallurgical industry, was such an executive under Stalin. The psychology of such managers was brilliantly portrayed by A. Bek in his novel Onisimov, for which Tevosian was the prototype. The novel did not see the light of day in the USSR but was published in the West.

17. In this connection, see the article by V. N. Bandera, "The New Economic Policy (NEP) as an Economic System," The Journal of Political Economy, vol. LXXI, no. 3, 1963, pp. 265-79. Here the author focuses on NEP as one possible model of the functioning of an economic system. NEP is usually regarded as a transitional period in the development of the Soviet economy.

18. In his day H. Heine made the following remark: "A communist who wants Rothschild to share his three hundred millions with him. Rothschild sends him his share, amounting to ten sou. And now, let me be." H. Heine, Sobranie sochinenii, vol. 9 (Moscow: Goslitizdat, 1959), p. 177.

19. I first understood the essence of this law in the following situation. Once a comrade and I took a taxi to visit some friends in Moscow. On the way we asked the driver to stop at a store. My comrade went in to buy a present while I stayed in the taxi. To pass the time I struck up a conversation with the driver. Jokingly I said to him that my comrade, who had all our money, was not coming back and thus I would be unable to pay the fare. The driver replied earnestly (naturally realizing that in this case it was a joke) that in general there were many instances in which passengers got out without paying.

I then asked him how long he had been driving a taxi. He replied that he had been driving about ten years. How many persons had gotten out of his cab without paying, I continued my question. "Five or six," was the answer. "So," I said, "assuming you have an average of two passengers per call, approximately forty calls a shift, and one hundred and fifty shifts a year, in ten years you have transported more than 120,000 passengers. Compared with the number of passengers transported, the percentage that got out without paying is negligible. Why do you think that so many got out without paying? After all, the overwhelming majority of people are honest and do not leave without paying!"

"What is more," I continued, "of the eighty passengers transported each day, eight or ten get out of the cab and ask you to wait for them so that they can buy something they need in the store, get luggage from their home, go get a person being released from the hospital, and so on. Of course, there is the danger that the person will leave without paying. But evidently there are extremely few such persons. If one does not trust people on the basis that there are many cheaters, then one must demand payment for the previous part of the trip. But in such a case the passenger may take offense at the mistrust shown in him and may not leave a tip. Therefore the best strategy for the driver is to trust the passenger (naturally with the exception of obvious attempts to get out without paying). The losses that can result from passengers who get out without paying will be repaid with interest in the form of tips."

Essentially, the driver I talked to followed this strategy intuitively. However, he was unaware of it. Moreover, if someone told the driver that the execution of passengers who failed to pay him would sharply increase his income, I think he would believe it!

20. In the USSR the photographs published on page one of Pravda are mostly still state leaders and leading workers and collective farmers. Photographs of intellectuals are usually published on pages three and four of Pravda.

21. Even today in the USSR one hears the opinion that heavy spending on banquets given by the leaders to honor foreign guests is one major reason for people's low standard of living.

22. P. N. Demichev, secretary for ideology of the Central Committee of the CPSU, addressed a closed meeting at Moscow State University in the late 1960s. One of the participants in the meeting asked him roughly the following question: "Why does the party tolerate samizdat [unofficial publication]?" Demichev replied: "The country has great difficulty with paper, and hence it is not possible to print many works by Soviet writers. However, a writer can reproduce his own works and give them to his colleagues and friends to read." Naturally, his reply suggested that all this referred to party works. But while the person who asked the question assumed that everything in samizdat was antiparty, to Demichev samizdat and antiparty literature at that time were not the same.

23. This discussion was confined to only two articles. The first was a conventional official article by P. N. Fedoseev, vice-president of the USSR Academy of Sciences, "XXIV s"ezd KPSS i osnovnye napravleniia issledovanii v oblasti obshchestvennykh nauk," Kommunist, 1972, no. 1, pp. 36-77. In this article Fedoseev defended the concept of the working class as those doing physical labor. It must be assumed that at the time it was advantageous for Fedoseev, as a very experienced politician, to defend specifically this position.

The journal Kommunist (1972, no. 11, pp. 102-14) printed an article by A. Cherniaev, a leading official of the International Division of the Central Committee of the CPSU, "Postoianno rastushchii i razvivaiushchiiisia klass, klassgegemon," which affirmed the need to include certain strata of the intelligentsia in the working class. The article was presented with the following note, which is unusual for Kommunist: "This article touches on certain questions pertaining to the social structure of modern capitalist society that are examined for purposes of discussion. The Editors." Yet Cherniaev's article did not directly criticize a single Soviet scientist working on this topic. Cherniaev chose a unique way to criticize Fedoseev, his main opponent. The article contains not one critical remark aimed at Fedoseev, but on the contrary, it does have references to the book Osnovy nauchnogo kommunizma, published in 1969 by a collective of Soviet scientists under the direction of P. N. Fedoseev. Of course, the definition of the working class in the book is completely different from the one in Fedoseev's article.

24. Thus at the end of the 1960s the Institute of Electronic Machine Building, which trains specialists for the leading defense branches, was also to have sharply increased the admission of students from families of workers and peasants. Professor F., an excellent mathematician and teacher, worked at the institute. His services to the institute were very great: he created one of the first applied mathematics departments in an engineering institute and assembled a large number of able mathematicians.

A group of about sixteen students at the institute who had come from a workers' faculty were unable to pass the examination in one of the mathematical disciplines taught by teachers of the applied mathematics department. The students were threatened with expulsion from the institute for failing grades. The rector of the institute demanded that Professor F. raise the grades of the students, assuming that they would catch up later. F. refused. Then the rector asked him to resign from the institute, which F. did.

I do not by any means think that the rector of the institute was an obscurantist. It is even possible that he highly valued the merits of Professor F., but he could not expel a group of workers' faculty graduates from his institute. If he had done so, he would have been immediately summoned to the Central Committee of the CPSU by the instructor in charge of his institute or by the head of the appropriate sector. They would have "explained" to the rector his misunderstanding of the party line and the antiparty character of his action. The director might then have been removed from his post if he persisted in his "error" or if he did not realize that "there are no poor students, only poor teachers."

Unfortunately, the rector of the Institute of Electronic Machine Building is no more than a man who prizes his job very highly. It is difficult to demand heroism from him. Woe in general to the country that can exist only through heroes — so, approximately, says one of the characters in Brecht's play Galilei.

Notes to Chapter 3

Chapter 3

1. Voznesenskii also had his own views on practical matters and carried them out as chairman of Gosplan. I was told by Sh. Ia. Turetskii, who worked in Gosplan for many years, that Voznesenskii had confided in him that his ideal was Catherine the Great. He believed that Russia should be a strict centralized state with an enlightened "monarch." Planning should encompass all links of the national economy, and everything should be planned down to the last bolt.

2. My ideas on the decisive role of the pragmatic aspect for the development of new trends in Soviet science and the ability to forgo ideology can be confirmed by M. T. Iovchuk's article "Razvitie sotsialisticheskoi ideologii i kul'tury," published in Kommunist, 1971, no. 15. This article is all the more interesting in that it was presented by the rector of the Academy of Social Sciences attached to the Central Committee of the CPSU, an experienced political functionary who has learned the harsh lessons of success and failure.

3. Since the position of this group of oppositionists is less well known, I shall explain it in somewhat greater detail through an example. Wages on collective and state farms are based on specified work performed by the collective farmer. For example, a tractor driver's pay depends on the number of hectares plowed. This system of wages means that collective farmers are not interested in increasing the end result, e.g., in increasing grain output. Thus in his quest for a greater number of hectares plowed, the tractor driver ignores the quality of plowing. It is difficult to monitor a tractor driver's work, and most importantly, it is often impossible even to fix gaps in his work that may spoil the results of the work of many collective farmers for the entire year.

(It was no accident that the following incredible thing happened in the USSR: in the tractor driver competition conducted in the 1960s at the Exhibit of Attainments of the National Economy in Moscow, one of the leading places was held by a tractor driver considered a laggard on his collective farm. The point was that in the competition the tractor drivers had to meet not only the plowing speed standard but also the quality standard. In real life, however, the latter is frequently ignored. And if a tractor driver, working honestly, meets the quality standard, then he, as was the case with the winner in this competition, may prove to be a laggard.)

On a number of collective farms there were enthusiasts who organized so-called "integrated links." These links include workers in different specialties who work on a given agricultural process from beginning to end. They are paid for the end result, e.g., for the quantity of grain sold to the state.

As shown by the experience of the leading workers, under certain conditions such labor organization produces a significant effect: the crop yield is sharply increased, labor productivity grows, and costs decline, since the members of a link are genuinely interested in the end result. In the mid-1960s I. Khudenko organized the work of the entire "Akchi" State Farm in Kazakhstan along the lines of integrated links and achieved good results.

Yet this system also causes complex sociopolitical problems. Under it there is less need for directives from higher-echelon agencies, and there is no need for instructions on when to sow and when to harvest. Hence such an organization of labor conflicts with the interests of the collective farm bureaucracy, which

211

has grown much stronger in the last two decades. Such links also weaken the role of rural district party committees, whose basic role is also to issue instructions on when to sow and when to harvest.

It was no accident that an article appeared in Pravda during the months when the party organizations of Kazakhstan, with the consent and approval of the party bosses from the Center, liquidated the unique "Akchi" State Farm. Its author described with delight one day in the life of the secretary of a rural district party committee. Early in the morning the secretary called the chairman of a collective farm on the telephone and asked him whether he had sown a certain area with winter crops. The chairman thanked the secretary for the call, since he had indeed forgotten to sow. All day long the secretary of the district committee somehow reminded, gave instructions, and called attention to the need to do some job. He was the true, zealous master of the district.

4. A serious understanding of the role of creating a decision-making mechanism can be seen among mathematicians and engineers who have undertaken the application of mathematical methods to economics. This is shown in particular by the publication in the USSR in 1972 of the remarkable book by the American scientist R. Ackoff, Planning in Large Systems. It examines the art of compiling a plan under conditions of uncertainty in combination with the possibility of using the ideas of optimal planning to solve individual problems. Engineers working in the field of control set up the translation of the book.

5. A similar situation could be seen in Soviet biology. For a long time T. D. Lysenko, who was the worst enemy of the geneticists, had a monopoly in biological science. After long battles Lysenko was overthrown. Academician Dubinin, a famous geneticist, triumphed and immediately began introducing an Arakcheev regime and suppressing new ideas at the institute of genetics he headed. Moreover, in elections to the USSR Academy of Sciences, Lysenko and Dubinin frequently formed a bloc against scientists who did not agree with their opinions.

6. Thus it seems that Rudakov, secretary of the Central Committee of the CPSU for heavy industry, was removed from the Presidium of the Council of Ministers in the late 1960s. This act symbolically stated that the Central Committee of the CPSU would not actively intervene in the compilation of the national economic plan.

7. Moreover, it must be assumed that Brezhnev does not have a powerful apparatus of his own for implementing his policy. During the first years of his rule, Brezhnev's policy consisted of maneuvering between various groups and resolving the conflicts that arose among them. When Brezhnev decided to intensify his role and proclaim a more independent policy in the early 1970s, he evidently encountered difficulties because he lacked his own powerful apparatus: the apparatus of the Central Committee was largely divided between two prominent figures — Kirilenko and Suslov. It is possibly for this reason that three ministers have recently been added to the Politburo; one of them is evidently supporting Brezhnev and has the necessary apparatus. The directors of two academic institutes — Academicians N. N. Inozemtsev and G. A. Arbatov — who have been enlisted by Brezhnev are exceeding their role as advisers; this is one more evidence that Brezhnev's own apparatus is weak.

8. The "marshals" of ideology continue the debate about unification and diversity in economic science. Thus S. P. Trapeznikov, the head of the Department of Science and Educational Institutes of the Central Committee of the CPSU, in

his article in Voprosy ekonomiki (1974, no. 3), "Ekonomicheskuiu nauku — na
uroven' sovremennykh zadach," resolutely demands a struggle against diversity
and the introduction of unanimity. Enumerating the reasons for further development of the political economy of socialism, Trapeznikov writes: "... Fourth, our
community of higher educational institutes, and especially teachers of the economic sciences, have begun to feel an acute need for the theoretical elaboration
of the political economy of socialism. This is all the more noticeable in that
higher educational institutes and technical secondary schools do not yet have a
standard textbook (my emphasis — A. K.) on the political economy of socialism. ... And the sixth and final point is that now as never before, economic science itself has begun to feel the need for a thorough analytical elaboration of the
theory of the political economy of socialism. After all, it is no secret that among
economists themselves there are often different interpretations of many important problems in economic theory. Take, for example, the problems of value,
commodity-monetary relations, price formation, and cost accounting under the
conditions of developed socialism. Or the question of applying mathematical
methods to economic science. All this indicates that we must again and again
very attentively examine all aspects in the development of our economic science
and elaborate a unified authoritative opinion (my emphasis — A. K.) on all problems of economic theory. And this must be done primarily by economists themselves who are called on to give a scientifically substantiated answer to the top-
ical questions advanced by economic construction, by the needs of today and the
demands of tomorrow.

"Thus life itself dictates to us the need to be self-critical in approaching the
analysis of the development of our economic science. It is essential to examine
the entire complex of theoretical and applied scientific problems, to make a
radical turnabout toward the study of the contemporary economic basis and of
the mature, developed socialism that actually exists. Now as never before there
arises the problem of elaborating a large-scale state plan for the development
of economic science to unite and concentrate the efforts of scientists (my emphasis — A. K.) on the solution of the urgent problems posed by our party" (p. 5).

And here is what was written in the same issue of the journal by Academician
P. N. Fedoseev, vice-president of the USSR Academy of Sciences in charge of
the humanities and then director of the Institute of Marx-Engels-Lenin under
the Central Committee of the CPSU, in his article "Ekonomicheskaia nauka:
nekotorye zadachi ee razvitiia":

"It should be noted that the indicated reorganization of the work of scientific
economic institutes entails a number of difficulties. For example, there still
remains a certain segment of economic scientists who could not change under
the new conditions and could not focus their efforts to solve the most important
problems confronting the national economy. They devote their basic attention
to abstract discussions about the subject of political economy, the essence of
commodity production, the nature of a commodity, etc. Of course, these questions in themselves are of great importance and certainly should be studied;
but the discussions that we have in mind are usually conducted by these economists at the same level, without any apparent progress being made. Naturally,
such fruitless debates can only be regarded as marking time. What is more,
some of these 'theorists' are often dogmatic in their approach to the work
launched by research economists in various directions of our economic theory

and practice. Upon hearing the word "goal," they are prepared to shout: 'That is teleology'; they are sure to tie the term 'needs' to vulgar political economy; and anyone who mentions 'utility' they immediately accuse of 'regenerating the theory of Böhm-Bawerk, the theory of marginal utility,' etc. In our view such an approach is not constructive and hinders the development of economic science, even though we must always keep our powder dry and wage an implacable struggle against bourgeois ideology and the spread of its influence.... Attention should be called to the lack of harmony in the work of our economic scientists which is, in particular, expressed in the contrasting of their approaches to others, which leads to a certain 'self-isolationism.' We must also deal with this. Some theorists sometimes demand the condemnation or even prohibition of certain approaches to the solution of scientific and practical economic problems, and conversely the legitimation of their own. Here, in our view, it is essential to display a certain adherence to principle in the sense of not permitting the monopoly of any approach, of not hastily stopping new efforts that may at first glance appear somewhat pretentious. It is better to criticize premature, hasty conclusions in a comradely way rather than to reject them out of hand.

"But most importantly, it is essential to check any advanced conception against the theory and practice of Marxism-Leninism, to check it strictly and objectively" (pp. 60-61. Emphasis everywhere is mine — A. K.).

Chapter 4

1. A. Katsenelinboigen, "On the Various Methods of Describing the Socialist Economy," Matekon, vol. X, no. 2, 1973, pp. 3-25; "Variations in Means of Description of Economic Systems," Collective Phenomena and the Applications of Physics to Other Fields of Science, prepared for delivery at a seminar, Moscow, July 1-5, 1974, Brain Research Publications, 1975, pp. 38-44.

2. Production functions can not only be used to describe an economic system as a whole. They are suitable for any level in the hierarchy of an economic system when the structural changes occurring at lower levels of production are not known explicitly. At the lowest level of the production hierarchy, the production function may be replaced by an engineering function, since the description of the processes here is based directly on physical, chemical, and biological laws. For example, finding the relationship between the crop yield and the amount of fertilizer applied in a certain place may be based directly on biological laws.

3. A. I. Anchishkin, Prognozirovanie rosta sotsialisticheskoi ekonomiki (Moscow, "Ekonomika" Publishers, 1973).

4. In this connection, see the article "Nauchnoe prognozirovanie v perspektivnom planirovanii" by Iu. Belik, consultant of the department of planning and finance agencies of the Central Committee of the CPSU, in the journal Planovoe khoziaistvo, 1973, no. 5, pp. 24-35. (See Chapter 3 for greater detail on the role of this article.)

5. E. Slutskii, "Sulla Teoria del Bialancio del Consumatore," Giornale Degli Economisti e Rivista di Statistica, 1915, no. 51, pp. 1-26. This work by the distinguished Russian mathematician-economist was first published in 1915 in Italian. Soon thereafter it was translated into English. The article did not

appear in Russian until the early 1960s. For the further development of these ideas, see J. Chipman, L. Hurwicz, M. Richter, and H. Sonnenshein, Preferences, Utility, and Demand: A Minnesota Symposium (New York: Harcourt Brace Jovanovich, 1971).

6. A comparison between Marxism and the concept of optimality developed by Soviet scholars was made from a Western point of view by R. Campbell. His article, "Marx, Kantorovich and Novozhilov: Stoimost versus Reality" (Slavic Review, October 1971), in spite of its very bad "ideological smell," was translated into Russian. The translation was not published but was disseminated among a restricted group of scholars (dlia vnutrenego pol'zovania). It was the first Western article in this field accessible not only to the bureaucracy.

7. V. V. Novozhilov, "Metody nakhozhdeniia minimuma zatrat v sotsialisticheskom khoziaistve," Trudy Leningradskogo politekhnicheskogo instituta (Leningrad, 1946).

8. Interesting criticism of Novozhilov's model, which is very close to mine, is contained in G. Grossman, "Scarce Capital and Soviet Doctrine," Quarterly Journal of Economics, LXII, 1953, no. 3.

9. L. V. Kantorovich, Ekonomicheskii raschet nailuchshego ispol'zovaniia resursov (Moscow: "Nauka" Publishers, 1959). Also see the English translation, The Best Use of Economic Resources (Cambridge, Mass.: Harvard University Press, 1965).

10. A. L. Lur'e, Ekonomicheskii analiz modelei planirovaniia sotsialisticheskogo khoziaistva (Moscow: "Nauka" Publishers, 1973), chap. 18.

11. Note that L. M. Dudkin was probably the first to introduce in Soviet economic-mathematical literature the utility function to describe the national economy. But he did not associate research on it with problems of pure economic theory, since for many years his interest lay in the area of practical applications.

12. V. A. Volkonskii, Printsipy optimal'nogo planirovaniia (Moscow: "Ekonomika" Publishers, 1973).

13. A. Bergson, "A Reformulation of Certain Aspects of Welfare Economics," Quarterly Journal of Economics, February 1968.

14. In a number of works by Soviet authors on the theory of the optimal functioning of a socialist economy (including certain earlier publications by the author of the present book), the concept of price was established as a partial derivative of the national economic criterion of optimality for a corresponding constraint, which moreover possesses stability vis-à-vis small changes. In my view such a definition of price — based not on its function but on certain properties — is not entirely apt. It is tied to one model — the model of scalar optimization under special constraints. The definition of price from the standpoint of its function in the system of organization of the autonomous decision-making of individual participants (local objects) has the advantage that it makes it possible to focus attention on a role of price invariant vis-à-vis the method used in the representation of the system and not strictly associated with certain properties, including stability.

15. V. I. Danilov-Danil'ian and M. G. Zavel'skii, "Sotsial'no-ekonomicheskii optimum i territorial'nye problemy narodnokhoziaistvennogo planirovaniia," Ekonomika i matematicheskie metody, vol. 11, 1975, no. 3, pp. 547-63.

16. Kompleksnaia programma dal'neishego uglubleniia i sovershenstvovaniia sotrudnichestva i razvitiia sotsialisticheskoi ekonomicheskoi integratsii stran-chlenov SEV (Moscow: Politizdat, 1971).

17. The growth of nationalism in the USSR can be "quantitatively measured" in the following way. In 1947 Moscow, as the capital of Russia, celebrated the 800th anniversary of its founding. In the mid-1950s Tbilisi celebrated its 1500th anniversary, and soon thereafter Erevan observed its 2750th anniversary. Although Samarkand celebrated its 2500th anniversary in the late 1960s, some archeologists supposedly found shortly before the celebration that Samarkand was 4,000 years old (these data were not published).

18. This issue was the subject of serious discussions during the drafting of the new Soviet constitution.

Chapter 5

1. A sophisticated grasp of prices as a phenomenon also inherent in a planned economy dates back to research on the scientific principles of centralized economic systems that began in the West in the 1930s. O. Lange and F. Taylor, On the Economic Theory of Socialism (Minneapolis: University of Minnesota Press, 1938); A. Lerner, The Economics of Control (New York: The Macmillan Co., 1947); of the later works illuminating this problem, see, for example, P. Samuelson, Economics (New York: McGraw-Hill Book Co., 1976).

2. O. V. Guseva, "Posledovatel'nost' obmenov v zadache vypuklogo program-mirovaniia," Ekonomika i matematicheskie metody, vol. 5, 1969, no. 6; V. M. Polterovich, "Ob odnoi modeli pereraspredeleniia resursov," Ekonomika i mate-maticheskie metody, vol. 6, 1970, no. 4, pp. 583-93.

3. V. M. Polterovich and G. Ia. Fridman, "O nekotorykh modeliakh funktsioni-rovaniia proizvodstvennykh sistem," Pervaia konferentsiia po optimal'nomu planirovaniiu i upravleniiu narodnogo khoziaistva. Tezisy dokladov, sektsiia I, issue 2 (Moscow: TSEMI AN SSSR, 1971), pp. 88-98.

It is interesting to note that the conditions of the problems changed in the course of the experiment. Utility functions or production functions of the partic-ipants were assumed to be variously differentiable and nondifferentiable, i.e., there was a change in the condition expressed in the fixed proportions of the consumption of commodities.

In the case involving differentiable functions, the reaching of an optimal state, although not a monotonic process, was nonetheless quite "calm." In the case in-volving undifferentiable functions, on the other hand, even in the vicinity of reaching a state of equilibrium there were "explosions" that led the system far away from a state of equilibrium. Facts of this type gave me the following speculative ideas. They concern the attempt to ascertain one of the reasons underlying the acuteness of the economic crisis of 1929-33.

The point is that such branches of industry as the automotive and tractor branches developed quite rapidly after World War I. These branches even be-came dominant during that period. They are characterized by the fixed propor-tions of the resources they consume. Yet the economic mechanism remained the same. It is likely that the increase in the role of such branches had some influence on the course of the cycle and aggravated the Great Depression.

4. V. M. Polterovich, "Blochnye metody vognutogo programmirovaniia i ikh ekonomicheskaia interpretatsiia," Ekonomika i matematicheskie metody, vol. 5, 1969, no. 6, pp. 865-76.

Notes to Chapter 5

5. G. Dantzig, Linear Programming and Extensions (Princeton: Princeton University Press, 1963).

6. L. G. Pliskin, "Dekompozitsionnaia dinamicheskaia optimizatsiia proizvodistva s ierarkhicheskoi strukturoi upravleniia," Avtomatika i telemekhanika, 1969, no. 3-4. It is interesting to note that, owing to their ignorance of economic theory, engineers starting to use the decomposition procedures to solve problems relating to the control of technical systems experience difficulty in analyzing the algorithm as an imitation of the management process. In particular, they cannot understand the independence of the form of the local criterion of optimality for a unit from the rather broad class of optimality criteria for a system. They find it strange that given the existence of a general criterion for an enterprise, e.g., in the form of maximum output or minimum time for the attainment of the goal, the same maximum profit can be the local criterion for an object within the framework of a certain algorithm.

7. S. Smale, "Global Analysis and Economics. I. Pareto Optimum and a Generalisation of Morse Theory," Dynamical Systems, ed. by M. M. Peixoto (New York: Academic Press, 1973).

8. A. Lur'e, "O znachenii nelineinosti pri analize sotsialisticheskoi ekonomiki," Ekonomika i matematicheskie metody, vol. 4, 1966, no. 1.

9. A. I. Katsenelinboigen, S. M. Movshovich, and Iu. V. Ovsienko, Vosproizvodstvo i ekonomicheskii optimum (Moscow: "Nauka" Publishers, 1972).

10. See K. Lancaster, Mathematical Economics (New York: The Macmillan Co., 1968).

11. A remarkable physical explanation of this fact on the basis of the example of the multiplication of particles in an atomic reactor is presented in J. Lewins, Importance. The Adjoint Function (New York: Pergamon Press, 1965).

12. For greater detail on the relationship of economic and physical concepts concerning the common nature of forces and prices, and on this basis of the law of conservation of energy and the law of conservation of values, see, for example, A. Katsenelinboigen, "General Systems Theory and Axiology," General Systems, vol. 19, 1974, pp. 19-26.

13. B. T. Poliak and N. V. Tret'iakov, "An Iterative Method for Linear Programming and Its Economic Interpretation," Matekon, vol. X, no. 3, 1974.

14. D. Gale, The Theory of Linear Economic Models (New York: McGraw-Hill, 1960).

15. The existing general models of economic equilibrium can also be interpreted as models with money as we understand the word. However, they also focus attention on the way in which the participant's money is formed. This is shown in great detail in the Arrow-Debreu model. See K. Arrow and G. Debreu, "Existence of Equilibrium for a Competitive Economy," Econometrica, vol. 34, 1966, no. 1.

16. A. I. Katsenelinboigen, "On the Various Methods of Describing the Socialist Economy," Matekon, vol. X, no. 2, 1973, pp. 3-25.

17. G. Debreu, Theory of Value (New York: John Wiley, 1959).

18. B. S. Razumikhin, "Metod fizicheskogo modelirovaniia v matematicheskom programmirovanii i ekonomike," Avtomatika i telemekhanika, 1972, nos. 3, 4, 6, and 11; 1973, nos. 2 and 4.

19. Generally speaking, contour money can be seen as an invariant of production systems. This can be the case when for some reason the system is unable

to use money as an absolutely universal means, i.e., to acquire any commodity. It would then seem necessary to introduce a rationing system for the distribution of resources.

However, palliative solutions in the form of contour money are also possible. For example, it is possible to form groups of products according to a certain feature, especially from the standpoint of the scale of consumption. For the purchase of products in every such group, the use of the corresponding money, i.e., contour money, is authorized. Something similar is partially in practice in the USSR. There certain lines in the scheduling cost, especially wages, are a means of purchasing the corresponding commodities.

20. In the USSR this was called the creation of "seamless" elements.

21. Tovarno-denezhnye otnosheniia v sisteme planomerno-organizovannogo sotsialisticheskogo proizvodstva (Moscow: Moscow State University Press, 1971), p. 110.

22. D. Valovoi, "O planomernom ispol'zovanii tovarno-denezhnykh otnoshenii," Planovoe khoziaistvo, 1974, no. 2.

23. M. Bornstein, "Soviet Price Theory and Policy," The Soviet Economy: A Book of Readings, 4th ed. (Homewood Ill.: Richard D. Irwin Publishers, 1974), pp. 85-116.

24. A. I. Katsenelinboigen, I. L. Lakhman, and Iu. V. Ovsienko, Optimal'nost' i tovarno-denezhnye otnosheniia (Moscow: "Nauka" Publishers, 1969).

25. G. Grossman, "Gold and the Sword: Money in the Soviet Command Economy," in Industrialization in Two Systems: Essays in Honor of Alexander Gerschenkron, ed. by Henry Rosovsky (New York: John Wiley, 1966).

26. A. Nove, The Soviet Economy (New York: Prager, 1969).

Chapter 6

1. Narodnoe khoziaistvo SSSR, 1973, p. 779.

2. The program of the Communist Party of the USSR envisaged a sharp improvement in the well-being of the working people primarily through "an increase in individual remuneration according to the quality and quantity of labor, in combination with the lowering of retail prices and the abolition of taxes on the population." Programma Kommunisticheskoi partii Sovetskogo Soiuza (adopted by the Twenty-second Congress of the CPSU) (Moscow: Politizdat, 1969), p. 91.

3. The attitude of Soviet economists and managers toward the problem of connecting incentives with the creation of proper conditions for the activity of personnel can be expressed in the following example. Let us assume that a circus wants to stage a cat race act. If he followed the existing incentive principles, the Soviet trainer would have to think first about finding a new type of subtance, stronger than turpentine, with which to rub the cats and thereby increase their running speed. Yet the preparation for this act could be done differently. First, the cats could be fed properly, allowed to rest, and so on. Then a lure could be found for them, e.g., in the form of a live fish or other attractive food suspended in front of them. In the former instance, it is also possible to achieve some results, but they will be short-lived: the cats will soon become exhausted and will have difficulty participating in subsequent races.

4. J. Chapman, "Soviet Wages under Socialism," working paper of the Department of Economics, University of Pittsburgh, October 1974.

Notes to Chapter 6

5. P. Wiles, "Recent Data of Soviet Income Distributing," in Economic Aspects of Life in the USSR. Main Findings of a Colloquim Held January 29-31, 1975, in Brussels (NATO Directorate of Economic Affairs), pp. 113-29.

6. For greater detail, see A. Katsenelinboigen, "Disguised Inflation in the Soviet Union: The Relationship Between Soviet Income Growth and Price Increases in the Postwar Period," The Socialist Price Mechanism (College Station, N.C.: Duke University Press, 1977), pp. 170-83.

7. Here we can draw an analogy with complex chemical processes that simultaneously use both a catalyst and an inhibitor. It may be that the reason for the simultaneous use of inhibitors and catalysts in a number of cases stems from the fact that by the nature of the chemical process, the initial rate that the existing catalysts can communicate to the process is more rapid than the rate required for the normal course of the process. In order to balance the process, inhibitors are used simultaneously that slow the process down to the required level. One of my Moscow friends figuratively compared this situation in economics and chemistry with the whip and the reins used by a horseman.

8. F. Holzman, "Soviet Inflationary Pressures, 1928-1957: Causes and Cures," Quarterly Journal of Economics, May 1960, no. 74, pp. 167-88.

9. It seems that a special decree of the USSR Council of Ministers was even issued in 1948 forbidding the mechanical growth of wages (i.e., the growth of salaries and basic wage rates). I know about this decree from the following sources. In 1951 I wrote a book (which was also my candidate's dissertation) on the organization of labor and wages in the USSR national economy. This work specifically analyzed the state of foremen's wages and showed that the practice — condemned in the prewar years by the government — whereby foremen received smaller wages than skilled workers had been restored. I proposed that the salaries of foremen be increased. Staff members of the Division of Labor and Wages of the Moscow Likhachev Automotive Plant (at the time it bore Stalin's name), to whom I had given my work to examine, said that there were serious political errors in it. Among these errors they noted the proposal to raise the wages of foremen, since this proposal was a revision of a decree of the USSR Council of Ministers of 1948, signed personally by Comrade I. V. Stalin, which forbade mechanical wage increases.

10. According to data presented in the work by A. G. Aganbegian and V. F. Maier, Zarabotnaia plata v SSSR (Moscow, 1959), by 1959 approximately three fourths of all workers in industry and approximately ninety percent of all workers in construction were being paid on a piece-rate basis (p. 149).

11. In his doctoral dissertation E. L. Manevich presented a very broad analysis of the status quo with respect to the organization of the wage rate system and the system for establishing norms. These findings were published in part in his Zarabotnaia plata i ee formy v promyshlennosti SSSR (Moscow: Gosplanizdat, 1959).

12. Here is how it is described in "scientific terms" in a very interesting work by two famous Soviet economists: "In the postwar period the Soviet state has pursued a policy of lowering retail prices. For this reason the factors that are related to money and are associated with the change in the scale of prices have ceased to determine the movement of monetary wages. Factors relating to labor and directly stemming from the economic nature of socialism have advanced to the forefront" (A. G. Aganbegian and V. F. Maier, Zarabotnaia plata v SSSR, p. 86).

13. The table was compiled on the basis of data cited in Narodnoe khoziaistvo SSSR. 1922-1972, p. 350, and Narodnoe khoziaistvo SSSR. 1975, p. 546.

14. A remark made by L. I. Brezhnev in the Report of the Central Committee of the CPSU to the Twenty-fourth Congress of the Communist Party of the Soviet Union confirms cases of artificial price increases: "We must resolutely stop the jacking up of prices, institute tighter controls on the establishment of retail prices and rates for consumer services, and call strictly to account those heads of enterprises and economic agencies who try to circumvent the order established by the state." Kommunist, 1971, no. 5, p. 72.

15. The revaluation also led to the artificial redistribution of the incomes of some groups in the population. Thus there was a sharp increase in expenditures in the service sphere, since many services are performed for tips. (If you do not give tips, you may lose the services.) If a tenant summoned a repairman from the housing administration to do minor repairs, he paid him three rubles before 1960, for example. Soon after 1960 he paid the repairman at least one ruble. On the collective farm market vegetables, the prices of which were measured in a few kopeks, were sold for approximately the same price after 1960.

16. To some extent this is also caused by the fact that the growth in production of television sets is dictated by the need to create military capacities for the radio industry, which in peacetime cannot be used for military purposes and production of the means of production.

17. Narodnoe khoziaistvo SSSR. 1922-1972, p. 373.

18. Narodnoe khoziaistvo SSSR. 1973, p. 634.

19. Thus since April 15, 1974, there have been regular clearance sales at reduced prices (prices cut approximately in half) of certain types of clothing, footwear, and haberdashery for a total of more than 1 billion rubles. See Pravda, April 17, 1974.

20. The table was compiled on the basis of Narodnoe khoziaistvo SSSR. 1922-1972, pp. 373, 404; Narodnoe khoziaistvo SSSR. 1973, pp. 634, 664; and Narodnoe khoziaistvo SSSR. 1975, pp. 599, 630.

21. The sensational Patricia Hearst case in the United States, which entailed extortion of money from the Hearst family to help the poor, is typical of the attempts in this type of struggle for the just distribution of income. The important point about this incident is not only that there were extremists who wanted to establish their principles of social justice by any means but that there were several tens of thousands of people who agreed to accept the money obtained by the extremists. What if the extremists had given out not $2 million but $2 billion, and not $70 a person but $700. How many candidates for this money would there have been in the United States then? Here is an interesting problem for sociologists!

22. P. Cazenave and C. Morrison, "Fonctions d'Utilité Interdépendantes et Theorie de la Redistribution en Economie de Production," Revue Economique, vol. 24, 1973, no. 5, pp. 725-60. Here it is especially important to call attention to the language of reflexive processes that any person can use to describe the awareness of his behavior depending on the awareness that other people have of his behavior and their own behavior. See V. A. Lefevr, Konfliktuiushchie struktury (Moscow: "Sovetskoe radio" Publishers, 1973). (A translation into English has already appeared.) Considerable interest is afforded by studies of the mechanism for distributing goods by using the aforementioned language. See V. A. Lefevr, P. V. Baranov, and V. E. Lepskii, "Vnutrenniaia valiuta v refleksivnykh igrakh," Tekhnicheskaia kibernetika, 1969, no. 4, pp. 29-33.

23. M. Matthews, "Top Income in the USSR," Economic Aspects of Life in the USSR, pp. 131-54.

Notes to Chapter 6

24. A. Yanov, Detente After Brezhnev: The Domestic Roots of Soviet Foreign Policy (Berkeley: Institute of International Studies, University of California, 1977).

25. The story has it that in the mid-1950s in the Ministry of Ferrous Metallurgy, a deputy minister stood out among his colleagues — a former director of the Magnitogorsk Metallurgical Combine. He demonstratively took his meals in the same snack bar used by the rank-and-file personnel, did not use a car to visit the numerous government institutions, and so on. This deputy minister was a thorn in the flesh of his colleagues. His fate following the abolition of the ministry when the regional economic councils [sovnarkhozy] were set up is unknown to me.

26. Given the low level of development of consumer goods production, the quite free replenishment of the work force, and the leader's command of enormous political power, he can invoke the strictest measures against those who fail to fulfill the plan in order to intimidate others. During the construction of the pyramids in Egypt there were cases in which slaves were buried alive because they did not meet the "plan" (output norm).

27. In a speech at the Council of the People's Commissariat of Heavy Industry on June 29, 1936, G. K. Ordzhonikidze noted: "The system of fines for engineers and technicians must be abolished (voices: 'Right!'). It must be abolished in all branches where it exists. (Applause)."

"Let us agree: Great attention must be devoted to the selection of engineers and technicians for various posts; but if they are not suitable, it is better to transfer them to work that fits their knowledge than to fine them. (Voices: 'Right!')" (G. K. Ordzhonikidze, Stat'i i rechi, vol. 2, 1926-37, Moscow, 1957, p. 789).

28. This point of view is presented in V. F. Pugachev's Optimizatsiia planirovaniia (Moscow: "Ekonomika" Publishers, 1968).

29. F. S. Veselkov, Stimuly vysokikh planovykh zadanii (Moscow: "Ekonomika" Publishers, 1968). Mathematical research on this topic has been carried out in the USSR under the direction of A. Ia. Lerner at the Institute of Control Problems. See V. Burkov and A. Lerner, "Open Control Principle for Active Systems," Automation and Remote Control, 1970, no. 8, pp. 1288-97.

30. J. Berliner, "Innovation in Soviet Industry," manuscript, 1974; M. Weitzman, "The New Soviet Incentive Model," The Bell Journal of Economics, Spring 1976, pp. 251-57.

31. Op. cit.

32. There are very serious reasons to assume that such a system of planning will be preserved in the future, since owing to the incompleteness of information, it is technically extremely difficult to obtain a rigorous plan from calculations. Planning from the attained level introduces realism to the planning process and builds a basis for plans from the experience amassed in the course of their fulfillment. Interesting ideas have been expressed in this regard by I. Ia. Birman in the manuscript of his work "Plan (teoriia i praktika)," a preliminary variant of which was presented in 1975 at General Electric, Tempo, Washington.

33. E. G. Liberman, Ekonomicheskie metody povysheniia effektivnosti obshchestvennogo proizvodstva (Moscow: "Ekonomika" Publishers, 1970).

34. The existence of such features in the purpose of the plan and in the responsibility for its fulfillment by central authorities and at the intermediate

levels has also been expressed in the organizational structure of the system of planning. The central authorities could not trust the ministries' reported production capacities as the basis for planning the most important indicator: output. Hence during the prewar era a special commission was created in USSR Gosplan to directly ascertain the capacities of enterprises. The commission had its own regional inspectorates for this purpose. Since the regional party organizations are responsible for the fulfillment of the plan by all regional enterprises, they are usually also interested in obtaining nonintensive plans for enterprises located on their territory. Therefore, as an exception, regional inspectorates of the commission on capacities were independent of the local party organizations. It seems that the commission on capacities was abolished when N. S. Khrushchev organized the regional economic councils.

35. V. S. Nemchinov, "Sotsialisticheskoe khoziaistvovanie i planirovanie proizvodstva," Kommunist, 1964, no. 5.

36. Given a prohibition on official travel for the "pusher," he performs his function in the guise of a "student of progressive know-how," etc. See works by H. Levine and J. Berliner for greater detail on the role of "pushers" and other negative aspects of Soviet material and technical supply.

37. A detailed critical analysis of the situation in which demand exceeds supply is given in J. Kornai's Anti-Equilibrium (New York: North Holland, n.d.). However, in my view a shortcoming of Kornai's work is that it does not pay proper attention to the formation of the mechanisms that limit the extreme excess of supply over demand.

38. This idea accords with proposals expressed in M. Ezekiel's Jobs for All Through Industrial Expansion (New York: Knopf, 1939), which is about the possible organization of offices in the United States to buy surplus commodities, especially during a depression period.

39. One can find the views of these managers in I. Shevtsov's Vo imia ottsa i syna (Moscow: "Moskovskii rabochii" Publishers, 1970). This book is an open program of Russian national socialism. But in it the author also provides a rare opportunity for direct rebuttal by proponents of the opposing point of view, which specifically entails introducing a competitive mechanism in the USSR.

40. Since this decree was not officially published (at any rate in the general press), we refer to the report on it in Pravda, October 23, 1968: "The decree outlines measures for developing broad competition in science and technology and for preventing monopoly in the solution of key problems in science and technology. To this end, it is recommended that in necessary cases ministries and agencies, councils of ministers of union republics, the USSR Academy of Sciences, and branch academies of sciences assign research and development work to several organizations pursuing different directions."

41. A. Fedoseev, Zapadnia. Chelovek i sotsializm (Frankfurt: Possev-Verlag, 1976), pp. 230-34.

42. P. Demichev, "Razrabotka aktual'nykh problem stroitel'stva kommunizma v resheniiakh XXIV s"ezda KPSS," Kommunist, 1971, no. 15.

Chapter 7

1. Folk sayings like "the law is a shaft: where it's aimed it goes" reveal the

general attitude of the people toward the law. The behavior of the defendant in a play by Sukhovo-Kobylin is another example. When the judge, placing his hand on a pile of books — the law code — asks the defendant: "How shall I judge you: according to conscience or according to the law?" the defendant replies: "According to conscience, sir, according to conscience."

2. Certain generalizations and facts about semilegal and illegal markets can be found in the text of the report by Dimitri K. Simes, "The Soviet Parallel Market," Economic Aspects of Life in the USSR, pp. 91-100.

3. The following is the definition of profiteering in the RSFSR Criminal Code (Moscow: "Iuridicheskaia literatura" Publishers, 1971): "Profiteering is the buying and reselling of commodities or other items for profit" (p. 59). The problem of creating a flexible mechanism for distributing the means of production in a planned system is considerably more complex, since for many commodities the number of consumers is not large enough to form a convex set.

4. As follows from the works by R. Auman, "Existence of Equilibria in Markets with a Continuum of Trades," Econometrica, vol. 34, 1966, no. 7, and V. Arkin, "An Infinite-Dimensional Analog of Non-Convex Programming Problems," Cybernetics, 1967, no. 2-3, given a continual set of participants and a certain number of commodities, it is possible to find the optimal equilibrium state of a system by means of prices and incomes constraining the participants even if the objective functions of the participants are nonconvex, etc.

5. A. Katsenelinboigen, "Constructing the Potential of a System," General Systems, vol. XIX, 1974, pp. 27-36.

6. Other less important sources of products on the collective farm market are fruits and berries from garden plots allotted to workers and employees of especially important enterprises and institutions in large cities.

7. Narodnoe khoziaistvo SSSR v 1972 g., p. 577.

8. Ibid., p. 573.

9. The New York Times, November 11, 1974.

10. In 1956 the practice of evicting workers from apartments received from an enterprise in the event a worker quit his job was discontinued. Manpower turnover is quite high in the USSR at the present time, and it is quite difficult to control with the available means. For this reason a number of enterprise managers have raised the question of returning to Stalinist methods of economic management that would enable them to hold on to manpower, particularly by means of eviction from houses belonging to the enterprise. As far as I know, in the late 1960s the Volgograd Tractor Plant attempted to return to the eviction practices that existed prior to 1956. But the USSR Procuracy halted the eviction of workers who quit their jobs at the enterprise.

11. For all practical purposes air conditioners are virtually not used in the USSR. Only in the last few years have provisions been made for air conditioners in the construction of some modern buildings. But as experience shows, these air conditioners are either of poor quality or the personnel servicing them have low skill levels. Hence these air conditioners generally do not work, which causes enormous problems for people working in buildings for which air conditioners were intended. Here we see quite a conventional picture for the Soviet Union: the clash between West and East. Imitating the West, Soviet architects build a new type of building with wide windows, etc. But the quality of the construction of these buildings and the servicing of them remain Soviet. As a result these

buildings are extremely hot in the summer, and cold winds blow through them in the winter. When there was an unusually hot summer in the later 1960s in Moscow, people housed in the new buildings found themselves in very trying circumstances. The air conditioners were not running, and the windows could not be opened, since they were airtight for the air conditioners.

12. As shown by events in the 1960s in the West, as well as in Yugoslavia and Poland, students are the most dynamic force in contemporary radical movements. Soviet leaders were frightened by the wave of the student movement that had already directly approached the Soviet frontiers. The introduction of courses — rabfaky — for the less well-educated (worker) youth entering higher educational institutions and the privileges conferred on them were designed to make these young people obedient defenders of the regime who would paralyze the actions of their better-educated and more independent classmates.

A child from an intellectual family is no longer grateful to the Party and the government for his opportunity to study: he accepts it as his right and sometimes even as an unpleasant duty, since his parents want to see him no less well educated than they are.

What I have said suggests that working youth admitted under preferential conditions to higher educational institutions are distributed among all groups. Thus in every group a nucleus is created that opposes student activism. Official propaganda attempts to explain the privileges conferred on working youth by saying that from the standpoint of social justice, the social composition of the student body should reflect the social structure of the population, that workers cannot afford to provide better knowledge for their children through private lessons, and thus naturally, bright working youth cannot compete with the less able but "coached" children of intellectuals, and so on. Even though they seem humane at first glance, all these arguments are demagogic. If the Soviet leaders were actually concerned about humane interests, they would create better educational conditions for schoolchildren, especially for bright schoolchildren from the families of low-income workers and collective farmers.

Note, by the way, that the average wage of intellectuals in the USSR in recent years has been almost equal to the wage of workers and collective farmers and that families in the various social groups now have the same number of children. Love of alcohol, indifference to the education of the children, the desire to see their children more affluent — these are the values that are dominant in workers' and peasants' families and that make it difficult to draw children from workers' families into higher educational institutions.

Finally, if the Soviet leaders were concerned with humane interests, they would create special groups at higher educational institutions for less prepared worker and peasant students where they would gradually acquire the knowledge they need. However, the penetration of these students into the general student body lowers the level of preparation. The attempts of individual professors to protest the positive assessment of these students' skills, since it poses the threat that unqualified specialists will be graduated from higher educational institutions, have ended in the expulsion of these professors from the higher schools. The rector of a higher educational institution knows that if he gives a negative certification to a student from a worker's faculty, this will be regarded as an antiparty act, since it would entail weakening the authorities' stability in the immediate future. (Also see Chapter 2.) And it is unimportant whether the quality of specialists deteriorates, since this decline will surface only in the more distant future, when the present leadership will no longer exist.

13. The New York Times, October 25, 1974.

14. In my view the operation of the subway system in the USSR is an example of what a state with a strictly centralized economy can achieve. Yet it should be borne in mind that such irreproachable operation of the subway system (if one does not count the crowds at rush hour and the deafening noise on some sections) has been attained under unusual conditions. The subway system functions as a type of transport not connected with other types of transport, and the number of disruptive factors in it has been reduced to a minimum: there are no intersections, there is no influence from the surrounding atmosphere (temperature, precipitation, etc.). A strict centralized control system experiences great difficulty in similar routine processes where it is necessary to coordinate different types of production processes operating in parallel and to eliminate the disturbances that arise. It goes without saying that such systems cannot organize effective production where there are nonroutine processes and where a special, flexible system of control is required.

15. During his tenure as chief of state, Khrushchev sharply reduced the number of passenger automobiles and with them the number of drivers at the disposal of the heads of enterprises and institutions, thereby evoking the wrath of the bureaucratic elite in no small measure. One of the first acts of the leaders who replaced Khrushchev was to restore these vehicles. In the last few years the Soviet leaders have attempted only to decrease the size of this group of drivers by requiring that the managers themselves learn to drive the cars the state is prepared to assign to them.

16. It appears that one of the new unofficial incentives for Soviet athletes to break records in the West is that record breakers may get through customs a virtually unlimited quantity of goods.

17. In Stalin's day one Mel'nikov (Mil'man), toiling in the Union of Writers, expressed the view that it would be a good idea to write a book about the best people in the USSR who are already living in the communist way. Stalin, of course, constantly exploited the idea that the victory of communism was close at hand. (Recall, for example, Babaevskii's novel The Cavalier of the Gold Star.) Therefore the proposed book was right in the vein of official propaganda. Upon securing the mandate of the Union of Writers and a black ZIM limousine, Mel'nikov set out for the bountiful southern regions (communism is evidently closer to the south). There he was wined and dined for months by the chairmen of the rich Kuban collective farms who very much wanted to see themselves portrayed as representatives of the communist tomorrow.

Among other things Mel'nikov undertook to help these chairmen get an automobile, which in those days was even harder than now. He faked telephone calls directly from the office of a collective farm chairman to a highly placed official in the Ministry of Trade in Moscow and explained to him how important it was to allocate a car for this chairman. Everything the Moscow writer did instilled trust in him, and people eagerly gave him money so that he would purchase the car upon his return to Moscow. Mel'nikov performed similar machinations with promises to deliver a car in the Donbass, where rather well-to-do groups of miners, who were to become the heroes of his book, eagerly gave him their money to buy cars.

After returning to Moscow, Mel'nikov continued to pull the wool over the eyes of the trusting southerners with his promises to ship their cars. In the mid-50s Donetsk miners meeting with Rudenko, their deputy to the USSR Supreme Soviet and chief procurator of the USSR, told him the story about the automobiles. Following this, Mel'nikov was convicted.

18. A. I. Katsenelinboigen, S. M. Movshovich, and Iu. V. Ovsienko, <u>Vospro-izvodstvo i ekonomicheskii optimum</u> (Moscow: "Nauka" Publishers, 1972).

19. V. Treml, "Alcohol in the USSR: A Fiscal Dilemma," <u>Soviet Studies</u>, vol. 27, 1975, no. 2, pp. 161-77.

20. In the USSR I was told about the exposure of a group of thieves stealing gold in the gold fields and selling it to wealthy people in Armenia. This group hired itself out to work in the gold fields, worked very intensively, overfulfilled its plan, and won the title of communist labor brigade. Under the terms of the competition for this title, the winners work without additional supervision — the administration trusts them (just as the best workers at machine-building plants are given their personal stamp). After winning the confidence of the administration in this way, the group began to systematically steal part of the gold produced.

21. This matter was entrusted to the Ministry of State Security: the Ministry of Internal Affairs, whose direct duties included such matters, was not trusted by Khrushchev (and for good reason) because he believed its personnel were corrupt. This case, by the way, created a precedent for the Ministry of State Security to begin dealing with matters outside its normal purview. Apparently finding this to their liking and desiring to enhance their prestige, personnel from the Ministry of State Security suggested that their services be enlisted in exposing other economic crimes. But the authorities evidently remembered in time how dangerous the strengthening of this punitive apparatus could be.

22. As far as I know, prostitution was legal in Czechoslovakia prior to 1968, but only for foreigners from capitalist countries who were staying in Czechoslovakia for more than a month. These foreigners were issued special cards entitling them to invite girls to a certain hotel. The girls were in state service and enjoyed special privileges, including a pension at the appropriate age for their profession. The argument for providing such a service to foreigners was that they would find prostitutes anyway. Thus it was better to control the business and get foreign currency for it rather than let it takes its course.

Index

Academy of Sciences of the USSR, 55, 60, 73
Aganbegian, A. G., 60
"Akchi" State Farm, 66
Anchishkin, A. I., 80
Armenia, 43
Azerbaijan, 200

Baibakov, N. K., 11, 73
Belashova, 151
Belik, Iu., 72
Belorussia, 96
Berliner, J., 157
Bernard, C., 31
Berri, L. Ia., 52
Böhm-Bawerk, E., 68
Bolsheviks, 23, 30, 33, 43
Brauer fixed point theorem, 19, 20
Breev, M. V., 52
Brezhnev, L. I., 66

Capital, 5, 31, 48, 123
Castro, F., 35
Cauchy, A. L., 32
Central Committee of the CPSU, 34, 57, 69, 72-74, 150, 163, 164
Central Economic Mathematical Institute [TSEMI], 55, 70, 72, 73, 80
China, 5, 28, 52, 66, 95, 124, 164
COMECON, 95
Common Market, 95
Communist Party of the Soviet Union, 34, 59, 72, 138, 156
Council of Ministers, USSR, 13, 50, 59, 144, 149, 163
Cuba, 35, 124

Dantzig-Wolf algorithm, 103, 104, 110, 114-17
Demichev, P. N., 164

Efimov, A. N., 61
Engels, F., 42, 88, 123, 125

Fedorenko, N. P., 60, 69
Fel'dbaum, A. A., 24
Finland, 193

Geil, D., 112, 118
Georgia, 195
Germany, 37
Germany, Federal Republic of, 44
Glushkov, V., 61, 62, 69
Gosplan, 11, 18, 61, 73, 80, 185
Great Britain, 37, 95
Grossman, G., 127
Gurevich, A. Ia., 56
Guseva, O., 101

Holzman, F. D., 144

Iakovlev, 69, 163
Israel, 31
Italy, 37
Izvestia, 60

Japan, 44
Jews, 43, 54, 72, 181

Kakutani, S., 19
Kantorovich, L. V., 51, 52, 85, 87, 88
Kapustin, E. I., 73
Kats, A. 71-73
Kazakhstan, 66
Keynes, J. M., 68
KGB, 57, 201
Khrushchev, N. S., 27, 34, 35, 40, 65, 69-71, 149, 166, 179, 195, 199, 200
Khudenko, I., 66
Klimenko, K. I., 52
Kolmogorov, A. N., 47, 54
Konstantinov, 56
Kornai-Liptak algorithm, 110, 116
Kossov, V. V., 61, 73
Kosygin, A. N., 59
Kozlov, F. R., 34, 35
Kronrod, A. I., 72

Index

Lagrange multipliers, 19, 51, 113
Laplace, P. S., 68
Lavrent'ev, M. A., 47
Lenin, V. I., 27, 33, 35, 84, 150, 155, 166
Leningrad, 193
Liberman, E. G., 60, 70, 158
Lorenz, K., 33
Lukomskii, Ia. I., 52
Lur'e, A. L., 51, 85, 88, 89, 105
Lysenko, T. D., 49, 50, 54

Malenkov, G. M., 52, 84
Marx, K., 5, 24, 29, 31, 36, 38, 41, 42, 62, 84, 88, 89, 123, 125, 150
Marxism, 5, 6, 23, 29, 37, 88, 89, 122-24, 165
Miasishchev, 69, 163
Mikhalevskii, B. N., 80
Mikoian-Gurevich, 69, 163
Ministry of Agriculture, 70
Mitchell, J., 79
Mitin, M. B., 56
Moiseev, N. N., 60, 68, 69
Monge problem, 51
Moscow, 141, 173, 179, 180, 193
Moscow State University, 54
Mussolini, B., 37

Napoleon, 68
Navoi, 96
Nekrasov, N. N., 73
Nemchinov, V. S., 51, 160
NEP [New Economic Policy], 40, 125, 165
Neumann, J. von, 19, 107, 109
Nobel Prize, 51
Novozhilov, V. V., 85-87

October Revolution, 33, 37, 45, 46
Odessa, 193
Ostrovitianov, K. V., 50

Pareto optimum, 91, 105
Paris Commune, 150
Planned Economy [Planovoe khoziai-stvo], 71-74
Polianskii, D. M., 67
Politburo, USSR, 11, 50, 59, 66, 68, 69, 71, 72, 74, 164

Polterovich, V. M., 101, 102
Pravda, 72-74

Rumiantsev, A. M., 56
Russell, B., 200
Russia, 23, 30, 37, 42-44, 96

Scarf, H., 19
Schaeffle, 37
Schumpeter, J., 68
Shevtsov, I., 67
Slutskii, E., 82
Smale, S., 105
Solov'ev, 72
Stalin, J. V., 23, 35, 40, 43, 45, 48-50, 52-54, 65, 69, 70, 82, 96, 156
State Committee on Prices, 13
Suslov, M. A., 35

Tallin, 193
Tinbergen, J., 33
Treml, V., 197
TSEMI, See Central Economic Mathematical Institute
Tsentrosoiuz, 175
Tugan-Baranovskii, M. I., 128
Tupolev, A. N., 69, 163
Turgot, A. R. J., 68

United States, 28, 36, 44, 55, 141, 145, 182, 198
Uzbekistan, 96

Venzher, V., 70
Voronov, G. I., 66
Voznesenskii, N. A., 50

Walras-Wald model, 82
Weitzman, M., 157, 158
Wieser, F. von, 68
Wiles, P., 141
World War I, 52
World War II, 48, 52, 82, 144, 171
World War III, 52

Yugoslavia, 40

Zeravshan, 96
Zhukov, G. K., 69

228

About the Author

Born in the Soviet Union in 1927, Aron Katsenelinboigen was educated at the Moscow State Economics Institute, from which he received his doctorate in 1966. From 1966 to 1973 he was head of the Department of Complex Systems at the Central Economic Mathematical Institute of the USSR Academy of Sciences, and from 1970 to 1973 he was a professor of economics at Moscow State University.

Since his emigration to the United States in 1973, Professor Katsenelinboigen has been a visiting scholar at the University of California at Berkeley and has taught at the University of Pennsylvania and Princeton University. The author of several books and dozens of articles in economics, his current research centers on theoretical problems of the functioning of planning systems, general systems theory, and axiological problems.